Europe's Crisis,
Europe's Future

Europe's Crisis, Europe's Future

Kemal Derviş
Jacques Mistral
editors

BROOKINGS INSTITUTION PRESS
Washington, D.C.

The Brookings Institution is a private nonprofit organization devoted to research,
education, and publication on important issues of domestic and foreign policy.
Its principal purpose is to bring the highest quality independent research and analysis
to bear on current and emerging policy problems. Interpretations or conclusions in
Brookings publications should be understood to be solely those of the authors.

Library of Congress Cataloging-in-Publication data is available.
ISBN 978-0-8157-2554-1 (pbk. : alk. paper)

9 8 7 6 5 4 3 2 1

Printed on acid-free paper

Typeset in Adobe Garamond

Composition by Circle Graphics
Columbia, Maryland

Contents

Part II. Cross-Cutting Issues

Foreword

JAVIER SOLANA

There is strong hope that 2014 will be a year of renewed growth in the eurozone, even in the countries that were in deep crisis for several years. The resumption of growth would of course be good news but will not resolve the tremendous pressures generated by high unemployment and social difficulties that remain widespread, even beyond Southern Europe. The year 2014 will also see elections to the European Parliament, with the prospect that euro-skeptic parties will find new support. The election campaigns will likely include a more vigorous debate about the future of Europe, which should be viewed as a positive side effect.

This book draws on the experience of a diverse set of authors and on two key workshops, one held at ESADE in Madrid in March 2013, and the other at the Robert Bosch Stiftung in Berlin in May 2013. It links a discussion of individual country case studies to the broader debate over reform in the eurozone and in Europe, with two chapters focusing in particular on the financial sector and on social policies.

Experience has shown that while it is difficult for Europe to launch a grand institutional reform in one dramatic stroke, progress has often been made in response to a crisis or to an accumulation of problems. When one looks back at what has happened since the eurozone crisis erupted late in 2009, first in Greece and then in Ireland, it seems fair to say that a lot has been achieved. There is a European Stability Mechanism (ESM) now in place with substantial financial firepower, and a new treaty has been agreed on, the Fiscal Compact, committing eurozone member countries as well as some others to increased fiscal policy cooperation.[1] The European Central Bank (ECB) is in the process of becoming the supervisor of the eurozone banking system; again, some non-eurozone members are also accepting ECB supervision, though they are not in the monetary union. Nobody would have predicted this amount of institutional progress in 2008; but then, of course, nobody had predicted the severity of the crisis that unfolded after 2009. These steps have all been incremental, and some of the most important advances, such as the new Fiscal Compact, have had to sidestep European Union law and be launched as intergovernmental agreements, mainly because of objections by the United Kingdom. Nonetheless, the reforms cover not only the eurozone, but in some cases the whole EU.

The achievements summarized above should not lead one to underestimate two big areas of challenge that remain. One is the gap between the needs of Europe in 2014 and the perception that large segments of the European population have about the EU and the eurozone. Clearly, politics is lagging behind the economics-driven institutional steps, and Europe faces the challenge of having to generate much more vigorous support among its citizens for the institutions it is creating and the degree of cooperation it wants to embark on. The second major challenge has to do with the institutional structure itself. The situation a few years ago was such that, by treaty, the euro became the currency of the EU, although the United Kingdom and Denmark were able to negotiate formal exemptions for themselves, and Sweden has managed to stay out of the eurozone, despite the absence of a formal exemption. Legally, nothing has changed, but there is an increasing need for clarity as to which institutions and mechanisms apply to the eurozone and which apply to the entire EU. There is an inherent tension between a vision of Europe that is essentially identical to the eurozone, and a vision of Europe with at least two concentric circles, where some countries would durably remain outside a more integrated eurozone while being full members of the EU.

The editors and the authors of this volume address these issues from different perspectives and backgrounds at a time when the debate on the future of Europe is reaching a new phase. Will the recovery from acute crisis lead to complacency and unwillingness to address the issues that the crisis brought to the fore? Or, will the lessons be learned and lead to decisive new steps, both in

---

1. Formally, this is the Treaty on Stability, Coordination and Governance in the Economic and Monetary Union, signed on March 2, 2012. It is also referred to as TSCG or the Fiscal Stability Treaty.

setting country policies and in renewing a European institutional design that can accommodate more advanced integration in some domains and by some countries, as well as greater flexibility for others?

There is unlikely to be a huge breakthrough in the form of a comprehensive new treaty. The message of this book, however, is that purely marginal and slow changes will not be enough to generate a new confidence in the European project and the prosperity that should come with it. Having worked closely with most of the contributors to this volume and supported its publication, I agree that 2014 and the near future should be a period of strong and open debate and citizen engagement, followed by some courageous decisions that would become the bedrock of Europe's future. The world needs a stronger Europe, and one is possible if we work toward it together.

Acknowledgments

The editors would like to gratefully acknowledge the Stavros Niarchos Foundation, the ESADE Business School, and the Robert Bosch Stiftung for supporting this collaborative research and providing a forum for all authors. We also thank the authors for their dedication and excellence in research, as well as their collaboration in finalizing the book. We would like to thank those who have provided invaluable comments in the editing process, including John Page, Charles Stewart, Guillermo Vuletin, and Brookings Press staff. Valuable comments on various parts of this volume were also received, often at roundtable meetings, from Bill Antholis, Josep Borrell, Sandra Breka, Matthew Browne, Jean Pisani-Ferry, Randall Henning, Fiona Hill, Jacob Kirkegaard, Donald Kohn, Reza Moghadam, Ernesto Talvi, Thomas Wright, Stelios Vasilakis, and Nicolas Veron. Our deep gratitude also goes to Javier Solana for his continued support and guidance. We also thank Soumya Chattopadhyay, Annick Ducher, Karim Foda, Edith Joachimpillai, and Galip Kemal Ozhan for their research support and management in putting together this work.

Brookings recognizes that the value it provides is in its absolute commitment to quality, independence, and impact. Activities supported by its donors reflect this commitment, and the analysis and recommendations here are not determined or influenced by any donation. Interpretations or conclusions in all Brookings publications should be understood to be solely those of the authors.

1

Europe's Crisis, Europe's Future: An Overview

KEMAL DERVIŞ AND JACQUES MISTRAL

The economic crisis that started in Greece in late 2009 quickly spread to Ireland and Portugal and then to Spain and Italy. After becoming a major eurozone crisis, it eventually came to threaten the global system in the autumn of 2011. And like the subprime crisis in 2008, no one had predicted it.

There had been, of course, many warnings in the 1990s, before the euro was launched, about forming a monetary union without a sufficient political union. But the first ten years of the euro seemed quite successful. The warnings and criticisms died down quickly. Interest rates inside the eurozone converged surprisingly rapidly, as if membership in this monetary union was a sufficient condition for an immediate equalization of sovereign creditworthiness; credit conditions became so favorable that growth in the periphery countries where there were more "catch-up" opportunities—those that would shortly become the crisis countries—was particularly strong; Spain, for example, was not far from being called a new economic miracle. As late as December 2008, *The Economist* published a spectacular assessment of what had been achieved, calling the "euro at ten" a "resounding success" and confirming to its readers the belief that the single currency had proved "demonstrably durable." The evolution of the euro-dollar exchange rate was a visible confirmation of these comments. Initially fixed at 1.19 dollars in 1999, the value of the euro declined during its two first years when "irrational exuberance" in the United States was fueled by the promise of the new information technology (IT) economy. But after the dot-com bubble burst, the value of the euro rose more or less steadily and exceeded 1.55 dollars in the spring of 2008.

We do not recount the details of the causes and the evolution of the eurozone crisis in this overview. The individual chapters in this volume describe the onset and evolution of the crisis in Greece, Italy, and Spain, as well as its effects in France and Germany; supporting comparative macroeconomic data are also available in the appendix. A chapter on the financial sector and one on social policies focus on two areas of particular importance for the eurozone.

A few words regarding the systemic aspects of the crisis at the eurozone level are nonetheless appropriate in this introduction. The global economic prosperity during the first ten years of the euro helped conceal a deeply rooted vulnerability that was fully exposed once the economic crisis set in. The global crisis that began in 2008 was not the *cause* of the eurozone's economic woes, but it was a tipping point for economies that had been operating on unsound foundations for a while. The monetary union and the way it had been managed had allowed a large build-up of public and/or private debt in many countries and a serious divergence of real unit labor costs, and therefore a loss of competitiveness. Regarding its *public debt* component, the crisis would have been much more manageable if the Maastricht Treaty, with its limits on public debt and deficits, had been fully enforced. Germany and France had been the first to violate the treaty, damaging the sense of discipline that was so essential to a proper functioning of the monetary union, and thereby set a bad precedent for others. It is also true, however, that the crisis in Ireland and Spain—countries that did not violate the Maastricht criteria—was not of a fiscal nature. It was due in both cases to a real estate bubble allowed by excessive increases in *private debt*—leading to a terrible banking crisis.

The dangers of excessive growth in private or public debt, despite being clearly reflected in large current account deficits, were not addressed in a timely way, as they would have been under the weight of the "external constraint" before the introduction of the single currency. Initially, the response to increasing levels of public debt was benign neglect. With regard to private debt, neither market players nor the eurozone's leadership imagined that private investors and financial institutions could make such huge mistakes. This blind belief in the infallibility of markets was similar to what had led to the subprime mortgage debacle that triggered the financial crisis in the United States. The currency union and the Maastricht Treaty alone did not have strong enough enforcement mechanisms to ensure adequate banking and fiscal restraint.

Have Early Critics of the Eurozone Now Finally Been Proven Right?

It starts with a very simple question: How did the (mis)management of a crisis in a marginal economy, Greece (whose GDP is 2 percent of that of the eurozone), become a continental and then a global systemic risk? Seen from the IMF headquarters in Washington, D.C., or the EU Commission's offices in Brussels, the Greek problem initially appeared to be just one more episode in a long history of debt-rooted financial crises. The international institutions had a long memory of countries that descended into similar financial disorder: Mexico, Argentina, Thailand, Russia, and Turkey, to name a few. And there was a well-known toolkit to deal with such situations. As unpleasant as it can be, an IMF-style rescue package is based on an adjustment program that, generally speaking, includes austerity measures, devaluation of the currency, and structural reforms to make the economy more competitive. These are accompanied by medium-term financing that gives the country time to restore its damaged international credit. The whole process is implemented under IMF surveillance. What made the Greek case so special is that Greece belongs to a monetary union. Greece cannot devalue its currency, and there was no Treasury in Brussels, no EU institution (like the IMF) in charge of dealing with a financial crisis in one component of the union. Exchange rates in the monetary union are irrevocably fixed; unrestricted capital mobility opens the way to massive capital exports at the earliest alert. The Maastricht Treaty includes an explicit no-bailout provision and bans any monetary financing of public deficits.

All this explains most of the hesitation in the first half of 2010—before the first European compromise was adopted. That first package of measures appeared to be a success because the creation of the European Financial Stability Fund (EFSF) opened the way to a rescue operation. But it was also the first error, because it was too little, too late, and visibly too reluctantly agreed upon. Doubts about the willingness of the eurozone countries to stick together were sown, and two years passed before the European Central Bank (ECB) president Mario Draghi delivered the final and convincing promise to do "whatever it takes to preserve the euro" (in July 2012). Meanwhile the situation had quickly deteriorated. In the years immediately preceding the crisis, the size of the problem in Greece had clearly been underestimated—partly due to Greece misreporting statistics before a new prime minister unveiled this deceit. The attempt to implement some adjustment and fiscal consolidation quickly exposed the weak public administration and the dysfunctional political system. In Brussels and the eurozone capitals, the response to the crisis had proved incoherent; future risks were faced with repeated indecisiveness; there was no serious attempt to elaborate a strategy that included support for growth alongside fiscal consolidation—and there were deep disagreements on burden sharing. By the end of the summer of 2010, the creation of a more powerful rescue mechanism became unavoidable.

In the eyes of many German voters, the Greeks were not only seen as having mismanaged their country: they were "sinners" who had betrayed the contract between the members of the European Monetary Union (EMU). Following two decades of effort to bring eastern Germany more or less in line with its western counterparts, German taxpayers, for understandable reasons, were not ready to pay for what they saw as the profligacy of the South. Moreover, citizens in Germany and elsewhere found it unacceptable that the reckless behavior of private banks should result in their having to bail out the shareholders and managers of these banks. After all, a credit transaction always has two sides to it: for someone to have borrowed excessively, there had to have been someone willing to lend excessively. This is why Germany found the first compromise hard to accept. Only a few months later, German chancellor Angela Merkel, with an eye on both the upcoming regional elections preceding the forthcoming national ones, and because of the genuine outrage prevailing in her country, felt that a more politically acceptable package was needed. A message had to be sent to both public and private actors that would reduce "moral hazard" not only for politicians but also for the private banks. The idea that gained traction in this context was to explicitly declare that the private sector would have to share the losses that would occur in bailouts, a mechanism known as "private sector involvement" or PSI. In the past, such PSI applied to previously incurred debt up to a clear cut-off date. It had been built into several IMF programs for emerging markets, always with fierce opposition from the private financial sector. The early discussion on Greece was unfortunately vague as to the cut-off date and, by presenting it as a general policy to be adopted by the eurozone, raised doubts about whether private debt restructuring would be confined to Greece.

Fearing destabilizing consequences for the financial markets, the ECB and most governments were not warm to this German proposal. The IMF, on the other hand, was supportive, and indeed IMF staff was pushing for very strong PSI. The fact that it was grudgingly adopted by the European Council in October 2010 relied heavily on the support of French president Nicolas Sarkozy after the so-called Deauville Compromise reached with Chancellor Merkel (what Paris got in this compromise was a suspension of pending pursuits by the EU Commission within the framework of a procedure against excessive public deficits).

The Deauville Compromise inflamed the markets and was followed by twelve months of chaos. The initiative had already received the label "haircut," and the financial markets immediately got the message: financing southern countries would be risky for all; be ready for investments in those countries to be valued at a possibly deep discount. The EU Commission, the Eurogroup (the eurozone finance ministers), and the IMF did not send the clear message that during the ongoing crisis at least (as opposed to future crises) insistence on PSI would be limited to Greece. On the contrary, the introduction of PSI as a general principle without clearly ring-fencing Greece, encouraged market panic. The contagion immediately spread to all southern countries; the country default spreads (CDS) became the daily measure of everything European; banks (where household savings are parked in Europe, and which in turn invest a large part of these resources into government bonds) were stuck in a vicious circle with a threat of depreciated portfolios. In an attempt to quickly fix their balance sheets, banks restricted their credits to the economy. Coming on top of fiscal austerity measures initiated by the governments, the credit squeeze pushed many economies into recession. Despite the fiscal consolidation measures, a declining GDP worsened the debt-to-GDP ratios. Credit ratings were finally downgraded for some countries, such as France and Austria, which, like Germany, until then seemed not to be mired in the worst of the crisis. In the autumn of 2011, the G-20 summit in Cannes—where national leaders were supposed to discuss the major problems of the world— was instead completely overshadowed by the intricacies and uncertainties of the eurozone crisis.

Did the Eurozone Emerge from This Vicious Circle?

Facing the abyss, the European Council, for the first time since the beginning of the debt crisis, took decisive and forward-looking action in December 2011, and the ECB forcefully backed its decisions. The ECB started by providing banks with huge refinancing funds with medium-term maturity. That move quickly eased financing conditions for the southern countries in the first quarter of 2012. The governments adopted a new "fiscal compact" that would significantly increase the power of Brussels to enforce fiscal discipline. A permanent financial institution, the European Stability Mechanism (ESM), was added to the temporary EFSF and endowed with greater power. A second Greek deal was successfully concluded; it was the largest haircut on privately held debt in history, in terms of the amount involved. But Chancellor Merkel clearly stated that Greece was "unique" and that "one euro was worth 100 cents." Plans for institutionalizing future PSI were temporarily shelved.

All of these initiatives and declarations were proof that the heads of states and governments had finally taken the measure of the crisis, had assessed the costs and benefits of different options, and had concluded that they would stick to the single currency and also keep Greece in the eurozone. The Council asked for a report to the "four presidents" (the presidents of the European Council, the European Commission, the Eurogroup, and the ECB) to design a plan that would create a better functioning monetary union. In June 2012, the Council adopted proposals that are known as the "four unions": a fiscal union, a banking union, an economic union, and a political union. Political "will" seemed to have been decisively formulated. And these political decisions were quickly followed up when ECB President Mario Draghi declared in July "The ECB is ready to do whatever it takes to preserve the euro." He added, "And believe me, it will be enough!" This was the announcement of the Outright Market Transactions (OMT) program committing the ECB to buying sufficient amounts of distressed sovereign debt in the secondary market to limit sovereign debt spreads to sustainable levels. This signaled possible massive intervention by the ECB in the sovereign debt market, in addition to the medium-term liquidity already provided to the banks. The markets had hoped for such a decision for months. The financial press had been asking over and over: "When will the ECB decide to use a big bazooka?" This declaration became the turning point in the evolution of the debt crisis. It is of course not in the power of the ECB alone to take responsibility for rescuing the single currency "at any cost": such a choice clearly lies in the hands of democratically elected officials. It took two years for the heads of states and governments to come to an explicit decision on this issue of vital importance to eurozone citizens. But once they had asserted their political will, it was the responsibility of the ECB and its president to do "whatever it takes" to make the project a reality. The ECB proved itself to be up to its task.

The acute debt crisis faded from sight during the months following the September 2012 meeting of the ECB board (the power of the declaration of intent proved sufficient; the ECB did not have to make any actual OMT purchases). In hindsight, it is now clear that the Greek haircut, which was politically unavoidable and no doubt helped send a necessary message to reckless private lenders, should have been accompanied from the very beginning with the credible "Believe me; it will be enough!" commitment from an ECB empowered by the Eurogroup to draw a clear and powerful line *separating* Greece from the other crisis countries. When managing a debt crisis, the key to success is to be decisive and rapid when restructuring has become unavoidable, as it was in the case of Greece, and just as decisive and quick in building a huge protective wall around that part of the debt that can be preserved from restructuring. Eurozone leaders built that wall two years too late, with the delay having led to huge social costs. While some "pressure" on the countries in crisis to move ahead with fiscal consolidation and structural reforms may have been necessary, it is doubtful that the size of these social costs was required, let alone desirable. On the contrary, it may be argued that the social costs made, and continue to make, it more difficult to pursue vigorous structural reforms.

The fading away of the acute debt crisis and the welcome signs of recovery in the eurozone do not imply that the path ahead is clear of dangers or that the deeper issues surrounding the successful functioning of the monetary union have been resolved—far from it. Europe and the eurozone are going through a deep "existential crisis" with huge social problems in the southern countries, a steep decline in public support for the European institutions, and difficult unanswered questions as to how the wider EU can relate to the smaller eurozone. Moreover, now (late 2013) that the acute crisis has receded, European leaders seem much more reluctant to implement the four unions they committed themselves to at the critical moment described above. At the time, they allowed the powerful OMT-related declaration of the ECB and promised a real banking union. But now there seems to be diminishing resolve to act with any urgency. The partial steps agreed to in late 2013 on the banking union are a step forward but fall short of what had been announced initially.

If the intragovernmental process fails to support the ECB in its new role as bank supervisor, a new crisis could develop. The bank stress tests that the ECB has launched are a typical—and worrisome—example. If the stress tests are to be serious and tough, which they should be, there will have to be resources for bank resolution to kick in for the banks that fail these tests. The political leaders must guarantee this. Otherwise they would repeat their "Greek mistake": questioning the value of some private assets without a commensurate public guarantee for similar types of assets that should be safe. Much remains to be done after the first difficult and socially very costly victory of the eurozone. The future of Europe remains at stake. This is what the essays in this book, written during 2013, the year before the European Parliament elections of May 2014, focus on.

Country and Sector Perspectives

The following chapters describe the crisis from the perspective of individual countries as well as from the perspective of broad policy areas, such as financial sector policies and social policies. The concluding chapter discusses the possibility of a renewed vision for the European Union in the 2020s, which would accommodate the need for greater political integration in the eurozone, with continued membership in the larger European Union of countries such as the United Kingdom (but others as well) that are not members of the monetary union and do not want the degree of sovereignty sharing that will be required in the eurozone.

Michael Mitsopoulos and Theodore Pelagidis, the authors of chapter 2, attribute the causes of the prolonged economic crisis in Greece and the continued deep economic hardship to the faulty design as well as the slow implementation of the stabilization and reform programs. They argue that the "troika" (the IMF, the ECB, and the European Commission) made a bad scenario even worse. They provide a detailed analysis of why some key initiatives have been counterproductive. Austerity measures were heavily skewed toward the types of indirect tax increases with high negative multiplier effects; these tax increases were front-loaded, while expenditure control was either postponed or not fully implemented; labor market reforms were enacted in a way that increased unemployment, while little was done to increase administrative efficiency or to implement product market liberalization or reform monopolistic market structures that were stifling competitive forces in the economy.

The "internal devaluation" was forced on the productive sector (which forms the tax base), while the root causes of Greece's problems—the profligate and weak bureaucracy and a dysfunctional political system—were shielded from the programs. The authors argue that this strategy of "least resistance"— being soft with the Greek government and private rent earners, and harsh with the productive private sector and the society as a whole—led to design flaws. There were no significant growth-oriented structural reforms focusing on product markets and oligopolistic market behavior or on the structure and quality of public expenditures. The "strategy of least resistance" exacerbated existing problems and compounded the challenges for a recovery: the competitive parts of the private sector weakened, the tax base shrank with high unemployment and business closures, the productive capacity of the economy eroded, and the prospect for political instability and unpredictability increased during the 2010–12 period. Looking ahead, Mitsopoulos and Pelagidis suggest that any appreciable and sustainable Greek economic recovery desperately requires a rebalancing of the policy priorities, with greater focus on product markets, support of sectors with competitive potential, changes in the structure of public expenditures and an even-handed public administration. Greece's international partners can play a crucial role in holding the Greek government to such a rebalanced set of commitments and in offering continued conditional but strong support that is needed to prevent any reemergence of redenomination (euro exit) risk.

In chapter 3, Angel Pascual-Ramsay tracks the Spanish economy through its remarkable riches-to-rags saga within the span of a decade. He identifies a comprehensive array of factors forming the structural flaws of the economy, in particular the steady and substantial loss of competitiveness over the 2000–08 period. In the years before the crisis, the current account deficit was increasing dangerously, with growth largely based on foreign financing of domestic consumption and housing construction. Toward the end of that pre-crisis period, far from being a miracle, Spain had become "an accident waiting to happen"; the global economic crisis in 2008 triggered the fall of the Spanish dominoes. A sustainable Spanish economic recovery requires a new growth strategy based on creating new long-term competitiveness. This would require persistent improvements in the education system and domestic R&D—both private and public. The author strongly supports comprehensive fiscal and public sector reforms. He cautions, though, that the recent increase in revenues through tax reform, while overdue, cannot go much further. A decline in government expenditure and efficiency improvements in the public sector—by streamlining administrative structures and strengthening independent regulatory institutions—offer greater promise in the long run. He recommends continuing with ongoing reforms in the labor market and in the financial sector.

Spain exhibited a spectacular turnaround in its current account balance over the 2011–13 period, running a small surplus in 2013. This positive development should not give way to new substantial deficits, as and when economic growth resumes. Spain requires continued emphasis on the production of tradable goods. Pascual-Ramsay concedes that recovery driven by remedying structural problems and developing a new growth strategy will be gradual, time-consuming, and with limited room for maneuver. Countries in the EMU with fiscal flexibility and large current account surpluses should facilitate overall rebalancing and adjustment in the EMU by stimulating their own domestic demand. The EU and EMU have critical facilitating roles as "external reformers" in this process. He argues that since the fortunes of the EMU and Spain are intertwined, Spain and the eurozone ought to strike a grand bargain: in return for Spain's strong commitment to structural reforms, guaranteed by the transfer of more economic policymaking powers to the EU, it would get additional time to reduce its fiscal deficit, with a continuation of the contingent ECB guarantee through the OMT program, and a credible commitment to transition to greater fiscal and economic union in the eurozone. The challenge for the Spanish economy is to make deep structural reforms that are decisive enough to free the country from its current economic doldrums, and yet not so drastic as to trigger economic upheaval and political chaos. If the EU and the Spanish government are prepared (and able) to cooperate, Spain could prove one of the major keys to dispelling the lingering doubts about the future of EMU.

In chapter 4, Domenico Lombardi and Luigi Paganetto offer a cautiously optimistic assessment of Italian attempts to stimulate an economic recovery. The bad news in this regard is that the economic crisis is structural in nature and is not amenable to a "quick fix." The good news is that policymakers seem to have taken the measure of the situation and have begun looking beyond one-shot fiscal adjustments to policies that can remedy the deeply anchored structural deficiencies. The authors cite detailed data to suggest that the current economic crisis in Italy stems from the absence of productivity gains for more than a decade before the global financial crisis of 2008. The global financial crisis triggered a massive economic slide, because the foundations of stability and competitiveness had already eroded. For example, despite steadily improving fiscal flows since joining the eurozone, Italy still had a stock of public debt above 100 percent of GDP in 2008. Slow growth made progress on fiscal indicators very difficult. The lack of fiscal space restricted the scope of policy responses to mitigate the effects of the crisis on the real economy. The fiscal consolidation measures that were initiated further reduced economic growth and worsened the debt-to-GDP ratio. Large tax increases, rather than ambitious and well-targeted expenditure cuts, led to large multiplier effects by depressing domestic demand, stifling investment flows, and raising unemployment levels.

The authors argue that the government is caught in a bind here: it cannot raise additional revenue without suppressing domestic demand, and it cannot curtail expenditures since large portions thereof are for social protection, pension, and health programs, which are growing as the population ages even more rapidly in Italy than in most European countries. This highlights the structural malaise in the economy: the lack of policies and investments in growth-oriented economic activity that creates and sustains market competitiveness. As a consequence, Italy has done much less than competing eurozone countries to exploit the opportunities of a closely integrated financial and goods market. Policies initiated by the government under Prime Minister Mario Monti had begun to remedy some of the deep-rooted deficiencies in Italy—in the labor market (that has the lowest efficiency among thirty-four OECD countries), in factor productivity and innovation (where Italy lags behind the average EU-27 levels), in efficiency of public spending (which the IMF contends is disproportionately large and inefficient), and in corruption. But the authors caution that these measures will require time to bear fruit. They also recommend some additional policy measures to augment existing initiatives. The strength of the Italian economy, they argue, rests on long-term growth strategies that eliminate embedded economic inefficiencies; additional short-term austerity measures are unlikely to foster sustainable growth or improve productivity. Policies should instead focus on improving the country's innovative capacity and competitiveness through reforms oriented toward structural and microeconomic performance.

In chapter 5, Jacques Mistral recalls that France, through the 1990s and into the early 2000s, consistently outperformed Germany, which was then perceived as "the sick man of Europe." The tables have turned over the past decade, so much so that, looking at France's fiscal and current account deficits of worrying proportions, *The Economist* recently wondered whether France was a "ticking time bomb within the eurozone." As the second largest economy in the eurozone, after Germany, France could be a driver of recovery for the region, or could mire itself deeper in crisis. What happens will be critical. Mistral emphasizes that the twin deficits are not the direct consequence of the eurozone crisis, but rather of policy complacency and the misplaced policies of the French government between 2000 and 2010—a period he calls the "lost decade." This period witnessed the steady and marked erosion of both non-price and price competitiveness of the French economy. This was masked by rapid global growth and booming financial markets in the 2002–07 period, but became fully visible with the crisis after 2008.

Looking ahead to the options and actions of the François Hollande presidency that began in 2012, Mistral approves of the new government's commitment to balance the budget by 2017. However, he disapproves of the mix of tax increases and spending cuts and argues that an over-reliance on tax increases with too slow an implementation of the spending cuts has lowered the efficacy of the budget deficit remedies. On the current account deficit, Mistral contends that restoring non-price competitiveness to invigorate exports requires a gradual and patient accumulation of wise and sustained investments in both the private and public sectors. The government until now has too frequently been perceived as fundamentally unsympathetic to private business. Nonetheless, Mistral explains that the Hollande government has begun to address some of the main hindrances to competitiveness, such as reducing labor costs and streamlining the industrial relations laws. Interestingly, the French government has until now enjoyed the continued support of the financial markets and has even reduced the sovereign bond spread between France and Germany. In brief, France is seen not to be in as precarious a position as some economists fear. But the twin deficits will take time to reverse, and the weakness of growth calls for more resolute action. Mistral also worries about the lack of political trust between France and Germany, two countries that have always been considered the engine of the European integration project. Restoring a good Franco-German partnership would be a great boost for the future of the eurozone.

Friedrich Heinemann wrote chapter 6 before the German general elections in September 2013. He argues that there is likely to be basic continuity in the policies advocated by Germany before the elections. At the time of his writing, the new government had not yet been formed. The pre-election German government's policy responses to the eurozone debt crisis have evoked strong negative perceptions in Europe and the rest of the world. The countries in crisis (and others) regard past German policies to have been guided by narrow national self-interest and an obvious lack of European solidarity. In contrast, large parts of the German population perceive the policies of the Merkel government during the 2010–13 period to have gone to the maximum justifiable extent, and beyond, in accepting financial risk for Germany and showing a willingness to compromise with the European partners. According to Heinemann, support for European integration remains robust from the grass roots of German society to the top of the government. Germany will not let the eurozone disintegrate. However, any (and all) German governments face some peculiar systemic and societal constraints that are typically not well understood by outsiders. These constraints restrict both the nature and the extent of German policy responses to any "bailout/rescue" of countries in a crisis and limit the room for maneuver in policy options and negotiations. As governments (and people and commentators) outside Germany underestimate these unique German constraints, it leads to misperception of the German policy position and its actions.

Heinemann identifies two key constraints in the design of German policies. The first is the Federal Constitutional Court in Karlsruhe. This court has been active in assessing the validity of ECB-guided policy interventions under the German Constitution and has refused to surrender its authority to review EU laws and agreements that affect German interests. The second is the perception of German academics and economists. On the one hand, the crisis has energized skeptics who have always doubted that the eurozone was ever an optimal currency area, and those who now fear that the introduction of eurobonds would render Germany a part of a "transfer union." The German Council of Economic Experts regards the existing eurozone crisis to be a structural malady that eurobonds or lowering the German current account surplus would not cure. They support a strictly conditional and limited financial engagement, with the debt redemption fund as a transitory instrument. On the other hand, the new euro-skeptic "Alternative für Deutschland" Party was unable to enter the German Parliament, having received less than 5 percent of the popular vote.

Heinemann's analysis has one clear bottom line, which relates to the hope that Germany will be willing to accept larger fiscal liabilities after the general election, or even open the door to solutions such as eurobonds. In light of the constitutional obstacles described and the clear position of voters expressed in the 2013 general election results, this would be an unrealistic hope, at least for the near future. Any future German government would face an uphill battle if it tried to push for joint and several guarantees of European debt, spending a lot of its political capital on a project with a highly uncertain outcome.

Heinemann is very clear on these limits to "fiscal union." He believes that *domestic* demand expansion and higher *domestic* wages, both long called for by most economic analysts outside Germany, have a better chance of being realized by the new coalition government. Recent developments show that there will be increasing pressure on Germany in this direction.

Chapter 7, by Douglas Elliott, is the first devoted to sectoral issues and is focused on the realization of a banking union that was endorsed by European leaders at their June 2012 council. In addition to being an organic evolution of the increasing economic integration within the eurozone, the banking union is seen as being at the heart of the recovery efforts. Its goal is to integrate regulation and supervision, provide a deposit guarantee system, and allow speedy resolution of troubled banks. Elliott scrutinizes the pros and cons of decisions already made in achieving this goal; he critically assesses whether the institutions involved are suited to perform meaningfully as a "union" by 2015; he explores some key unresolved issues, both existing and anticipated, that could restrict the potential benefits, or even derail the process, as this union begins to take shape. He offers suggestions for how some of these hurdles could be effectively overcome. The author lauds the central idea of a "banking union." It offers clear benefits for an economic recovery in the eurozone; it helps counter doubts about the continued viability of a monetary union, and it paves the path for efficiency gains in European financial services. In Elliott's assessment, what is planned is definitely an improvement over the existing system of loosely and informally linked national banking authorities.

The devil, however, lurks in the details of the design and in the implementation of the plans. Since creating and running this banking union involves different stakeholders with divergent preferences and priorities, and different entities with competing politics and ideologies, it requires difficult compromises and trade-offs. The absence of clear theoretical guidelines for making these policy choices adds to the complexity of the process. Elliott mentions the choice of the ECB as the principal supervisory authority of this banking union, and the necessity of restricting this authority to just the eurozone countries, as two illustrations of second-best outcomes achieved through compromises, when perhaps the European Banking Authority (EBA) with a jurisdiction spanning the entire EU would have been the ideal regulatory structure. A critical and recurring issue still unresolved is the distribution of responsibility and the allocation of authority among competing European and national institutions with overlapping jurisdictions while performing key banking union functions. The author presents a set of normative principles that should form the foundations for a robust banking union architecture (from supervision institutions to banking resolution mechanisms). He uses the same principles to evaluate the merits and shortcomings of alternatives and to offer thoughtful recommendations. The desirability of a banking union is settled; the chapter lays out guidelines to help policymakers create the most effective set of institutions that realizes the constructive potential of such a union.

In chapter 8, Jacques Mistral focuses on social policies. He first emphasizes the surprising history of convergence of social conditions in Europe, with the exception of the United Kingdom, before the crisis. There was no explicit "European social policy": social policies remained fully national. However, looking at the *outcomes,* one can see a common philosophy and ambition at work, clearly setting continental Europe apart from the rest of the world and fundamentally contributing to the present European identity based on three pillars: a market economy, a political democracy, and strong social solidarity. Interestingly, the social insurance schemes in continental Europe were, before the debt crisis, more robustly financed than the taxation-and-redistribution schemes dominant in the Anglo-American world. The eurozone financial crisis has, however, become a serious threat to this process of convergence: the southern countries have suffered serious losses of GDP and employment, a brutal surge in poverty, and a dramatic deterioration of social conditions not experienced since the war years. As a result of very strong austerity policies, some of the policy measures taken by the countries in crisis are opening a new gap in social outcomes between themselves and the rest of Europe.

Mistral then investigates the logic of policy reforms implemented in southern countries. Are they preparing a dual Europe where the North would have access to social benefits from which southern countries would be excluded? Or are they, on the contrary, setting the stage for a convergence of social policies in the future (similar retirement conditions, equivalent unemployment schemes, comparable access to health care)? This is a methodologically difficult but politically central question. Based on available evidence, Mistral describes pension reforms as clearly directed toward a convergence of pension rules and parameters, making the eurozone of tomorrow even more homogeneous than it has been. The situation is less clear-cut with regard to unemployment and health care benefits. There is no macro-social indication of excessive "generosity" in the southern countries; but ongoing spending cuts in these areas have been driven by austerity policies. These measures could have future undesired consequences by increasing social differences among European countries. It appears that whatever excesses there were that made the existing social protection network unsustainable in the South have essentially been corrected. Presently diverging social conditions in different countries mostly reflect differences in the macroeconomic situation. A return to more convergent social conditions is thus based on a proper resolution of the austerity-versus-growth debate and an economic recovery in the southern countries. In this context, it would be wrong to force further reductions to the safety net in countries such as Spain and Greece; doing so would undermine confidence in the euro rather than contribute to a better functioning of the monetary union. On the contrary, consolidating the single currency now requires rebuilding a sense of sustainable social progress in the eurozone.

In a final section, Mistral explores what "Social Europe" could look like in 2025. Most policies would remain based on national preferences and institutions, but a much stronger eurozone framework would have been designed in order to make these evolutions coherent and compatible—both with the requirements of a well-functioning monetary union and with the vision of a common destiny on the continent. In addition to national policies, part of the social protection network (constituting, say, 20 percent of social expenditures) would be based on an extension of European competencies that could range from unemployment insurance schemes to measures to enhance labor market mobility, with special focus on an ambitious program that would pave the way for a better future for young Europeans.

The fiscal responses to the debt crisis in the Southern European countries have all involved some form of austerity. Understandably, no one was ready to offer their credit card to pay for the excesses of the past without a strong signal that they would not be repeated. Accompanying these austerity measures, however, the forgotten "Keynesian multiplier" came back with a vengeance: recent experience confirms that austerity has a strong negative impact on economic activity. There is, at least in the short run, nothing in a depressed economic environment like a "deflationary expansion." The degree of austerity, as well as the "mix" of fiscal policies adopted, further worsened the crisis in Europe and has both complicated and delayed the recovery. All contributors to this book, in line with IMF recommendations, propose a more gradual and balanced fiscal consolidation, with greater emphasis on reductions in public expenditure—particularly in the most inefficient parts of public sector/ government expenditures—reductions that would have a smaller dampening effect on the domestic economy, in contrast to large indirect tax increases, and would better succeed in lowering debt levels. What is needed is a more carefully designed policy mix that would be rigorous enough to have the support of Germany and growth oriented enough to avoid the risk of a Japanese-style lost decade. In short, the eurozone economy needs a Germany-supported and even a Germany-inspired policy mix, not a Germany-imposed across-the-board austerity.

A common theme emerging from the chapters dealing with the three ailing southern European economies—Greece, Italy, and Spain (as well as France, which so far has been treated with benevolence by the markets)—is the gradual erosion of non-price competitiveness as a key driver in causing and prolonging the economic downturn. Restoration of better competitiveness cannot rely only on price and wage competitiveness, but it requires long-term investments—which require sustained financing for extended periods of time. That, however, is a luxury that these countries cannot afford because of their accumulated debt. Lagging competitiveness is also clearly attributed to the lack (or at least the insufficiency) of structural reforms in the past. The authors also point to a common theme of poor public management. In particular they point to inefficient government expenditures of which too small a proportion is in initiatives to generate growth and enhance competitiveness. So while there is scope for national government efforts to remedy these pervasive conditions, it is still doubtful whether they will have the capacity and political support to do so, unless confidence in future growth can be increased. "Structural reforms" are not perceived by most citizens as preparation for a better future; they are identified with increasing unemployment and reduced social protection. People in the eurozone will not adhere for long to an economic future painted just in somber colors. Beware of nationalist, populist reactions! Younger generations in Europe need a new political-economic vision that would extend into the twenty-first century the peace-and-prosperity promise offered in the second half of the twentieth century.

A well-functioning monetary union, in Europe or elsewhere, clearly needs a degree of coordination and harmonization of economic policies that either do not allow large imbalances to arise—the correction of which cannot be facilitated by nominal exchange rate adjustments—or provide for the possibility of fiscal transfers through which surplus countries can make up for possible shortfalls in private capital flows to deficit countries. A combination of both types of arrangements is probably necessary, with the need for larger fiscal transfers if or when economic policy coordination is not sufficient.

The macroeconomic equation is as simple as that, and it can easily be made more concrete: If Germany were to agree to reduce its current account surplus (close to 7 percent of GDP) by expanding domestic investment and wages, and were confident that this would not trigger a relaxation of structural reform in southern Europe, the southern countries would need less actual or contingent transfers from the North. Both—this type of macroeconomic policy coordination and the organization of some fiscal transfers—require a fairly advanced degree of sovereignty sharing, for which the eurozone countries were not ready, either in the 1990s at the creation of the euro, or in 2010, and still are not sufficiently ready for in 2014! This remains the most delicate issue for the eurozone if it wants to successfully exit from its recent economic troubles and achieve sustainable growth. Now that more fiscal discipline is the norm in the eurozone, now that more powerful tools are in place in Brussels to enforce this discipline, and now that the European Parliament will be endowed with more democratic supervision, the time may be ripe to move further in the direction of a more integrated eurozone—both in terms of financing, including the introduction of well-specified eurobonds, partially mutualizing some debt, and with regard to a more institutionalized economic governance of the eurozone. The eurozone already has a federal institution, the ECB, which has served the continent well. What is still missing is a strong European executive arm, a Treasury that is able to manage the large financial flows and the tricky political constraints that come with the integration of a continent-wide economy. The eurozone is waiting for its Hamiltonian moment.

The final chapter, by Kemal Derviş, deals with the need for such a renewed overall political vision for Europe that would make the Hamiltonian "leap forward" possible. His key argument is that a broad vision, and its political acceptance, has to *precede* the detailed institutional reforms and possible treaty changes needed for the Europe of the twenty-first century. Succinctly stated, the horse has to come before the cart, not vice-versa. Or, as Strobe Talbott puts it in his Brookings essay "Monnet's Brandy and Europe's Fate," the political "locomotive" has to drive the institutional and legal "train," not the other way round. The "Monnet method" has been seen as one where technical detail and economic decisions bring about or even "force" political integration. But the Monnet method worked as long as there was a broad and accepted political vision for Europe. It worked "within that vision" to bring about institutional change. A renewed vision is needed for the twenty-first century. And only if such a vision emerges and gains political legitimacy can institutional reforms really succeed. If the political process can generate such a vision, Europe can again embark on a path toward renewed success, and the crisis of 2010–13 may turn out to have been the opportunity for a renewal and the start of a new future.

PART I

Country Perspectives

2

Greece: Tax Anything That Moves!

MICHAEL MITSOPOULOS AND THEODORE PELAGIDIS

"I should note, as we have said before, the government that came into office last year was in a different position. There was no more scope for relying on revenue measures. It had to focus on expenditure measures and difficult expenditure measures. It did so, and it has implemented this program as agreed, and there was only need for a minor adjustment of fiscal policy to keep it on track"—Poul Thomsen, July 30, 2013[1]

Open markets with clear and properly enforced rules support competition and the growth of productivity. Recent works, such as that of Cacciatore, Duval, and Fiori (2012), now indicate that product market reforms can also create growth with minimal downside, especially in depressed economies. Their results seem to confirm the more intuitive suggestion made by Mitsopoulos and Pelagidis (2012) that product market

We thank Guillermo Vuletin and the participants in the Brookings-ESADE workshop in Madrid, March 12–14, 2013, and the Brookings–Robert Bosch Stiftung workshop and conference, Berlin, May 23–25, 2013, especially Kemal Derviş, Jacques Mistral, Javier Solana, Domenico Lombardi, and Karl-Heinz Paqué, for comments and suggestions on an earlier draft of this chapter. The usual disclaimers apply.

1. From "Transcript of a Conference Call on Greece," Washington, July 30, 2013 (www.imf.org/external/np/tr/2013/tr073013a.htm). Poul Thomsen is deputy director of the IMF's European Department, in charge of programs with Greece and Portugal.

reforms in Greece should have taken precedence over labor market reforms, especially since there is strong evidence that Greece has much to gain from such reforms.[2]

Furthermore, available research suggests that, for heavily indebted countries, fiscal consolidation through large and untargeted tax increases seems to entail more risks and fewer rewards than a strategy based on a well-targeted reduction of expenditure. New research and debate on fiscal consolidation have contributed both evidence and arguments. While discussions about the size of the overall fiscal multiplier have received the most public attention,[3] the issue of the composition of any fiscal adjustment effort also benefits from the insights provided by high-quality research.

Such research deals with (1) the definition of such adjustments, (2) whether announced or implemented adjustments should be assessed, (3) the timing of announcements, (4) the credibility of the announced policies, (5) the formation of expectations, (6) the composition and accuracy of the data measuring tax increases or expenditure cuts, (7) the qualitative details of both announced and implemented policies, (8) the level of government debt, (9) the perceived condition of the economy at the time of the consolidation effort,[4] (10) the evolution of interest rates in view of monetary policy, and numerous other methodological and conceptual issues. This increasing body of work indicates that the expenditure-control side of fiscal consolidation, and more significantly, the composition thereof (for example, expenditure items marked for government consumption as opposed to public investment), is of great significance for the success and durability of fiscal consolidation efforts.[5] The *World Economic Outlook* (IMF 2010c) empirically determined that spending-based deficit cuts had smaller contractionary effects than tax-based adjustments. And among expenditure cuts, those that reduced government transfer programs had a more benign detrimental impact on economic performance in the short run than did expenditure cuts on government consumption or

2. See, for example, Arnold, Nicoletti, and Scarpetta (2008); Conway and others (2006); and similar studies by numerous other authors.

3. See, for example, Batini, Callegari, and Melina (2012); Delong and Summers (2012); Blanchard and Leigh (2012, 2013); and European Commission (2012).

4. See Taylor (2013).

5. See, among others, Alesina (2010); Alesina, Favero, and Giavazzi (2012); Alesina and Ardagna (2012); Auerbach and Gorodnichenko (2012); ECB (2009, 2010); Guichard and others (2007); IMF (2010a); and Tsibouris and others (2006).

investment of matching magnitude.[6] In contrast, revenue increasing austerity achieved by increasing indirect taxes has markedly large immediate and secondary costs.[7]

This chapter investigates the effectiveness of the policy prescription as suggested and approved by the official lenders of the Greek government (the "troika," consisting of the European Central Bank (ECB), the International Monetary Fund (IMF), and the European Commission (EC), as well as its implementation by the Greek government. We do not argue that measures to increase tax revenue should not have been part of the program; despite available research indicating the negative impact of tax increases on GDP, Greece's government debt and fiscal deficit was so high by 2009 (see appendix tables A-5 and A-6) that it could not have been tackled except through a combination of both cost-cutting and revenue-increasing measures. In addition, in some areas, such as recurring property taxes, the personal income taxes, and consumption taxes when adjusted for the composition of GDP, data made available by the Organization for Economic Cooperation and Development (OECD) and the European Commission Tax Database (ECTD) clearly suggested scope for revenue increases. We focus instead on (1) the implemented policy mix between revenue increases and expenditure cuts and (2) the role of growth-enhancing structural reforms in both the business environment and crucial network industries on the one hand, and reforms in the private sector labor market on the other. Our goal is to determine whether the priority given to tax increases and labor market deregulation, and the relative neglect of targeted expenditure-cutting and growth-enhancing structural reforms, is responsible for the failure of the troika to anticipate the depth and length of the recession in Greece. The deep recession, the recurrence of uncertainty about the sustainability of Greek debt and, more important, whether Greece can return to growth stem from that failure. And it has resulted in multiple revisions of the program.

In the following section we address the implementation of the agreed program of reforms and fiscal measures (the "conditionality program") that was

---

6. See IMF (2010c, chap. 3) for a discussion on the mechanism of the differential effects of spending-based versus tax-based fiscal consolidation programs and their impact of output and unemployment in the short and long run. It, however, also points to some special implications for countries in a monetary union, such as Greece, where the adverse effect of expenditure cuts would be larger.

7. See Riera-Crichton, Vegh, and Vuletin (2012) for a discussion on the effects of direct and indirect taxes on output through their respective associated tax multipliers.

part of the official assistance that the Greek government received from the troika. In particular, we investigate the fiscal consolidation since 2010 and how it failed to maintain balance between spending cuts and tax increases that had been initially agreed to.

In the next section we focus on producer prices, using concrete evidence indicating how heavy taxation and the lack of substantial growth-enhancing reforms have impeded growth, especially in the export manufacturing sectors.

We next discuss incomes and consumer prices, before and after taxation. As in the preceding section, we pay particular attention to data supporting the arguments that (1) the fall of incomes and asset values (termed "internal devaluation"), which was a policy priority for the troika, did not lead to the expected increase in competitiveness, because of price increases due to taxation and the lack of reforms in product markets, and (2) uneven implementation of this "internal devaluation" in the productive sector resulted in a dramatic 23 percent fall in GDP (including in 2013) and thus eroded the tax base.

In the final section we offer policy guidelines for Greece and other EU member states that face similar challenges.

The Conditionality Program: Spending Cuts versus Revenue Increases

At the center of the criticism of the austerity measures imposed on Greece by the troika was their initial emphasis on tax increases, and less on cost-cutting measures that could have increased the non-wage competitiveness of the productive sector. Making things worse, an item-by-item comparison of those initial measures and the measures taken by the Greek government shows that the implementation of the conditionality program emphasized increasing revenue rather than cutting costs (see table 2-1), especially since the numbers initially budgeted did not reflect the recessionary impact of the implemented policy mix. Much of the cost cutting in 2010 reflected simply the dropping of large expenditure items of 2009 by both the outgoing and the incoming governments in pursuit of their respective political agendas. Thus, as the crisis hit, fiscal consolidation in Greece was not "expenditure driven," as is often erroneously claimed: rather the expenditure cuts of 2010 and 2011, compared with the benchmark year 2009, were, for the most part, accomplished by simply avoiding the extraordinary expenditures of 2008, and especially 2009.

The rush to implement a front-loaded approach to increase revenue, and a reluctance to cut costs, can be seen again in the Medium Term Fiscal Strategy (MTFS) adopted in late June 2011 (see table 2-2). The MTFS had to be

Table 2-1. *Fiscal Measures Foreseen by the Memorandum of Understanding (MOU) and Measures Actually Implemented by the Greek Government*

Fiscal measures that apply from January 2010	2010	2011	2012	2013	2014
A. Government revenue—budgeted increase					
According to MOU **Total, million euros**	**1,250**	**7,150**	**7,975**	**8,050**	**7,000**
According to MOU *% of estimated GDP*	*0.5*	*3.2*	*3.5*	*3.5*	*3.0*
Measures actually taken **Total, million euros**	**5,886**	**11,763**	**11,713**	**11,833**	**11,033**
Measures actually taken *% of estimated GDP*	*2.6*	*5.3*	*5.2*	*5.1*	*4.7*
B. Decrease in government expenditure					
According to MOU **Total, million euros**	**−4,550**	**−6,600**	**−10,850**	**−11,150**	**−11,150**
According to MOU *% of estimated GDP*	*−2.0*	*−3.0*	*−4.8*	*−4.8*	*−4.7*
Measures actually taken **Total, million euros**	**−4,567**	**−4,754**	**−4,754**	**−4,754**	**−4,943**
Measures actually taken *% of estimated GDP*	*−2.0*	*−2.1*	*−2.1*	*−2.1*	*−2.1*
C. Measures not specified, and remaining to be specified later					
According to MOU **Total, million euros**	**6,017**	**4,617**		**4,200**	**9,950**
According to MOU *% of estimated GDP*	*2.64*	*2.08*		*1.82*	*4.23*
Measures actually taken **Total, million euros**			**3,117**	**3,117**	**3,117**
Measures actually taken *% of estimated GDP*			*1.38*	*1.35*	*1.32*

(continued)

Table 2-1. *Fiscal Measures Foreseen by the Memorandum of Understanding (MOU) and Measures Actually Implemented by the Greek Government (continued)*

Fiscal measures that apply from January 2010	2010	2011	2012	2013	2014
Expenditure reductions for which laws have been legislated as a percentage of reductions foreseen in the MOU	**100.4%**	**72.0%**	**43.8%**	**42.6%**	**44.3%**
New tax revenue for which legislation was passed as a percentage of the revenue increases foreseen in the MOU. For 2010, only those measures legislated after the signing of the MOU or those measures explicitly mentioned in the MOU, even if they had already been legislated shortly before, are added—effectively those are measures taken up to mid-April 2010. Numbers are given according to the sums budgeted by the Greek government.	*101.0%*	*164.5%*	*146.9%*	*147.0%*	*157.6%*

Source: Item-by-item analysis of MOU (Memorandum of Understanding) and central purser's office assessment that accompanies laws passed by Parliament, as well as official announcements and government presentations.

Table 2-2. *Revenue and Expenditure Measures in the 2011 Medium-Term Fiscal Strategy (MTFS) for Greece, June 2011*
Million euros

Year	Revenue	Immediately legislated	% of MTFS total	Of these, investment budget cuts	Expenditure	Immediately legislated	% of MTFS total
2011	3.095	2.882	93	850	3.650	1.553	43
2012	3.877	3.691	95	−500	3.004	1.260	42
2013	2.069	154	7	…	2.664	440	17
2014	3.153	809	26	…	2.783	415	15
2015	1.896	4	0	…	2.222	130	6
Total	14.090	7.540	54	350	14.323	3.798	27

Source: Central purser's office estimates of the budgeted impact of the measures legislated, where available, and alternatively government official announcements and presentations.

completed as part of the European Semester;[8] it remains a requirement for member states benefiting from the conditionality program.

Furthermore, when additional measures had to be taken in October 2011 to close the existing financing gap, which was caused by the failure of the administration to deliver the budgeted revenue increases, the Greek government again chose to introduce new taxes, in particular an additional property tax on top of the already excessive property tax introduced in 2010.

The delay in acknowledging the importance of cost-cutting measures as a crucial ingredient of success is particularly puzzling given that, from 1990 onward, both the technical reports and the IMF Article IV reviews for Greece that accompanied these technical reports consistently refer to the inability of Greek governments to control expenditures. These IMF reports also criticize the perceived preference of all Greek governments for revenue-increasing measures to meet fiscal targets. In particular, the IMF Staff Report for the 2006 Article IV Consultation stresses this issue; it refers to international experiences analyzed by the IMF staff that suggest the benefits of expenditure cuts. Furthermore, recent IMF research suggests an awareness, around the time of the engagement of the organization in the Greek program in May 2010, that expenditure control is an important part of fiscal consolidation efforts. The IMF also states that "Consolidation is more painful when it relies primarily on tax hikes."[9] It stated, "The findings also suggest that spending-based deficit cuts, particularly those that rely on cuts to transfers, have smaller contractionary effects than tax-based adjustments"[10] It adds, "[a] rise in net exports mitigates the impact of the consolidation on GDP in both cases. However, there is a considerably larger improvement in exports associated with spending-based measures than with tax-based measures."

In this research, interest rates appear to be very important for growth. The documented importance of interest rates does raise the question as to why Greek interest rates in the private sector, which have risen as a result of the large country risk premium that emerged along with the questions about Greece's future in the eurozone, have not been scrutinized more closely by the troika. In the past, acts and statements by Greek officials have definitely added to this uncertainty. Statements by European officials linking Greece's future in

---

8. The "European Semester" is a six-month cycle of economic and fiscal policy coordination within the EU, starting at the beginning of each year.
9. See IMF (2010b, chap. 3), "Will It Hurt? Macroeconomic Effects of Fiscal Consolidation."
10. See IMF (2010b, p. 113).

the EU with the poor reform record of successive Greek governments also did little to reassure markets even while debt sustainability exercises were based on variables that are directly affected by private sector interest rates.

One can only wonder why the Greek government never warmed to the idea that a balance between expenditure reductions and tax increases, as agreed upon in the initial conditionality program, was necessary to constructively implement the strategy of "internal devaluation" that the troika so vigorously supported. It is just as baffling that the troika expressed no concern about front-loading tax increases and postponing the cost-cutting actions in the program. Concerns about the excessive reliance on tax increases in the fiscal adjustment strategy appeared, really, only in December 2011. But even in March 2012, almost two years after the time of the initial agreement between the troika and the Greek government, there was no full assessment of the implications of the policy mix of the fiscal adjustment program (IMF 2012). The only clear reference states: "The focus of the program is therefore to restrain spending while strengthening the core social safety net. Social transfers will need to be better and more efficiently targeted so as to allow measures that protect the most vulnerable people in society to be strengthened. There is ample scope to do this: existing social benefit programs are unequally distributed and poorly targeted—for instance, 60 percent of all family benefits go to the 40 percent with the highest incomes." (See appendix figure A-9 for the sectoral distribution of general government expenditures in Greece in 2012.)

Producer Prices

Another major problem with the program was the absence of focus on product market reforms. Not until the fourth quarter of 2012 did the troika finally start to press the government to implement structural reforms in product markets and professional services and to cut waste. But the damage to the productive economy had already been done. The heavy emphasis by the troika on reducing labor costs in Greece, rather than reducing administrative costs and government-sponsored restrictions on competition, is puzzling since available evidence showed that the cost of wage-earning labor was lower in Greece than in any other European country, while regulatory costs and restrictions on competition were the highest among all EU countries (see figure 2-1).

The fact is that growth-oriented reforms never became a high priority for either the Greek government or the troika. In all of the IMF reports on the implementation of the conditionality program, even in late 2011, structural reforms are primarily analyzed with respect to the labor market, while reforms

Figure 2-1. *Gross Wages and Salaries, and Administrative Cost, 2003*

Percent

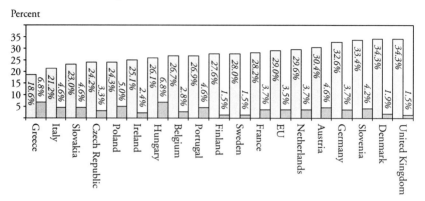

☐ Ratio of gross wages and salaries, all sectors except public administration, to GDP
▨ Estimated total administrative cost as percent of GDP

Source: Eurostat, 2003; Kox Report for the European Commission, 2005, based on 2003 data.

in product markets, professional services, and the business environment are always relegated to the last paragraph of the conclusions. Yet OECD econometric analyses of fiscal consolidation strategies, such as that by Cacciatore, Duval, and Fiori (2012), suggest that liberalizing the labor market in the midst of a deep recession, or even depression, can actually lead to a short-term worsening of economic performance. (See appendix figures A-7 and A-8 for overall unemployment and youth unemployment trends in selected European economies since 2000.) This seems to have happened in Greece, where the gains from increased flexibility introduced by labor market reforms had a less positive and immediate impact owing to the predominance of highly flexible self-employment and the low share of wage-earning employment in the cost structure of the economy. And it is useful to recall that during the 1990–93 period, amidst aggressive product market reforms, the government actually took measures such as the extension of unemployment benefits using the same rationale as Cacciatore, Duval, and Fiori (2012).

Indeed, labor market reforms will undoubtedly make wage-earning employment more attractive in the long run. And data from the social security fund of the private sector, Idrima Koinonikon Asfaliseon (IKA) [Institute of Social Security], already indicate that wage reductions and other measures to reduce personnel costs in the private sector are taking precedence over lay-offs in the wake of the reforms implemented since 2012. Yet producer prices conspicuously fail to reflect the fall in labor costs because the (quantitatively) more important costs associated with country risk, the numerous indirect tax increases, and other costly distortions introduced by the state have persisted and increased. Those sectors that contribute significantly to exports (like metals) have been hit by large energy cost increases (gas, heavy fuel, and electricity), which are entirely due to excise tax increases and government policies (figure 2-2).[11] Especially for the energy-intensive production of basic metals, where energy costs may exceed 50 percent of total production cost while labor costs are less than 20 percent, the divergence between the import price index and the production price index that reflects the domestic producer prices, both for the domestic market and their export activity, clearly demonstrates a strong disparity that can only be explained by the large increase in energy prices due to the government-sponsored pricing strategies and the high excise taxes.[12] Similarly, other energy-intensive exporting sectors, such as refineries and the cement industry, have also suffered. In 2011, exports of

11. Electricity bill A150 was increased 10 percent in mid-2008, and during the summer of 2010, an excise tax was imposed that increased the cost of electricity another 4 percent for industrial consumers. In September 2011, the excise tax on heavy fuel was doubled and extended to include natural gas. The latter was relevant because, following the clear incentives and policy guidelines given by the government in previous years, many energy-intensive industries had invested heavily in infrastructure that uses natural gas, and in some cases they had even invested in electricity-generating infrastructure that uses natural gas. The excise tax that was imposed on natural gas actually leads to a higher tax burden per calorie (heavy fuel tax €3.35/MWh vs. natural gas tax $5.4 \times 1.111 = $ €6/MWh LHV), and thus it led to an increase of €2.65/MWh or 80 percent on the base price of €2.65/3.35. In addition, contrary to the practice adopted in many European countries, large consumers of energy cannot negotiate separate agreements with energy suppliers, a fact not reflected in Eurostat tables that compare energy prices for industrial consumers.

12. Producer prices are also known as output prices. Although the short-term statistic Regulations (STS Regulations) use the term "output prices," in practice the commonly used term is "producer prices." The definition in this paragraph reflects the terminology used in the Commission Regulation 1503/2006.

The non-domestic price index shows the average price development (expressed in the national currency) of all goods and related services resulting from that activity and sold outside of the domestic market. When combined, these two indexes show the average price development of all goods and related services resulting from an activity. It is essential that all price-determining characteristics of the products are taken into account, including quantity of units sold, transport provided, rebates, service conditions, guarantee conditions, and destination. The indexes of domestic and non-domestic prices require separate output price indexes to be compiled according to the destination of the product. The destination is determined by the residency of the third party that has ordered or purchased the product. Output prices for the non-domestic market are further subdivided into output prices for products dispatched to eurozone countries and all other output prices.

Figure 2-2. *Index, Producer Prices, Manufacture of Basic Metals*

January 2007 = 1

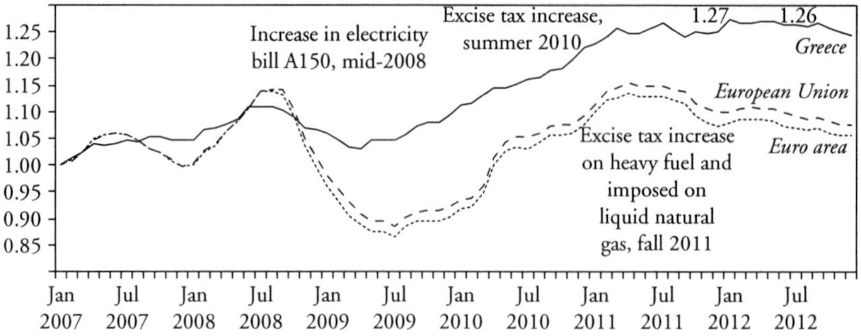

Source: Eurostat.

refined fuels exceeded 6 billion euros,[13] exports of metal products and cement were well over 1.5 billion euros, receipts from tourism were 10.5 billion euros, and receipts from transportation (largely shipping) 14 billion euros. These numbers highlight the importance of the export-oriented sectors that have actually been undermined by the implemented policy mix.

In figure 2-3 one can see how the producer price of electricity and gas has risen in Greece in comparison with the rest of the EU; a comparison of producer prices for energy (except electricity and gas) reveals the origin of the increase in this index.

Similarly, the impact of state policies restricting product market competition can clearly be seen in the Eurostat data for many product and service subgroups. For example, the producer price for bread has been affected by institutional developments concerning the blatant violation of EU law by Greece with respect to the operation of bakeries that sell pre-frozen bread. Under a new national law that continued to contravene EU laws, these cheaper bakeries were forced to stop operating, leading to the complete write-off of multimillion-euro investments in many instances. Even though the national law has now been adapted to the EU law, the product lines have shut down and the accumulated losses remain on the weakened corporate balance sheets.

13. Hellenic Foreign Trade Board, *Statistical Report on Exported Goods* (www.hepo.gr/portal/site/ope/menuitem.49d7d1e66f46c766e733a789c51000a0/?vgnextoid=0cdccfc567112 210VgnVCM100000d4cb10acRCRD&lang_choosen=el [in Greek]).

Figure 2-3. *Index, Producer Prices, Electricity, Gas, Steam, and Air Conditioning, 2007–12*

January 2007 = 1

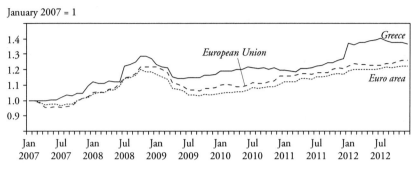

Source: Eurostat.

Consumer Prices versus Income

Greek consumer prices have been directly and disproportionally affected by the increase in indirect taxes. In addition to the distortions that increase producer prices, as reflected in related Eurostat data, one can see the impact of the increased consumption taxes by comparing the evolution of the Harmonized Index of Consumer Prices (HICP) for Greece and the eurozone, with and without taxes (see figures 2-4, 2-5, 2-6).

Goods, especially energy goods, are strongly affected by the tax increases, as is reflected in the Eurostat data. Food, including alcohol and tobacco, is also affected by the tax increases at the consumer level. It should also be noted that the remaining difference "with constant taxes" (especially for energy and food, including alcohol and tobacco) could be the result of secondary effects of the tax increases, which may not have been fully accounted for in Eurostat data. The fact that consumer prices do not reflect the fall of producer prices, relative to the eurozone average, even with constant taxes, demonstrates the persistence of the market distortions resulting from state interventions and the problems of scarcity and high cost of financing, the collapse of trade credit, and the increase of uncertainty in transactions between manufacturers and retailers. In addition, utilities such as water and sewage services, postal services, and railroad services, which are mainly state controlled, tend to have implemented above-average fee increases in spite of the crisis and the supposed determination of the government to reduce consumer prices.

Tellingly, the price of unprocessed food not burdened with the high costs that affect production processes (red tape, cumbersome licensing, and other

Figure 2-4. *Harmonized Index of Consumer Prices, All Items, Greece and Euro Area, 2003–12*

January 2003 = 1

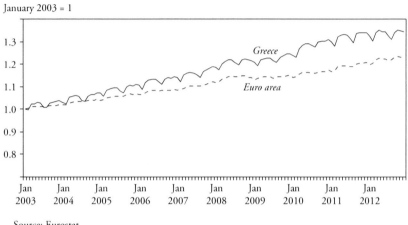

Source: Eurostat.

Figure 2-5. *Harmonized Index of Consumer Prices, All Items, with Constant Taxes, Greece and Euro Area, 2003–12*

January 2003 = 1

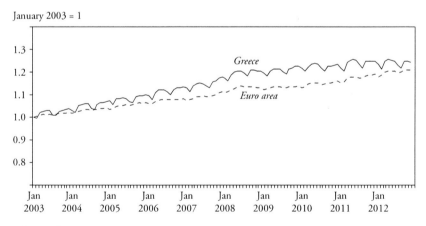

Source: Eurostat.

Figure 2-6. *Harmonized Index of Consumer Prices, All Items, with and without Constant Taxes, Greece, 2003–12*

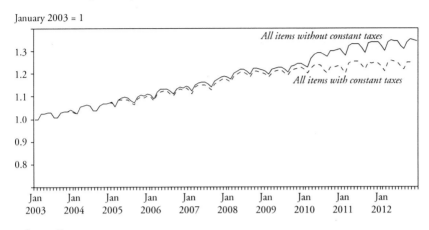

January 2003 = 1

Source: Eurostat.

costs associated with the hostile business environment), increased after 2003 at a lower rate than in the rest of the eurozone. This is even clearer from the HICP with constant taxes (see figure 2-7). Similarly, prices of non-energy industrial goods, which are disproportionally affected by the negative aspects of the business environment, have increased relative to the rest of the eurozone even with constant taxes, although this tendency has decreased since the onset of the Greek crisis (see figure 2-8). This fact—that Greek manufacturing has been at a significant disadvantage simply because it was harmed more severely by the failings of the business environment—was never stressed by the troika. Yet research such as that in *The Atlas of Economic Complexity* (Hausmann and others 2011) suggests the crucial importance of maintaining a healthy export-oriented manufacturing base with a pool of skills that permit a country to climb up the value chains, irrespective of the fact that Greece should take advantage of its value as a tourist destination, for example.[14] One wonders therefore, once more, how the troika expected the Greek economy to recover, and pay its debts, while the elements that have put its productive base at such a disadvantage were not only not addressed, but were also intensified by ill-conceived tax policies as well as the increase in the country risk premium

14. See also Bustos and others (2012); Hausmann, Rodrik, and Sabel (2008); and Rodrik, Hausmann, and Hwang (2006).

Figure 2-7. *Harmonized Index of Consumer Prices, Unprocessed Food, at Constant Taxes, Greece and Euro Area, 2003–12*

January 2003 = 1

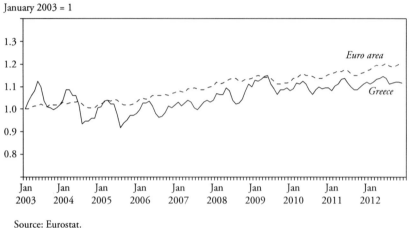

Source: Eurostat.

Figure 2-8. *Harmonized Index of Consumer Prices, Non-Energy Industrial Goods, at Constant Taxes, 2003–12*

January 2003 = 1

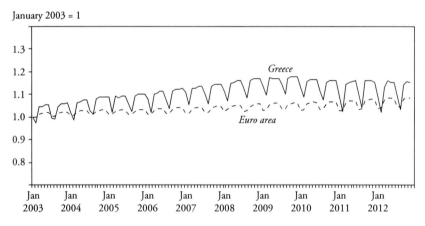

Source: Eurostat.

Figure 2-9. *Nominal Compensation per Employee, Total Economy, Greece and Euro Area, 2000–13*

Thousands of euros

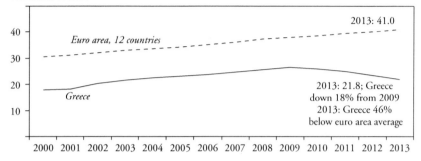

Source: Annual macro-economic database (AMECO), HWCDW series, European Commission. EU-12: weighted mean.

linked to public doubts by the European leaders with respect to Greece's continued membership in the eurozone.

The evolution of wages and labor costs with respect to benchmark years, such as 2000, as is favored by many analysts, cannot reflect the real issues that determine the competitiveness of a country. One reason is that, following a country's accession to the eurozone, "convergence" of incomes was a stated EU policy. Structural programs sought to achieve this convergence often with complete disregard of the fact that the inflow of large amounts of EU money in the context of weak institutions would lead to a "Dutch disease" in the country. Phillipopoulos (2001) explicitly worried about such a danger, and Malliaropoulos (2011) shows that unfortunately these fears were well founded.

In spite of the relative increase in unit labor costs since Greece's accession to the eurozone, wages and total employee compensation remained well below the pre-crisis European averages. By 2013, after the reductions that began in 2009, they were even lower. Eurostat data reveal that the average gross income of employees fell by over 18 percent between 2009 and 2012, and by 2013 was 46 percent below the eurozone average (see figure 2-9). Yet these averages do not reveal that detailed Eurostat data on wages for different sectors of industry prove that wages in competitive sectors, such as food and manufacturing, are much lower, both domestically and in comparison with European averages, than in sectors that benefited from state sponsorship and protection, like electricity production or water utilities.

Figure 2-10. *Employee Compensation, Greece, 1999–2013*

Billions of euros

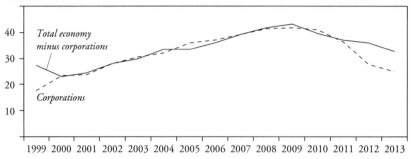

Source: Annual macro-economic database (AMECO), European Commission.

In the end, it is a fact that the internal devaluation "was pushed" predominantly onto the private and tradable sectors because of (1) the much larger decline in wages and employment in the private sector than in the public sector, (2) the lack of counterbalancing product market reforms, (3) the complete financial suffocation of the productive sector resulting from the default of the Greek government, elegantly labeled Private Sector Involvement (PSI), (4) the impact that official statements that cast doubt on the European future of Greece had on the financing of the private economy, and (5) the fact that the inefficient public administration, due to the multibillion-euro official support it was receiving, did not face sufficient pressure to reform itself while the private sector was suffocating from lack of liquidity. Therefore, it comes as no surprise that the corporate wage bill shrank much more than that of the non-corporate sector (predominantly the government, see figure 2-10). Looked at in one way, the "internal devaluation" was forced on the productive sector (which forms the tax base), while the root cause of Greece's problems— the profligate and corrupt state, rent-seeking private groups, and the political system—were shielded from an equally aggressive "internal devaluation" by the official support of the troika.

Policy Guidelines for an Economy in Depression

Nicoletti and Scarpetta (2005) and Mitsopoulos and Pelagidis (2012) examine the way product and labor market rigidities complemented each other, and how they reinforced each other in Greece until 2009. Unfortunately, this analysis still applies, at the time of writing, to crucial network industries and the business environment in Greece. The state is still restricting competition on a broad range of economic activities, creating rents, as defined by "public choice theory," and maintaining equilibrium among various interest groups and the political establishment that guarantees these rents. Thus, even as taxes increased and labor market reforms were implemented during 2010–12, under increasing pressure from the troika, the Greek government still tried to direct the burden of these reforms toward private sector employees, while shielding privileged groups, trade unions, and public sector employees. To be fair, one has to acknowledge that some progress has been made in the liberalization of product markets, network industries, and professional services. But since pressure by the troika was much weaker in those areas than with respect to labor market reforms and tax increases, overall they still fell short of what was needed.

It is hoped that the troika has now recognized the futility of pushing for ever more taxes and will demand more progress on the improvement of the business environment and the privatization program, for which they are now offering extensive technical assistance. But because this assistance still has not yielded any concrete results, the delay in recognizing the importance of measures to enhance growth may yet prove to be crucial.[15] Even if useful reforms can still be implemented—and given the social and political dynamics resulting from the devastation of the productive economy, that is now a big if—they will be applied to a devastated economic landscape, where healthy companies have succumbed to the depression of the economy, over-taxation, a high country risk, financial strangulation, and customer and supplier insolvency. In addition, in the context of the over-taxed Greek families that are unable to offer their traditional support to the unemployed young, the collapse of employment may lead to political developments with unpredictable results. Such events could prevent the implementation of reforms that could create jobs and improve cost competitiveness through an increase in the denominator (GDP) rather than the much advocated decrease in the numerator (wages), which happens also to be the tax base.

It should be mentioned here that exactly this strategy—to counterbalance the increase in taxes with cost cutting, privatization, structural reforms, and innovative market-friendly concepts like concessions for public infrastructure projects—was implemented during the 1990–93 period. At the time Greece was also on the brink of bankruptcy, but with the above-mentioned strategy

---

15. See "Transcript of a Conference Call on Greece" (www.imf.org/external/np/tr/2013/ tr073013a.htm), and in particular the quotation on the first page of this chapter.

the county avoided the worst-case scenario and the need to ask for an IMF bailout.

The Greek case is illustrative for others with similar problems. Thus an analysis of "what went wrong in the Greek case" may avoid a repetition of the same mistakes elsewhere. The experience gained in Greece can be hoped to have a positive influence in shaping more efficient policies to make "internal devaluation" work better, faster, and most importantly, with much less collateral damage in the future. The Greek case indicates that tax increases, and in particular increases in indirect taxes that undermine competitiveness, and labor market reforms should not take precedence in the implementation of a conditionality program, with the reduction of public expenditure and product and professional services market reforms left as an afterthought. On the contrary, especially in countries such as Greece, with obvious and significant failures of business regulation and with increased labor market flexibility as a result of widespread self-employment, concentrating predominantly on revenue increases and labor market reform will most likely worsen the depth and duration of the resulting depression.

On the basis of this analysis, we believe that the Greek reform agenda should include the following:

—Completion of the reform of business licensing, business park legislation, and spatial planning (currently about 40 percent complete).

—Completion of commercial trucking deregulation (currently about 50 percent complete). For example, there remain issues with truck fleets that are owned by companies, and market entry still faces barriers.

—Completion of the meaningful deregulation of professional fees and mandatory services (public notaries, lawyers for larger real estate transactions, and others) and thus consolidation of the significant advances already made.

—Establishment of working one-stop shops for company startups and gradual improvement in their operation (as the current complicated process still does not work well).

—Export facilitation mainly through administrative simplification.

—Rationalization of the complex system of fees that benefit third parties in numerous economic transactions and that increase costs, as they are effectively adding up at each layer of production. For example, when selling a sack of cement a fee of 2 percent of the value has to be paid to the fund of workers in the cement industry; similar fees apply to fuel and flour used by mills or even to the certification of a university degree, for which a small fee has to be paid to the farmers' fund.

—Rationalization of regulation and lowering prices for producers and indirect taxes in the energy sector.

—More aggressive implementation of the privatization program, emphasizing assets crucial for competitiveness like ports, and not assets such as gaming licenses that do not affect productivity. The good example of the Port of Piraeus should be used as a positive benchmark.

—Identification and implementation of meaningful structural reforms of the business environment beyond the usual benchmarks. A related project with the OECD needs to receive the maximum of political support and be nurtured to success.

—Meaningful tax reform that ensures effective tax collection without resorting to unfair and unreasonable practices.

—Measures that will facilitate the immense reallocation of assets that has to happen in the country. These measures range from the rationalization of the high and uncertain taxes on transfers of property and companies to the streamlining of bankruptcy procedures in a way that will facilitate the continued operation of companies that are basically sound but weakened by the depression.

—On the European side, two issues remain crucial and may contribute significantly and positively: (1) raising the perceived threshold of exit from Europe and the eurozone by making it clear that, to use an analogy, "if California does not reach an agreement with the teachers' union, the Valley will not be kicked out of the dollar zone." Thus, the productive base of the economy will no longer be the primary victim of the policy failures of the Greek governments; and (2) completing the banking union in a way that will ensure to a reasonable extent that capital that flows into Greece will not be "bailed in" for as long as the country remains in a depression.

Appendix. Selected Tax Measures Implemented in Greece during 2010–12

Abolition of several tax exemptions

Increase in annual estate tax, up to 2 percent of administratively set value, and then additional estate tax through electricity bills

Multiple VAT increases

New personal income tax with higher rates, lower tax-free income

Three successive tax increases on tobacco and alcoholic beverages and a VAT increase on non-alcoholic beverages

Further increase of tax on mobile communications—the highest in the EU

Three successive gasoline/petrol tax increases

Multiple tax increases on electricity, especially for businesses, giving Greece what are probably the highest industrial energy prices in the EU

Introduction and subsequent increase of luxury tax

Recurring extraordinary tax on profitable companies and increase in tax on dividends

Introduction and subsequent increase of recurrent extraordinary tax on high personal incomes

Tax on bank deposits and increase in tax on interest earned

Tax on television advertisements

Tax on violations of building permits

Green tax

Income tax on leased cars and private sector company cars (but not on official government cars)

Introduction and subsequent increase of tax on assumed income

Increase in train and bus fares

Fee to receive medical treatment in hospitals

Highest recurring real estate taxes in the OECD, and probably the world

References

Alesina, A. 2010. "Fiscal Adjustments: Lessons from Recent History." Prepared for the Ecofin meeting in Madrid, April 15.

Alesina, A., and S. Ardagna. 2012. "The Design of Fiscal Adjustments." Working Paper 18423. Cambridge, Mass.: National Bureau of Economic Research.

Alesina, A., G. Favero, and F. Giavazzi. 2012. "The Output Effect of Fiscal Consolidations." Working Paper 18336. Cambridge, Mass.: National Bureau of Economic Research.

Arnold, J., G. Nicoletti, and S. Scarpetta. 2008. "Regulation, Allocative Efficiency and Productivity in OECD Countries: Industry and Firm-Level Evidence." Economics Department Working Paper 616. Paris: OECD.

Auerbach, A., and Y. Gorodnichenko. 2012. "Measuring the Output Responses to Fiscal Policy." *American Economic Journal: Economic Policy* 4 (2): 1–27.

Batini N., G. Callegari, and G. Melina. 2012. "Successful Austerity in the United States, Europe and Japan." Working Paper WP/12/190. Washington: International Monetary Fund.

Blanchard, O., and D. Leigh. 2012. "Are We Underestimating Fiscal Multipliers?" *World Economic Outlook* (October). Washington: International Monetary Fund.

———. 2013. "Growth Forecast Errors and Fiscal Multipliers." Working Paper 18779. Cambridge, Mass.: National Bureau of Economic Research.

Bustos, S., C. Gomez, R. Hausmann, and C. Hidalgo. 2012. "The Dynamics of Nestedness Predicts the Evolution of Industrial Ecosystems." Working Paper Series. Cambridge, Mass.: Harvard University, John F. Kennedy School of Government.

Cacciatore, M., R. Duval, and G. Fiori. 2012. "Short-Term Gain or Pain? A DSGE Model-Based Analysis of the Short-Term Effects of Structural Reforms in Labor and Product Market." Economics Department Working Paper 948. Paris: OECD.

Conway, P., D. de Rosa, G. Nicoletti, and F. Steiner. 2006. "Regulation, Competition and Productivity Convergence." Economics Department Working Paper 509. Paris: OECD.

DeLong, J. B., and L. H. Summers. 2012. "Fiscal Policy in a Depressed Economy." *BPEA*, no. 1 (Spring): 233–74.

European Central Bank (ECB). 2009. "Experience with Government Debt Reduction in Euro Area Countries." *ECB Monthly Bulletin* (September).

———. 2010. "The Effectiveness of Euro Area Fiscal Policies." *ECB Monthly Bulletin* (July).

European Commission. 2012. "Fiscal Consolidation and the Economic Outlook." European Economic Forecast, *European Economy* 7 (Autumn).

Guichard, S., M. Kennedy, E. Wurzel, and C. André. 2007. "What Promotes Fiscal Consolidation: OECD Country Experiences." Economics Department Working Paper 553. Paris: OECD.

Hausmann, R., D. Rodrik, and C. Sabel. 2008. "Reconfiguring Industrial Policy: A Framework with an Application to South Africa." Working Paper RWP08-031. Cambridge, Mass.: Harvard University, Kennedy School of Government.

Hausmann, R., C. Hidalgo, S. Bustos, M. Coscia, S. Chung, J. Jimenez, A. Simoes, and M. Yildirim. 2011. *The Atlas of Economic Complexity: Mapping Paths to Prosperity*. Cambridge, Mass.: Harvard Center for International Development (CID), Harvard Kennedy School, MIT, and MIT Media Lab.

IMF. 1990–2009. Annual Chapter IV Consultations. Washington: International Monetary Fund.

———. 2010a. *World Economic Outlook: Recovery, Risk, and Rebalancing*. World Economic and Financial Surveys (October). Washington: International Monetary Fund.

———. 2010b. "IMF Approves 30 Bln Loan for Greece on Fast Track." Greece Program. Washington: International Monetary Fund, May 9.

———. 2010c. *World Economic Outlook: Recovery, Risk, and Rebalancing*. World Economic and Financial Surveys (October). Washington: International Monetary Fund.

———. 2012. *IMF Country Report* 12/57. Washington: International Monetary Fund.

Malliaropoulos, D. 2011. "The Loss of Competitiveness of the Greek Economy after EMU Accession." In *The International Crisis, the Eurozone Crisis and the Greek Financial System*, edited by G. Hardouvelis and C. Gortsos. Athens: Hellenic Bank Association. In Greek.

Mitsopoulos, M., and T. Pelagidis. 2012. *Understanding the Crisis in Greece*. Rev. ed. Houndsmills, United Kingdom: Palgrave Macmillan.

Nicoletti, G., and S. Scarpetta. 2005. "Product Market Reforms and Employment in OECD Countries." Economics Department Working Paper 472. Paris: OECD.

OECD. 2012. *Consumption Tax Trends 2012*. Paris: OECD.

Phillipopoulos, A. 2001. Comment on J. Spraos, "EU Transfers and Greece's Real Exchange Rate: A Naked Eye View." In *Greece's Economic Performance and Prospects*, edited by R. Bryant, N. Garganas, and G. Tavlas. Athens and Washington: Bank of Greece and Brookings Institution.

Riera-Crichton, D., C. A. Vegh, and G. Vuletin. 2012. "Tax Multipliers: Pitfalls in Measurement and Identification," Working Paper 18497. Cambridge, Mass.: National Bureau of Economic Research.

Rodrik, D., R. Hausmann, and J. Hwang. 2006. "What You Export Matters." CEPR Discussion Paper 5444. London: Centre for Economic Policy Research.

Taylor, A. 2013. "When Is the Time for Austerity?" July 20 (Voxeu.org, [November 2013]).

Tsibouris, G., M. Horton, M. Flanagan, and W. Maliszewski. 2006. "Experience with Large Fiscal Adjustments," IMF Occasional Paper 246. Washington: International Monetary Fund.

3

Spain: A New Quest for Growth

ANGEL PASCUAL-RAMSAY

Over the past six years, Spain has suffered a severe economic, social, and institutional crisis. A country that for over a decade showed impressive growth figures and came to be seen as a poster child for eurozone growth suddenly found itself mired in an economic recession of unprecedented proportions in its recent history. At the time of this writing in early 2014, the economy seems to be improving, having undergone some key adjustments and with growth and employment showing encouraging signs. Yet as we will see, the crisis in Spain is more structural than cyclical, and much remains to be done if the country is to put itself on a path to sustainable growth.

The Origins of the Spanish Crisis: An Unsustainable Growth Model

The global recession of 2008–09 crystalized a much graver crisis in Spain: the collapse of its unsustainable growth model. Between 1997 and 2008 the Spanish economy enjoyed annual growth rates above 2.5 percent of GDP for fifty-one consecutive quarters, growing 23 percentage points more than the accumulated growth of the euro area (Ferreiro and Serrano 2012). (See

I would like to thank the members of Brookings Institution's Europe's Crisis, Europe's Future project, and in particular Kemal Derviş and Jacques Mistral, as well as Guillermo Carlomagno, José Ignacio Conde Ruiz, and Angel Saz, for their comments and assistance.

appendix tables A-1 and A-2.) Yet this growth showed clear signs of unsustainability: it was based mainly on private consumption, which accounted for 62.8 percent of growth from 1997 to 2007 (Ferreiro and Serrano 2012); imports, which went from 25 percent to 41 percent of GDP, resulting in a change in the current account from a 0.5 percent surplus to a 10.5 percent deficit (see appendix tables A-3 and A-4); and very low interest rates that led to a massive, externally financed credit bubble, which in turn led to asset price bubbles, most notably in the construction sector, and excessive infrastructure investment.

This growth model would have been shown to be unsustainable even earlier had it not been for three seemingly positive developments that allowed the model to perpetuate itself and permitted necessary restructuring to be delayed. These three *positive external shocks* were: access to the European Union, which attracted foreign direct investment and opened new markets for Spanish firms; access to the euro and low interest rates (Fernández-Villaverde, Garicano, and Santos 2013), which flooded the country with cheap credit; and a massive increase in low-skilled labor through immigration, which supported low-productivity sectors, especially construction.

By 2007, the factors noted above had created a set of imbalances that made Spain "an accident waiting to happen": an extremely high and unsustainable current account deficit, high dependence on foreign financing, very high levels of private debt, excessive concentration on low-productivity sectors and tasks, and diminishing competiveness (Ortega and Pascual-Ramsay 2012). Excess credit led to asset price bubbles, especially in housing. When the financial crisis hit, it shut down the international financial and credit markets on which Spain was so dependent, resulting in a recession from which the country has just barely started to recover.

The impact of the recession led to an increase in public spending to offset the recessive effect of the credit crunch and the slowdown of consumer spending and investment. Together with a major decrease in tax revenues, the result was a dramatic increase in the budget deficit, from a surplus in 2007 to an 11 percent deficit in 2009. Although fiscal policy was reversed in 2010, there was such a large decline in tax revenues as a result of the recession that the deficit continued at over 9 percent in 2010 and 2011 and over 10 percent in 2012, according to Eurostat. (At the time of writing, the figure for 2013 was not yet known, although, according to the European Commission, it is expected to be around 7.2 percent.) When the cheap and easy credit disappeared, the supposed miracle of infrastructure development and modernization was shown to have been based, at least in part, on

Figure 3-1. *Divergence in Unit Labor Costs, in Selected EU Countries, 1999–2012*

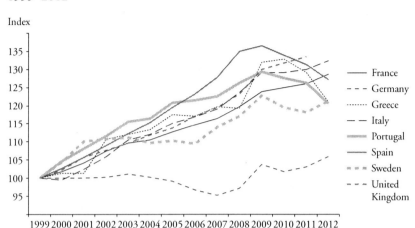

extraordinary revenues and unsustainable financing, a situation that had not been recognized by the government or private markets.

This deterioration of public finances converged with very high levels of private debt. Lending to households and companies by private financial institutions was 170 percent of GDP in 2008 (93 percent of GDP to companies and 77 percent to households). Total debt (households, companies, financial institutions, and the public sector) was 342 percent of GDP in 2008, and external debt was 168 percent of GDP the following year (1.7 trillion euros), as can be seen in the comparative tables in this book's appendix. This dependence on foreign financing and high level of private debt were all fed by the assumption that debt could be financed forever. The crisis shattered that illusion.

The crisis also revealed the lack of competitiveness of many sectors. Between 2000 and 2009, unit labor costs grew by 33 percent, while in Germany they barely increased (see figure 3-1). Productivity was also far worse than the EU average. Yet, contrary to widespread belief, during the previous growth cycle, high profit margins contributed more to Spain's chronically high inflation than did unit labor costs. From 1999 to 2007, Spain's annual average inflation differential with the eurozone was 1.85 percentage points (pp), of which profit margins represented 0.88 pp, with salaries contributing 0.30 pp and productivity subtracting 0.45 pp. (See table 3-2 on p. 57; also see appendix figures A-4 and A-5 for comparative labor productivity and labor compensation trends within selected European economies.)

The consequences of this crisis have been devastating for Spain, as reflected in three particularly worrying problems:

—A lack of growth, leading to an economic downturn that is more structural than cyclical. The country has experienced two recessions since 2009, with 2013 being the fifth year of negative or very low growth. In 2012, GDP contracted by 1.4 percent, domestic consumption dropped by 3.9 percent, and investment dropped by over 10 percent. The year 2013 is expected to close with a 1.3 percent contraction, according to the IMF (2014).

—Chronically high levels of unemployment: over 26 percent among the working population, or just under 6 million people; over 55 percent among youth. (See appendix figures A-7 and A-8 for overall unemployment and youth unemployment trends in selected European economies.) This unemployment is increasingly structural, with almost 3.5 million long-term unemployed, 1 million young people who did not finish secondary school and who will be extremely difficult to retrain or reemploy, and almost 2 million households in which no family member earns any income.

The combined effect of the foregoing factors has led to a severe deterioration of public finances. Public debt skyrocketed from 37 percent of GDP in 2007 to over 93 percent of GDP in the third quarter of 2013. The resulting cuts in investment and social expenditures have led to a profound social crisis, as well as levels of income inequality not seen in three decades and discontent with existing politics and institutions (Martinez 2013).

How Do We Fix It? Real Reforms to Unleash Spain's Growth Potential

By the end of 2013 there were some signs that the Spanish economy might be finally turning the corner; after nine consecutive quarters of negative growth, the country came out of recession in the third quarter of 2013. Yet the situation remains difficult. Despite the improvement in some key economic indicators and the positive impact of an apparently incipient European recovery, which has led the IMF to improve its GDP growth estimate for 2014 from 0 to 0.6 percent (IMF 2014), Spain's problems are more structural than cyclical, making any short-term recovery deceptive. The Spanish economy has serious deficiencies: an excessive concentration in low-productivity tasks and sectors, chronically high unemployment, high levels of public and private indebtedness, lack of competition in many non-tradable products and service markets, an inefficient tax system, low investment rates, meager research and development (R&D) levels and poor connections between the R&D centers and businesses, weak internationalization of small and medium-sized enterprises, an inefficient public sector, poor economic and regulatory governance, and a pervasive absence of entrepreneurship culture.

Furthermore, four idiosyncrasies of the Spanish economy are often misunderstood in policy debates:

—While unit labor costs grew significantly up to the crisis, corporate margins also contributed significantly to Spain's loss of competitiveness, a phenomenon that has received far less attention in the international press coverage of the origins of the crisis in Spain.

—A persistent trait of Spain's economic structure is the lack of competition in many non-tradable products and service sectors, owing to Spain's unhealthy corporatism and ineffective competition regulation.

—The main problem of the labor market is its "duality": the high proportion of temporary (not part-time) labor, which leads to low investment in human capital.

—The highly inefficient tax system results in a low tax base and low tax revenues; thus fiscal adjustment has to be accomplished primarily on the expenditure side.

Spain therefore needs to (1) complete the adjustment of the disequilibria accumulated before and during the crisis and (2) make serious structural reforms to unblock its growth potential.

Adjustment: Competitiveness, External Financing, and Fiscal Consolidation

Spain required a threefold adjustment. First, it had to recover competitiveness. This has already been achieved to a significant degree thanks to the steep decline in unit labor costs. From 1996 to 2008, productivity in Spain grew well below the EU average. Between 2005 and 2008, however, this trend started to change, and Spain has continued to improve, mainly through the loss of employment but also through the decrease in weight of low-productivity sectors, especially construction. Unit labor costs have also adjusted: in 2012 they decreased by a remarkable 5.8 percent over the previous year. In the last quarter of 2012, and for the first time in recorded statistics, corporate profits accounted for a higher percentage of gross income than salaries (46.1 percent versus 44.2 percent).

Second, Spain's need to close its current account deficit and diminish its dependency on foreign financing has also largely been achieved. Again, the current account deficit narrowed dramatically from 2008 to 2013 as a result of the drop in imports, increased exports, and of course the closing of foreign credit markets to Spain. It went from 10 percent in 2007 to 0.8 percent in 2012. In fact,

Table 3-1. *General Government Primary Fiscal Balance*
Annual averages, percent of GDP

	2000–07	2008–11	2012
France	0.1	−3.2	−2.3
Germany	0.6	0.6	2.6
Greece	−0.1	−5.7	−5.0
Italy	2.3	0.8	2.5
Portugal	−1.4	−3.8	−2.0
Spain	2.7	−6.8	−7.7
Sweden	3.7	1.6	0.2
United Kingdom	0.4	−6.0	−3.4
Euro area	1.4	−1.8	−0.6
European Union	1.2	−2.3	−1.0

Source: Eurostat.

in 2012 there was a current account surplus if energy was excluded. In the first seven months of 2013 the current account yielded a surplus for the first time since 1997 and is expected to have reached 1.4 percent by the end of the year. (See appendix tables A-3 and A-4.) Closely linked to this adjustment is private deleveraging, which is also progressing and declined by 24 pp of GDP after 2008, dropping from 170 percent of GDP then to 146 percent in March 2013.

This is the third adjustment: the reduction of the debt burden, both through private deleveraging and fiscal consolidation, the latter being the most daunting and controversial aspect of the management of the crisis. As elsewhere in Europe (and the United States), there has been a heated debate in Spain on the merits of austerity and on how fast the economy should close its primary fiscal deficit (see table 3.1). Economic history shows that the most efficient way to correct large debt/GDP ratios is through sustained growth, and current economic conditions in Spain are not encouraging for GDP growth in the short run. Deferring fiscal adjustment by borrowing at low cost in the open markets is not an option for Spain, and some fiscal effort is therefore required. But this adjustment should be gradual so as not to depress stagnant domestic consumption even more, as even the IMF country report for Spain of July 2012 acknowledged, following on evidence presented in the October 2012 IMF *World Economic Outlook* suggesting that fiscal multipliers may be larger than was previously assumed.

The fiscal consolidation efforts thus far have been insufficient. Most measures, such as payroll cuts, are, according to the government, only temporary. Revenue increases have also come from temporary measures, such as the two-year increase in income tax rates. If they are not made permanent, the government will have to find other budget items to reduce; either option will face strong social and political resistance. Most of the adjustment up until now has been in public investment, cut by over 60 percent, to around 2 percent of GDP, the lowest possible level to maintain existing capital stock. The second-largest cut was in public payrolls, to around 4 percent. The largest increase in expenditure came from debt service payments, which increased by over 70 percent and in late 2013 accounted for around 4 percent of GDP. Current expenditure, including pensions, health, education, and social benefits, increased by 2 percent from 2009 to 2013. It will inevitably have to be reduced, since investment cannot be cut much further if growth is to pick up. The reduction of the deficit will have to be achieved mainly through expenditure cuts rather than tax increases, since the Spanish tax system is highly inefficient and does not collect enough to finance current expenditure levels. The unavoidable expenditure reductions will be painful, since they will affect the core of public services and social safety nets.

In deciding how to most effectively make fiscal adjustment, let us first look at the composition of public expenditures and how efficiently it achieves its objectives. This leads us to the first of a number of structural reforms Spain must undertake: the reform of the public sector.

Public Sector Reform

The much-needed efficiency improvements in public expenditure and public administration can only be catalyzed by a profound reform of the public sector. Four areas should have priority: efficiency of public administration, efficiency of public expenditure, reform of the regional territorial structure, and good economic regulation.

With respect to the first, the two key issues are (1) wage expenditures and (2) the ratio of public sector employment to total employment. Spain's public sector is smaller than the OECD average when measured in terms of the number of public sector employees as a percentage of the total labor force. However, it has low productivity, at least in part because public employment is bloated at the lower, less productive levels, and thin at the more senior and value-creating positions. Thus, it is not size and expenditure, but productivity and composition that is the issue. The three levels of public administration— central, regional, and local—must adopt more effective management and performance assessment tools, developing a customer-oriented attitude and a culture of accountability to their users. The private sector should be involved in the provision of public services where it is effective to do so and does not endanger the public nature of the welfare state. Private sector involvement should be rejected when it does not provide efficiency gains; when it is driven only by ideological motives; or when it runs the risk of endangering afford-able, quality, and universal public services.

The second area ripe for an increase in efficiency in the public sector is public expenditure. Alfonso, Schuknecht, and Tanzi (2005) found significant differences in public sector performance and efficiency indicators in twenty-three industrialized countries, including Spain. This finding suggests a large potential for expenditure savings. The implications are obvious: any fiscal stimuli that entailed greater but inefficient public expenditure would have a limited impact on growth.

The third area for reform is the "Estado de las Autonomías," the decentral-ized regional governance model the constitution established in 1978, which has led to redundancies in administrative structures and lack of control on spending by the regional and local governments. Administrative structures must be streamlined, effective coordination mechanisms created, and the responsibility for raising tax revenues (and not merely for spending) developed at the regional level. There was a reform to this effect of the regional fund-ing system in 2010, and the Budgetary Stability Law passed by the current administration establishes deficit limits. These reforms, however, have led to criticism that the central government is imposing stringent deficit limits on the regions while being more relaxed with its own targets. Further reform of the financial arrangements underpinning the regional system is needed, and a number of proposals have been suggested to overhaul the regional governance model itself, not least in response to increasing frustration with the present arrangements in certain regions, especially Catalonia. But the constitutional amendment required for such an overhaul is a big obstacle, since the legislative process is extremely cumbersome.

Finally, Spain's economic and competition regulation and supervision must be improved, with particular attention given to strengthening inde-pendent regulatory authorities. Two newly created bodies, the Independent Fiscal Responsibility Authority and the National Markets and Competition Commission, are, however, not encouraging in this respect. The first, sup-posedly an independent fiscal authority for budgetary oversight in the style of the Office of Management and Budget in the United States, has been clearly politicized: responsibility for it is not in the legislature but in the Ministry of Finance, which will appoint its president, making a mockery of its supposed independence. Similarly, the structure of the newly created competition com-mission goes against prevailing best regulatory practice in the EU by creating a centralized single supervisor of competition, with area directors to be named by the executive, and depriving it of regulatory power by transferring most regulatory authority to the ministries.

Tax Reform

The Spanish tax system is simply ineffective, with overall tax income as a portion of GDP at 35 percent, the lowest in the EU-15. One of the reasons for this low rate is the inability to capture significant parts of economic activity, taxing instead other volatile items that are either not part of GDP, such as real estate transactions, or are unsustainable, such as the consumption and investment that led to a 10 percent current account deficit. This is evidenced by the fact that during the crisis fiscal revenues collapsed by 6 pp of GDP, from 41 percent to 35 percent of GDP, while one would normally expect the ratio to remain constant.

This thin tax base hampers growth by imposing marginal tax rates that are among the highest in the EU (52 percent; 56 percent in Catalonia). The corporate tax rate is also high, at 30 percent. These act as a disincentive to economic activity, consumption, and investment, distort the attraction of human capital, and create a significant deadweight loss. Tax deduction schemes are both wasteful and ineffective; while Spain had among the most generous tax benefits for research and development investment in the EU, private R&D in the country is among the lowest. Marginal rates are therefore effectively irrelevant for most large corporations, whose effective tax rates are among the lowest in the EU, thus punishing wage earners and small and medium-sized enterprises (SMEs).

These are crucial factors in Spain's current predicament, since they imply that with a proper fiscal system Spain's deficit could be significantly lower. It must therefore be a priority to incease tax revenues. Yet it is not possible to do so quickly in the absence of fiscal reform. Tax reform should entail, at least, simplification of the tax structure, a reduction of marginal rates, elimination of tax deductions and loopholes so as to expand the tax base, and tougher penalties for tax fraud. Some progress has been made already by the elimination of the homebuyers' tax deduction and other inefficient corporate tax deductions.

Labor Market Reform

Employment is the first priority for Spanish policymakers. It is a major problem on both the supply and the demand sides. The productive structure has been notoriously unable to create sufficient quality employment in the past

Figure 3-2. *Percentage of Employees with Temporary Contracts*

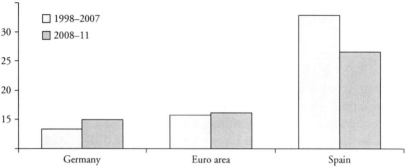

Mean of the periods 1998–2007 and 2008–11

□ 1998–2007
▨ 2008–11

Source: Eurostat.

several decades. At the same time, with a 26 percent unemployment rate, Spain's labor market is highly dysfunctional and susceptible to chronically high unemployment. Even during the previous growth cycle, after twelve years of continuous growth, Spain's unemployment rate never fell below 8 percent (see appendix figures A-7 and A-8). Thus, in addition to the cyclical component of current unemployment, there is a structural element. For this reason, labor market reform has been on the agenda of every government since the transition to democracy. The key objective has been to increase flexibility. One of the most relevant changes has been the promotion of temporary contracts (full-time contracts of short duration), by creating a two-tier labor market as a politically viable way of introducing flexibility in the face of union resistance. As figure 3-2 shows, temporary contracts are much more frequent in Spain than in the euro area, resulting in an insider-versus-outsider dynamic in the labor market, with strong protection for the former and very weak protection for the latter.

Yet, despite the high flexibility expected from these policies, the Spanish labor market has performed very poorly in the current crisis. Figure 3-3 shows the evolution in employment between 2000 and 2013 in Spain and selected euro area countries. Bentolila and others (2012) note that, although temporary contracts promote job creation during expansionary economic periods, they increase job losses in downward economic cycles. They also argue that job losses resulting from temporary contracts are even greater if the difference in termination costs between temporary and permanent contracts is significant, as has been the case in Spain.

Figure 3-3. *Unemployment Rate in Selected EU Countries, 2000–13*

Percent

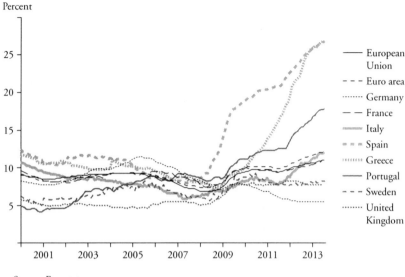

Source: Eurostat.

It thus seems reasonable to assume that the poor performance of the Spanish labor market during the crisis can be explained in large part by the lax regulation of temporary contracts and the difference in termination costs with permanent contracts, resulting in extensive use of the former. Bentolila, Dolado, and Jimeno (2012) estimate that better regulation of temporary contracts would have avoided approximately 45 percent of the increase in Spanish unemployment.

The 2012 reform aimed to tackle this situation. The principal goal was to permit internal flexibility by encouraging employees to accept salary reductions by making it easier to fire them. Yet there is the risk that employers will fire existing employees in order to hire younger and less-expensive employees and lose the accumulated human capital in the process. The availability of highly qualified unemployed young people has traditionally motivated Spanish firms to place employees in temporary cheaper contracts, and not to invest in human capital. It is still early to know whether the reform is working or having this detrimental effect, although toward the end of 2013 the pace of job creation was starting to pick up. However, the main effect thus far has been to depress wages, but it has not managed to decrease the high incidence of temporary contracts.

Collective bargaining was another target of the 2012 reform. The new labor law decentralizes collective bargaining, giving priority to firm-level agreements and facilitating the lowering of salaries when justified by economic reasons. This permits firms to adapt their labor costs to the market and to business needs. Termination benefits have also been made less generous. If a firm can demonstrate a persistent fall in income or sales over three consecutive periods, severance pay is twenty days per year worked, with a maximum of twelve months of salary. If economic reasons cannot be shown, termination benefits are thirty-three days per year worked, with a maximum of two years of salary. For temporary contracts, severance pay is eight days per year worked.

Employment protection is another concern, with OECD indicators showing very high levels of protection in Spain. But although overall employment protection legislation (EPL) may look high, it hides the large gap between temporary and permanent workers. Until the latest reform, Spanish firms tended to go down the disciplinary dismissal route, as courts were very stringent in accepting that dismissals were economically motivated. Firms were therefore forced to pay a higher severance pay penalty than they would have if dismissals could have been justified for economic reasons. Thus severance pay rose significantly. It is precisely this dynamic that the latest labor reform has tried to stop.

Pension Reform

Two factors make the sustainability of the pension system an issue of particular concern in Spain: the country's demographics, with a rapidly aging population and low employment participation ratios, and the worrisome state of its public finances. Pension expenditure currently accounts for over 10.5 percent of GDP.

As a result of this concern, this is an area where measures are indeed being adopted. The year 2011 saw the first major pension reform in years, when the government of Prime Minister Jose Luis Rodriguez Zapatero raised the retirement age to 67 from 65, and a minimum of thirty-seven years of contribution will now be required to qualify for a full pension. This new regulation is being introduced gradually, with full effectiveness scheduled for 2027. The contribution period was increased from the last fifteen years of employment to the last twenty-five years. This will also increase incrementally, with a one-year increase every year until 2022.

The government of Prime Minister Mariano Rajoy (elected in late 2011) has announced another major pension reform that will significantly reduce pension payments in order to make them more sustainable over time. It will

Table 3-2. *Inflation Breakdown, EU-12 Countries, 1999–2007*
Contribution to change, rate of annual change in percent

	Total	Salaries	Productivity	Profit margin	Taxes
EU-12	1.96	1.26	0.45	0.87	0.28
Deviation from the EU-12 average					
Belgium	−0.05	0.17	0.06	−0.03	−0.13
Germany	−1.13	−0.31	0.48	−0.33	0.00
Ireland	1.57	1.03	0.51	0.78	0.27
Greece	1.56	0.69	0.19	0.95	0.10
Spain	1.85	0.30	−0.45	0.88	0.22
France	−0.15	0.17	0.00	−0.20	−0.13
Italy	0.46	−0.14	−0.45	0.13	0.02
Luxembourg	1.26	0.35	0.01	0.81	0.11
Holland	0.64	0.65	0.32	0.18	0.13
Austria	−0.45	−0.22	0.30	0.31	−0.24
Portugal	1.13	0.66	−0.05	0.15	0.27
Finland	−0.55	0.25	0.44	−0.17	−0.19

Note: Total is the sum of salaries, margins, and taxes minus productivity.
Source: BBVA Research Department, from AMECO (in *Estudio Situación España,* March 2009, Servicio de Estudios BBVA).

have two main components: an "intergenerational equity factor" that links pensions to life expectancy, and an "annual growth factor" that links pension increases to cyclically adjusted revenues and expenses of the public pension system. Such a reform will bring Spain's replacement rate, the percentage of a worker's pre-retirement income that is paid out by a pension program upon retirement, in line with the rate in the European countries that have already conducted significant pension reforms.[1]

Liberalization and Competition

Spain has traditionally suffered from relatively high levels of inflation, to which corporate profit margins were an important contributor. In fact, during the previous growth cycle they were the most important one. Table 3-2 shows, as has already been noted, that between 1999 and 2007 profit margins contributed 0.88 percentage points to the annual inflation differential of 1.85 percentage points with the eurozone, compared to 0.30 percentage

1. See chapter 8 by Jacques Mistral for comparative analysis. See also comparative tables in this book's appendix.

points for salaries and −.45 percentage points for the decrease in productivity. Although low productivity and wage increases played a role in generating unsustainable unit labor cost increases and slowing competitiveness, since 2010 wage growth has been lower than productivity, making a negative contribution to the inflation differential, while profit margins have still made a significant positive contribution. In the fourth quarter of 2012, salaries decreased by 8.5 percent year over the previous year, yet margins kept growing. If profit margins had remained constant, Spain would have had the lowest inflation in the euro area (except for Ireland).

These high profit margins are in part the result of the low level of competition in many non-tradable product and service sectors. While domestic demand contributed during the boom years to record profits, the fact that in 2012 gross operating surplus grew by 1.6 percent while domestic consumption fell by 5.8 percent indicates that there is something more at play. The difficulty of firms in accessing finance is certainly a factor behind increased margins, which are the only source of funds to finance operations in the absence of credit. Yet even after five years of stagnant or negative growth, and with falling wages, inflation was still 2.4 percent in 2012—a plausible symptom of price rigidity and lack of competition in some key products and service markets. It has taken nine consecutive quarters of negative growth to finally bring about the substantial reduction in inflation observed in 2013.

In this respect, it is important to note the difference between tradable and non-tradable sectors. On the tradable side, the Spanish economy has been performing extremely well. Since 2009, export growth, in real terms, has been higher than that of France, Italy, or the United Kingdom. In the first half of 2013, exports grew by 8 percent. This gave Spain a ratio of exports to GDP of 32 percent, higher even than the United Kingdom. A key reason for this has been the increase in the number of exporting firms, which grew by 11.4 percent in 2012.

If the necessary internal devaluation is taking place in the tradable sectors and growth is still lacking, the non-tradable sectors must be inhibiting it. It is reasonable to assume that these sectors are not adjusting sufficiently because there is no competition, especially in the utilities sector. This is consistent with past empirical evidence, as well as with recent research on price collusion in the energy sector.[2]

---

2. See FedeaBlogs (Nadaesgratis.com), "La misteriosa caída de la inflación en noviembre," December 6, 2012 (www.fedeablogs.net/economia).

Lack of competition in the non-tradable sectors is thus a serious obstacle to growth in Spain. As Wolf and others (2009) have argued:

> More intensive competition in product markets tends to boost economic growth: empirical studies show that competitive product markets force companies to be more efficient and to increase productivity, a key component of growth in GDP per capita. Through a number of different mechanisms, including entry by new firms and changes in real wages, stronger competition in product markets may also have a positive effect on employment, another key component of growth in GDP per capita.

Not only does a lack of competition prevent new and more dynamic firms from entering the market, but it also affects the competiveness of the export sector, which must pay higher prices for inputs such as energy or communications.

Other empirical evidence substantiates the assumption that the Spanish marketplace lacks competition, such as the difference in markups in Spain in comparison with other economies. Estrada García (2009) has conducted such an exercise, measuring the level of markups over marginal costs as an indicator of the degree of market competition. The median markup for the seven economies studied is 22.8 percent, with Spain on the upper end of the ranking. Not surprisingly, the manufacturing sector has the lowest markups because of its higher tradability. As would be expected, the least tradable sectors, electricity and gas and services, are the ones with highest markups. Although Spain has ten sectors with markups above the median of the seven countries, four of them are the most relevant, since the distance to the median is substantial. These sectors are electricity and gas, transport, health, and personal services.

In sum, Spain is in dire need of liberalization in many sectors. In addition to its impact on prices, lack of competition is both a cause and a consequence of the poor dynamism in Spain's private sector, characterized, with some notable and growing exceptions, by low innovation, insufficient R&D investment, low investment in human capital, ineffective taxation (71 percent of tax evasion is estimated to be carried out by wealthy individuals and corporations), weak corporate governance, and, what is perhaps most significant, an unhealthy collusion between the public and the private, resulting in a corporatist business culture.

The tools for increasing competition are well known: effective regulation of competition, strong and truly independent enforcement, removal of barriers to entry, a reduction in the restrictive power of professional associations, less tolerance of the concentration of economic power protecting vested interests, and no tolerance of public and private collusion, especially of corrupt practices to gain administrative favors. All of these require political will; unfortunately, the highly political nature of the new competition regulatory scheme proposed by the current administration is not an encouraging sign for increased competition in Spain.

Financial Sector Reform and Access to Finance

The financial sector has been an obstacle to the recovery of the Spanish economy since the beginning of the crisis and is at the heart of a credit crunch that continues to be lethal to many firms. This reform must be completed in order for credit to flow again. The principal obstacle is doubt about the valuation of property assets, which many analysts think are still valued at unrealistic prices on the banks' balance sheets. Significant progress has been made in restoring the health of the financial sector, however; two major reforms forced institutions to raise capital provisions for doubtful assets, imposed the consolidation of the savings banks (*cajas*), recapitalized problematic institutions with European financial assistance, and transferred toxic assets to an asset management company (the SAREB).

Despite steady improvement, access to credit is still restricted. In 2013, credit to firms was at 2006 levels and dropped by almost 10 percent between the second quarter of 2012 and the second quarter of 2013. The fact that in Spain most credit is intermediated through banks increases the impact of this credit crunch. SMEs are affected in particular, because unlike large multinationals, they cannot tap the international markets. At the sovereign level, although the Treasury is able at present to tap international markets, it is completely dependent on the European Central Bank (ECB) guarantee. In any case, the salutary effect of the ECB's Outright Monetary Operations is unquestionable. Bond yields dropped significantly in 2013, and Spain's risk premium, measured by the difference with Germany's ten-year bond yield, dropped below 200 basis points for the first time since mid-2011.

Industrial Policy

Beyond the aforementioned reforms, the Spanish quest for growth will also require active investment. The "horizontal" structural reforms aimed at creating a more growth-oriented business environment must be complemented with "vertical" measures to spur economic growth. Spain must adopt an active industrial policy to channel national savings and foreign direct investment to higher-value-added sectors that have good future demand prospects and are capable of creating quality employment in sufficiently large numbers, and not to low-productivity sectors like construction, as happened during the bubble.

Such an industrial policy must have two pillars: (1) the "reinvention" of traditional sectors in which Spain has a leading position and that might yet have growth potential, such as tourism, infrastructure management (where six of the top ten world firms are Spanish), or textiles and (2) the development of new sectors in which Spain might have a comparative or competitive advantage, such as renewable energy, biotechnology, aeronautics, agro-business, or the creative and cultural industries (such as fashion and cuisine). Spain must also leverage the presence of Spanish firms that are global leaders in their sectors. Only with such a committed industrial policy can Spain hope to reverse the drop in investment in industrial activities, especially since 2009.

Innovation: Education and R&D

Probably the most important key to Spain's success in the long term will be its ability to innovate. Improving this ability will entail action in two areas: education and R&D.

Much has been achieved in education over the past two decades, not least in the number of higher education graduates, but much remains to be done. Cross-party national consensus is necessary to prevent each new government from adopting new educational reforms. This has been the historical norm, and it is extremely destabilizing for education, which requires long-term planning and stability. It is also important to align better educational qualifications with the professional needs of a modern economy.

R&D is much lower in Spain than in other developed economies. This is true for public R&D, but even more so for private investment. With some exceptions, Spain's private sector shows insufficient R&D investment and little innovation. In 2007, at the outset of the crisis, private Spanish R&D investment was just 61 percent of the EU average and 67 percent lower than the OECD average, while public R&D was *only* 61 percent lower than the OECD average. German companies invested three times and French firms twice as much as Spain's, even though Spain had one of the most generous tax deduction schemes for R&D in the EU. This low R&D investment is particularly acute among SMEs.

Education and innovation are intimately connected in the Spanish case. At present the instruments that enable innovation and the centers where it is replicated are accessible to a relatively small base of firms, entrepreneurs, and workers, thus preventing the country from deploying its full human capital for economic growth. This concentration of economic opportunities is in part the result of the excessive corporatism and lack of openness that dominates Spanish economic life. The country's overarching economic and social goal must be to "democratize innovation," to make the instruments that enable innovation more accessible to a broader base. In addition to breaking down vested interests through the fight against corporatism, education is the most effective way to change this status quo and unleash innovative power for economic growth. To do so, it is essential to make top-quality and experimental, rather than encyclopedic, education available to all who qualify and to improve professional training, including life-long learning and retraining, which are not sufficiently developed in Spain.

Conclusion: A Grand Bargain with the EU

Spain has an immense challenge ahead: to transform its growth model by undertaking deep structural reforms while simultaneously dealing with the effects of cuts in social expenditures that weaken the very social nets needed to make those structural reforms palatable and dampen consumption. Its room for maneuver is limited. Past episodes of internal devaluation have shown that structural reforms may produce future growth but do not generate immediate growth and employment, which is what Spain needs now. A less front-loaded adjustment would be preferable. The pressure from the EU and international financial markets to restrain public spending, however, has made austerity the priority. Spain is very much at the mercy of Brussels, Berlin, and Frankfurt, which still demand an austerity-driven economic policy. Although Spain has been granted an extension of the deadline for meeting its budget deficit targets, social cuts have already started to create social conflict, and disillusionment with the EU is growing.

Spain and the EU need to work together to turn this situation around. The European Monetary Union (EMU) and the EU will only be sustainable if there is growth in the European periphery, which will allow richer EU nations to overcome their fear of a dysfunctional monetary union in which they would have to finance the recurring fiscal deficits of the southern periphery. For this reason, it is in the interest of the EU to help Spain achieve sustainable growth. The EU and Spain should therefore strive for a "grand bargain": in return for Spain's real commitment to growth through structural reforms, guaranteed by the transfer of more economic policymaking powers to the EU, it would get more time to reduce its deficit, with a continuation of the ECB implicit funding guarantee while necessary and a credible commitment on the part of its EU partners to transition over time to a fiscal and economic union that would offer light at the end of the tunnel in return for so many sacrifices. Those countries in the EMU with fiscal flexibility and large current account surpluses should facilitate overall rebalancing and adjustment in the EMU by stimulating their own domestic demand.

The EMU and the EU have essential roles to play in this process. They should act as "external reformers," forcing reform on unwilling Spanish political and economic elites and breaking vested interests. This would help in unblocking barriers to enterprise and unleashing the growth potential of a country with a highly qualified young population and good infrastructure, as well as a dynamic export sector, a privileged geographic location connecting Europe, Africa, and Latin America, and world-class multinationals, all of which give it a competitive advantage to benefit from growth markets in Latin America and Africa. It will be a challenge, but there is reason for optimism. As in previous crises, the Spanish economy has quickly corrected some of the imbalances that led to this crisis. If the EU and the Spanish government are prepared to work together, Spain could prove to be the key to dispelling the lingering doubts about the future of EMU.

References

Alfonso, A., I. Schuknecht, and V. Tanzi. 2005. "Public Sector Efficiency: An International Comparison." *Public Choice* 123 (3): 321–47.

Bentolila, S., P. Cahuc, J. J. Dolado, and T. Le Barbanchon. 2012. "Two-Tier Labour Markets in the Great Recession: France versus Spain." *Economic Journal* 122 (562): F155–F87.

Bentolila, S., J. Dolado, and J. F. Jimeno. 2012. "Reforming an Insider-Outsider Labor Market: The Spanish Experience." *IZA Journal of European Labor Studies* 1 (4).

Estrada García, A. 2009. "The Mark-Ups in the Spanish Economy: International Comparison and Recent Evolution." Documentos de trabajo del Banco de España 5: 5–54.

Fernández-Villaverde, J., L. Garicano, and T. Santos. 2013. "Political Credit Cycles: The Case of the Euro Zone." Working Paper 18899. Cambridge, Mass.: National Bureau of Economic Research.

Ferreiro, J., and F. Serrano. 2012. "The Economic Crisis in Spain: Contagion Effects and Distinctive Factors." In *The Euro Crisis,* edited by P. Arestis and M. Sawyer, pp. 235–69. London: Palgrave Macmillan.

IMF. 2014. *World Economic Outlook.* January. Washington.

Martinez, J. 2013. *Estructura y desigualdad social en España.* Madrid: Catarata.

Ortega, A., and A. Pascual-Ramsay. 2012. *Qué nos ha pasado: el fallo de un país.* Madrid: Galaxia Gutenberg.

Wolf, A., I. Wanner, T. Kozluk, and G. Nicoletti. 2009. "Ten Years of Product Market Reform in OECD Countries—Insights from a Revised PMR Indicator." Economics Department Working Paper 695. Paris: OECD.

4

Italy: Strategies for Moving from Crisis to Growth

DOMENICO LOMBARDI AND LUIGI PAGANETTO

The current economic crisis in Italy stems from a period of stagnating growth and little progress in total factor productivity that began, it should be stressed, a decade before the global financial crisis of 2008. The governor of the Bank of Italy (2013) stated that the country "failed to respond to the extraordinary geopolitical, technological, and demographic trends of the last quarter-century" (p. 10). This is evident from the exceptional growth in other major advanced economies in the late 1990s and early part of the 2000s, growth that was absent in Italy.

From 1991 to 2013 the economies of the United Kingdom and the United States grew by more than 60 percent (see figure 4-1). Italy's eurozone partners, notably France, Germany, and Spain, experienced economic growth of over 30 percent. Italy's economy, however, fell well below the European average of 37 percent, growing by a modest 15 percent. Many members of the eurozone realized exceptional growth by taking advantage of the more integrated European capital markets, but Italy failed to undertake significant investments using long-term loans available at low interest rates.

The authors acknowledge comments on an earlier draft presented at the Brookings–Robert Bosch Foundation Workshop, "A Growth Strategy for Europe," held in Berlin on May 24 and 25, 2013. They also wish to acknowledge the outstanding research assistance of Samantha St. Amand.

Figure 4-1. *Economic Growth in Selected Advanced Countries*[a]

Index: 1991 = 100

GDP at constant prices

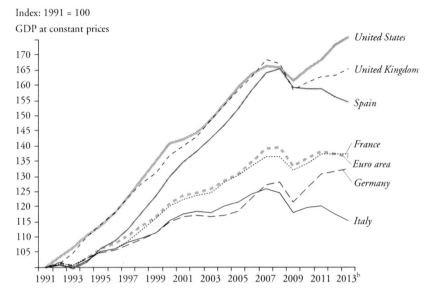

Source: International Monetary Fund, *World Economic Outlook* (WEO) database, 2013 (www.imf. org/external/pubs/ft/weo/2013/02/weodata/index.aspx).
a. Unless otherwise noted, all tables and figures that use data from IMF WEO are from the October 2013 WEO database.
b. Values for 2013 are estimates.

The global financial crisis emphasized the structural problems underlying Italy's stagnant growth and productivity. As such, Italy was hit particularly hard by the recession and is weathering one of the slowest recoveries within the eurozone. The country entered the recession with aggregate debt above 100 percent of GDP. Despite steadily improving its fiscal position since joining the eurozone, a deep recession in 2008 and 2009 caused a sharp increase in the debt-to-GDP ratio. After the implementation of austerity measures in 2012, further economic losses amplified by fiscal multipliers drove the debt ratio even higher. Debt-to-GDP is expected to peak in 2014 at 133 percent.

Fiscal sustainability should be achieved by implementing structural reforms that adopt a long-term strategy and that emphasize growth and productivity. Short-term strategies may encourage government deficits that hinder growth and promote rent-seeking behaviour. In order for the Italian economy to improve its competitiveness and adapt to economic shifts, it must foster balanced and strategic growth opportunities.

In this chapter we first review debt dynamics, the size of fiscal multipliers, and the effectiveness of the government's budget and consider the appropriate path to fiscal sustainability. Next we highlight structural impediments in the product and labor markets and finally discuss effective long-term growth strategies that improve productivity by expanding the stock of human capital, encouraging innovation, and deterring corruption.

Fiscal Consolidation Policy and Macroeconomic Strategy

As in many other advanced economies, Italy's public debt as a percentage of GDP skyrocketed after the onset of the global financial crisis. While other advanced economies—for example, Greece, Ireland, and Spain—experienced a surge in their debt levels due to large primary deficits in the form of fiscal stimulus, Italy has maintained relatively sound fiscal expenditures. This section explores the reasons for the deterioration of Italy's fiscal position and considers the appropriate path to consolidation.

Debt and Deficit Dynamics

Upon joining the eurozone in 1999, Italy's debt-to-GDP ratio was 114 percent, higher than that of France, Germany, Greece, or Spain. Italy's high public debt makes its fiscal position particularly vulnerable to downside risk in the rate of growth, inflation, and interest on public debt. After gradual improvement in its fiscal position, with public debt falling to 103 percent of GDP in 2007, Italy's debt-to-GDP ratio began rising again in 2008 (see table 4-1). A contraction in the economy by 5.5 percent of GDP was the primary contributor to the sharpest one-year rise in the debt-to-GDP ratio, by approximately 10 percent in 2009 (see figure 4-2). Despite the implementation of a consolidation plan in 2012, Italy's public debt rose sharply again owing to a contraction in the economy of 2.4 percent of GDP.

Italy's debt service costs are a consistently large burden on its fiscal position (see figure 4-2). Debt service costs are likely to remain high unless the authorities generate much greater confidence that the debt ratio is on a significant downward path and uncertainty about the future of the single currency is reduced. Before the crisis, inflation, real growth, and primary surpluses all contributed to improving Italy's fiscal position. However, Italy's shrinking economy, from 2008 to 2009 and again in 2012 and 2013, has resulted in an escalation of the debt-to-GDP ratio to over 130 percent.

Despite Italy's high level of public debt, its fiscal deficit is not as unfavorable as that of some of its principal European partners, even though it exceeded

Table 4-1. *Fiscal Variables, 2000–13*
Percent of GDP

	2000	2001	2002	2003	2004	2005	2006	2007	2008	2009	2010	2011	2012	2013[a]
Government gross debt														
France	57.4	56.9	59.1	63.3	65.2	66.8	64.1	64.2	68.2	79.2	82.4	85.8	90.2	93.5
Germany	60.2	59.1	60.7	64.4	66.2	68.5	67.9	65.4	66.8	74.5	82.4	80.4	81.9	80.4
Greece	103.4	103.7	101.7	97.4	98.9	101.2	107.5	107.2	112.9	129.7	148.3	170.3	156.9	175.7
Italy	108.6	108.3	105.4	104.1	103.7	105.7	106.3	103.3	106.1	116.4	119.3	120.8	127.0	132.3
Spain	59.4	55.6	52.6	48.8	46.3	43.2	39.7	36.3	40.2	54.0	61.7	70.4	85.9	93.7
EU-17	69.3	68.2	68.1	69.3	69.7	70.3	68.6	66.5	70.3	80.1	85.7	88.2	93.0	95.7
Government fiscal deficit														
France	-1.5	-1.7	-3.3	-4.1	-3.6	-3.0	-2.4	-2.8	-3.3	-7.6	-7.1	-5.3	-4.9	-4.0
Germany	1.1	-3.1	-3.8	-4.2	-3.8	-3.3	-1.7	0.2	-0.1	-3.1	-4.2	-0.8	0.1	-0.4
Greece	-3.7	-4.4	-4.8	-5.7	-7.4	-5.6	-6.0	-6.8	-9.9	-15.6	-10.8	-9.6	-6.3	-4.1
Italy	-0.9	-3.2	-3.2	-3.6	-3.6	-4.5	-3.4	-1.6	-2.7	-5.4	-4.3	-3.7	-2.9	-3.2
Spain	-1.0	-0.5	-0.2	-0.4	-0.1	1.0	2.4	1.9	-4.5	-11.2	-9.7	-9.6	-10.8	-6.7
EU-17	-0.1	-1.9	-2.6	-3.1	-2.9	-2.5	-1.3	-0.7	-2.1	-6.4	-6.2	-4.2	-3.7	-3.1
Government structural balance														
France	-3.0	-3.1	-4.2	-4.3	-4.1	-3.9	-3.4	-4.2	-4.1	-5.7	-5.7	-4.6	-3.5	-2.1
Germany	-1.8	-3.0	-3.3	-3.2	-3.3	-2.6	-2.3	-1.1	-0.9	-1.1	-2.2	-1.0	0.1	-0.1
Greece	-2.1	-3.1	-3.6	-6.1	-8.4	-6.7	-8.7	-10.8	-14.3	-19.1	-12.3	-8.3	-2.6	0.6
Italy	-3.2	-5.0	-5.1	-5.5	-5.2	-5.4	-4.2	-3.5	-3.8	-4.1	-3.6	-3.5	-1.3	-0.2
Spain	-1.1	-1.8	-1.1	-1.0	-1.0	-1.6	-1.3	-1.1	-5.3	-9.3	-8.1	-8.1	-6.3	-4.9
EU-17	-1.9	-2.8	-3.1	-3.3	-3.3	-3.0	-2.7	-2.6	-3.3	-4.7	-4.6	-3.7	-2.3	-1.4

(continued)

Table 4-1. *Fiscal Variables, 2000–13 (continued)*
Percent of GDP

	2000	2001	2002	2003	2004	2005	2006	2007	2008	2009	2010	2011	2012	2013[a]
Government revenues														
France	50.2	50.0	49.6	49.3	49.6	50.6	50.6	49.9	49.9	49.2	49.5	50.6	51.8	53.3
Germany	46.2	44.5	44.1	44.3	43.3	43.6	43.7	43.7	44.0	45.2	43.7	44.3	44.8	45.2
Greece	43.0	40.9	40.3	39.0	38.1	39.0	39.2	40.7	40.7	38.4	40.6	42.4	44.6	43.5
Italy	45.0	44.5	44.0	44.4	44.0	43.4	45.0	46.0	45.9	46.5	46.1	46.1	47.7	48.2
Spain	38.2	38.1	38.6	38.1	38.8	39.7	40.7	41.1	36.9	35.1	36.7	36.2	37.1	36.8
EU-17	46.0	45.2	44.8	44.8	44.5	44.8	45.3	45.3	45.0	44.9	44.8	45.3	46.3	46.8
Government expenditures														
France	51.7	51.7	52.9	53.4	53.3	53.6	53.0	52.6	53.3	56.8	56.6	55.9	56.6	57.2
Germany	45.1	47.6	47.9	48.5	47.1	46.9	45.3	43.5	44.1	48.3	47.9	45.2	44.7	45.4
Greece	46.7	45.4	45.1	44.7	45.5	44.6	45.3	47.5	50.6	54.0	51.4	52.0	53.6	47.3
Italy	45.9	47.7	47.1	48.1	47.5	47.9	48.5	47.6	48.6	51.9	50.4	49.8	50.6	51.1
Spain	39.2	38.7	38.9	38.4	38.9	38.4	38.4	39.2	41.4	46.2	46.3	45.7	47.8	43.3
EU-17	46.2	47.2	47.5	48.0	47.4	47.3	46.7	46.0	47.1	51.2	51.0	49.5	49.9	49.7

Source: Government gross debt, fiscal deficit, and structural balance from IMF, *World Economic Outlook* (WEO); total government revenues and expenditures from Eurostat Statistics Database (2000–12) and Eurostat (2013), General Government Data Time-Series.

a. Values for 2013 are estimates.

Figure 4-2. *Decomposition of Italy's Debt-to-GDP*

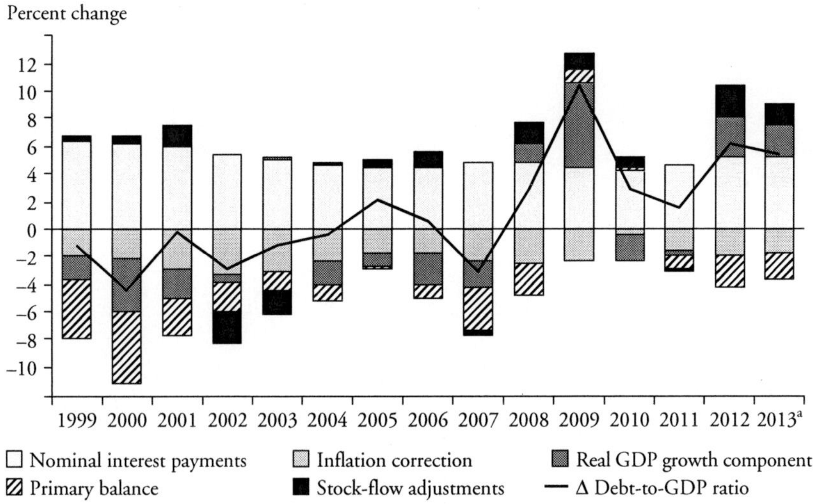

Percent change

Source: Authors' elaboration on IMF WEO database (2013).
a. Values for 2013 are estimates.

the 3 percent Maastricht threshold in all but four years from 2000 to 2013. Italy compensated for its large debt service costs by consistently maintaining primary surpluses in every year except 2009 and 2010. More specifically, when looking at the structural balances that take into account the relative position of its economy in the economic cycle, Italy has been gradually but steadily improving its fiscal position since 2006 (see table 4-1). Other countries, including Spain and Greece, have seen their fiscal positions deteriorate.

In fact, the sharp rise in government debt as a percentage of GDP of many European countries after the financial crisis, including Portugal, Ireland, and Spain, were predominantly caused by large primary deficits (see table 4-1 and appendix table A-5). Italy, however, saw a significant rise in its debt ratio, not because of its primary balances, but because of a particularly sharp recession such that the burden of the debt service costs could no longer be mitigated.

Despite facing sluggish growth rates and being hit particularly hard by the crisis, Italy's primary surpluses were larger than those of the EU-17 average before the crisis and have been the largest among its European counterparts since 2008. Furthermore, as table 4-2 shows, Italy is expected to run one of the highest primary surpluses among its European counterparts in every year from 2014 to 2018.

Table 4-2. *Government Primary Balance*
Percent of GDP

	1999–2007	2008–13	2014	2015	2016	2017	2018
France	−0.1	−3.0	−1.5	−0.7	0.1	0.9	1.7
Germany	0.3	0.8	1.8	1.9	1.9	2.0	2.0
Greece	0.3	−4.8	1.4	3.0	4.5	4.5	4.3
Italy	2.6	1.1	3.1	3.5	4.4	5.0	5.4
Spain	2.3	−6.9	−2.6	−1.7	−0.6	0.4	1.4
EU-17	1.2	−1.7	0.2	0.6	1.2	1.6	2.0

Source: IMF WEO database (2013).

The austerity measures implemented in 2012 were designed to place Italy on a path toward fiscal sustainability; they appear, however, to have prolonged the recession, which will further hinder improvements in Italy's fiscal position. Figure 4-3 illustrates projected and counterfactual public debt dynamics in Italy based on different real GDP growth scenarios. As it stands, Italy's debt-to-GDP ratio rose sharply in 2012 and 2013; it is expected to peak in 2014 at 133 percent and gradually fall thereafter. Public debt dynamics change significantly under different growth paths, all else being equal (see figure 4-3). If there were zero growth from 2011 to 2018, or if growth followed its projected potential path, the debt-to-GDP ratio would peak no higher than 128 percent and fall to 122 percent by 2018, 1 percentage point lower than the base case projection. If Italy's economy were to continue to grow at pre-crisis levels,[1] public debt would take a radically different path, peaking at 122 percent in 2013 and falling 14 percentage points to approximately 108 by 2018.

Austerity measures will aid in reducing the debt ratio from 2015 onward. However, Italy's high level of debt makes its fiscal position particularly vulnerable to fluctuations in the growth rate. Debt-to-GDP dynamics are strongly dependent on GDP growth and interest rates: when growth rate is equivalent to the interest rate, the denominator of the debt-to-GDP ratio, GDP, is growing at the same pace as the numerator, the level of debt, under a balanced primary budget. However, if the interest rate on debt exceeds the growth rate, then even with a balanced budget the debt ratio will rise indefinitely. Accordingly, with negative growth, Italy needs to run large primary surpluses in order to offset the cost of its debt service payments. Alternatively, strong and sus-

---

1. Pre-crisis growth refers to the average annual real GDP growth from 1999 to 2006, equal to 1.53 percent.

Figure 4-3. *Sensitivity of Italy's Debt-to-GDP Ratio to Real GDP Growth and Primary Balance, 2011–18*

Public debt (% GDP)

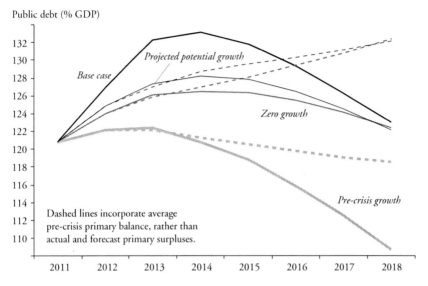

Source: Authors' elaboration on IMF WEO database (2013).

tained growth could stabilize debt dynamics without requiring extensive austerity measures.

Figure 4-3 shows the dynamics of the debt-to-GDP ratio under different growth scenarios, assuming that the government runs primary surpluses at pre-crisis levels.[2] Under this assumption, the zero-growth scenario generates continuously rising debt that could escalate to unsustainable levels. Using the projected potential growth path, the debt ratio would increase to 132 percent by 2018. However under a pre-crisis growth scenario, debt-to-GDP would move gradually, would not surpass 122 percent of GDP, and would fall in the medium term to approximately 5 percentage points below the base case projection in 2018.

In sum, primary surpluses are expected to contribute greatly to the decrease in Italy's debt ratio from 2015 onward. Given Italy's high public debt, Italy's fiscal position is vulnerable, however, to fluctuations in the growth path. Maintaining healthy rates of growth by focusing on long-term productivity

2. Pre-crisis primary surplus refers to the average value of the primary balance from 1999 to 2006, equal to 2.26 percent of GDP.

enhancers, rather than short-term deficits, is a much more effective and politically sustainable method for placing Italy on a path to fiscal sustainability. The austerity measures may appear to be chipping away at the stock of public debt through large primary surpluses, but sluggish growth rates are impeding significant improvements in Italy's fiscal position.

What Went Wrong with the Recent Consolidation?

The disappointing performance of the debt ratio despite the substantial fiscal tightening in 2012 points to the impact of fiscal consolidation on growth through multiplier and composition effects. The literature suggests that austerity measures lead to significant economic contractions when: the key monetary policy interest rates are low; other countries, especially trading partners, consolidate simultaneously; agents are constrained in their access to credit; and the economy is emerging from a recession.[3] These conditions were all present when Italy began consolidation: the European Central Bank already had a relatively accommodating stance;[4] the euro area was moving toward simultaneous consolidation well before twenty-five EU countries signed the Fiscal Stability Treaty; and credit growth in the non-financial private sector had dropped from an annual 3.5 percent in November 2011 to an annual 1.6 percent in April 2012.[5] Finally, Italy was just emerging from a strong contraction at the height of the international financial crisis: in 2009 its GDP had fallen by 5.5 percent. In contrast, the U.S. economy, where the crisis originated, contracted by 3.2 percent of output in that same year.

Based on this evidence, Blanchard and Leigh (2013) argue that fiscal cutbacks have, on average, had larger than expected negative short-term multiplier effects on output. This may explain the substantial growth shortfall. Relying on an econometric analysis covering twenty-six European economies, they find that "actual multipliers were substantially above 1 early in the crisis" (p. 19).

We calculated fiscal multipliers for a sample of European countries using the most recent data in order to assess the marginal impact of recent fiscal consolidation. While acknowledging that multipliers typically vary greatly by

3. See, among others, IMF (2010); Alesina and Perotti (1997); Darby, Muscatelli, and Graeme (2005); and Alesina and Ardagna (1998).
4. See, for instance, European Central Bank press release, November 3, 2011 (www.ecb.int/press/pr/date/2011/html/pr111103.en.html).
5. See IMF Italy 2013 Article IV Consultation Report. Moreover, Italy's rank in the category of "getting credit" in the World Bank's "Doing Business" survey deteriorated by 7 positions from 2012 to 2013, ranking 104 out of 185 countries.

period and country, our results are consistent with the analysis of Blanchard and Leigh (2013) and show a value for Italy's fiscal multiplier substantially above 1. We find highly asymmetric costs of fiscal adjustment at the margin: the fiscal multiplier is higher in Italy and Spain (close to 2) and lower in Germany (close to 0).

As Blanchard and Leigh (2013) note, however, this evidence does not deny in any way the challenges posed by a high public debt or by a significant structural deficit. Yet it does point to the importance of devising a gradual but steady consolidation plan over the medium term by containing its harmful short-run impact on growth, especially when aggregate output is already well below potential, as it has been in Italy.

Another stream in the literature suggests that fiscal consolidation has much smaller contractionary, or even expansionary, effects when consolidation is expenditure-based—that is, when it relies on cuts to primary current expenditures, including government wages, transfers, and subsidies.[6] In Italy, however, approximately 80 percent of the recent fiscal adjustments have been revenue-based, as opposed to expenditure-based, adding to its already-high tax burden, and rely mainly on raising tax rates rather than broadening the tax base. Specifically, the expansion of revenues over the period 2009–13 was more than double the amount achieved through the consolidation of expenditures. Substantial gains were realized from taxes on production and imports and from direct taxes on households (OECD 2012). These sources of revenue may have the effect of further depressing domestic demand, impeding investment, and keeping unemployment high. As a result, tax revenues will increase further to 48.2 percent of GDP in 2013, 3 percent higher than in Germany, but 5 percent lower than in France (see table 4-1).

Sources of Rigidities in Fiscal Policy

Government expenditures in Italy are 1.5 percentage points higher than the EU average; Eurostat estimates that expenditures were higher in Italy than in Germany, Greece, and Spain in 2013, but lower than in France (table 4-1). Government expenditures in Italy increased by approximately 5 percent of GDP from 2000 to 2013. Most EU countries have seen a rise in government expenditures as a percentage of GDP since 2000; the rise in government

---

6. Among many others, Alesina, Perotti, and Tavares (1998) and Alesina, Favero, and Giavazzi (2012) find that adjustments based on spending cuts are much less costly in terms of output losses than tax-based ones.

Figure 4-4. *Government Expenditure Breakdown by Function, 2011*[a]

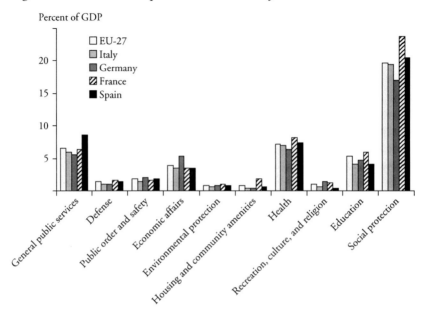

Percent of GDP

Source: Eurostat.

a. Eurostat uses the United Nations Statistics Division definitions to classify the various functions of government. The division's definition of "general public services" includes expenses related to executive and legislative organs, financial and fiscal affairs, external affairs, foreign economic aid, basic research, and expenses related to debt management.

expenditures is due to a contraction in the economy and to an increase in both discretionary and automatic fiscal expenditures.

Turning to the composition of public expenditures, illustrated in figure 4-4, we see that spending on social protection is higher than on other items, especially because of Italy's aging population—which will only grow in years to come—and is not especially efficient. For instance, although in per inhabitant purchasing power parity (PPP) terms Italy spends more than all other eurozone countries, second only to France,[7] it does not have the highest ratio of persons over 65 to the total population. Germany has the highest ratio

7. Pension expenditure by country in 2010, in purchasing power standard (PPS) per inhabitant (and percentage of the population aged 65 and over): France 3,996 (17.5); Italy 3,976 (20.8); Germany 3,840 (21.1); EU-17 3,628 (18.9); Sweden 3,552 (18.9); United Kingdom 3,196 (17.2); Greece 3,025 (19.4); Portugal 2,819 (18.5); Spain 2,646 (17.5). Eurostat (2013), Pension expenditure; World Bank (2013), Population aged 65 and over.

at 21.1 percent and Italy's was 20.8 percent in 2012; yet Germany's pension expenditures are lower. Overall pension expenditures—a key component of social protection expenditures—are 16 percent of GDP in Italy, the highest of any eurozone country (see appendix figure A-9 for a comparison of general governmental expenditures in Italy and a larger selection of European countries).

Against this background, in 2011 the Italian government implemented important reforms to the pension system. The pension reforms change the age of eligibility for full benefits, extend the contribution-based system, and decrease the value of benefits. The retirement age increased from 60 to 62 for women and from 65 to 66 for men. By 2018 the retirement age for both men and women who have worked in the private sector should converge at 66 and should be above 70 in 2060. The reforms change the method of calculating pensions, moving to those based on contributions and away from those based on earnings in order to reduce the number of high pension payouts. According to the IMF (2012), such reforms are expected to generate savings of around 1.2 percent of GDP annually from 2020 to 2030.

Italy's social protection absorbed 20.5 percent of GDP in 2011, almost one percentage point higher than the EU average. Health expenditures were also relatively higher in Italy than in many of its European counterparts. In contrast, the average EU expenditures in growth-enhancing areas, such as education, are much higher than in Italy. In 2011, Italy allocated 4.2 percent of GDP to education, considerably less than the EU average of 5.3 percent. For economic affairs, Italy's government expenditure of 3.6 percent of GDP was generally in line with the EU average of 4 percent, and more similar to that of Germany (3.5 percent of GDP) than Spain (5.3 percent of GDP). In other categories, Italy matched, or nearly matched, EU average expenditures as a percentage of GDP. In defense and environmental protection Italy spent the same proportion of GDP as the EU average (1.5 percent of GDP and 0.9 percent of GDP respectively).

Government expenditures on general public services, social protection, and health are higher than the EU averages. As the population ages, the burden of programs within these expense categories will only increase. Although expenditures in these categories are relatively high, the IMF notes that "[p]ublic expenditure remains very inefficient . . . Italy scores poorly in terms of the quality and efficiency of public expenditures" (IMF 2011, p. 18). According to the IMF staff, "shifting further the composition of adjustment towards expenditure cuts and lower taxes would better distribute the burden of adjustment and support growth" (IMF 2012, p. 22).

To sum up, while looming pension expenditures—a source of longer-term risk to fiscal sustainability—have been effectively managed with the reform enacted by the government of Prime Minister Mario Monti, the broader composition of Italy's public expenditures is not growth-enhancing. Since they are, moreover, relatively inefficient, public expenditures act as a further drag on growth by diverting resources that could be more effectively deployed either in growth-enhancing areas or in the form of lower taxation.

Competition and Markets

Stagnating growth in Italy stems from deep-rooted structural problems that have hindered its ability to remain competitive in light of the rise of competitiveness of emerging economies. Heavy regulation, red tape, and labor market frictions impede the efficiency of firms and their incentive to expand and commit to long-term strategies. In this section we examine the roots of stagnant growth in the product and labor markets and the reforms that were implemented from 2009 to 2013 to address structural problems.

Competitiveness and Product Markets

Italy ranks thirty-third among the thirty-four OECD member countries in the World Bank's "Ease of Doing Business" survey, placing it ahead of only Greece, and seventy-third in the overall ranking of 185 countries surveyed (see figure 4-5).[8] Before the financial crisis, Greece and France were further from the frontier of business regulation than Italy: Italy had an index value of 64.4, France at 62.8, and Greece 55.1 (see figure 4-6).[9] But Greece and France have made significantly more progress in improving their regulatory environment than has Italy since 2006: France has moved closer to the frontier by almost 9 index points, Greece by 7, while Italy has budged by less than 1.5 points. The main elements of the inefficiency in Italy's regulatory environment are to be found in the judicial system, financial markets, and electricity markets, and through the tax burden.

Italy performs a little better in the "global competitiveness" ranking by the World Economic Forum, ranking twenty-eighth among the thirty-four

8. The World Bank's "Ease of Doing Business" survey is intended to measure the regulation and red tape involved in owning and operating a domestic medium-sized firm. Information is retrieved from legal practitioners and professionals involved in the administrative and legal practices being evaluated.

9. "Distance to the frontier" is a measurement of how well a country's regulatory landscape performs in comparison with the best performance in each "Doing Business" category for all countries and years surveyed. The frontier is equal to 100.

Figure 4-5. *World Bank "Doing Business" OECD Rankings*[a]

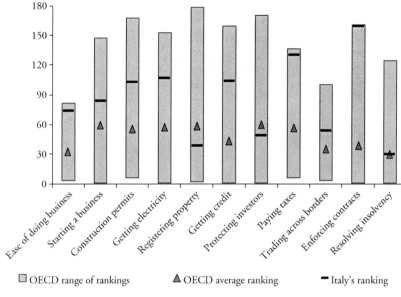

OECD range of rankings   ▲ OECD average ranking   ▬ Italy's ranking

Source: World Bank (2013).
a. A total of 185 countries were ranked.

Figure 4-6. *World Bank Progress toward the Frontier*

Distance to the frontier

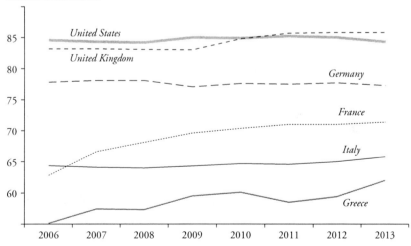

Source: World Bank (2013).
a. "Distance to the frontier" is a measurement of how well a country's regulatory landscape performs in comparison with the best performance in each "Doing Business" category for all countries and years surveyed. The frontier is equal to 100.

Figure 4-7. *Value-Added Trends for Macro-Sectors*[a]

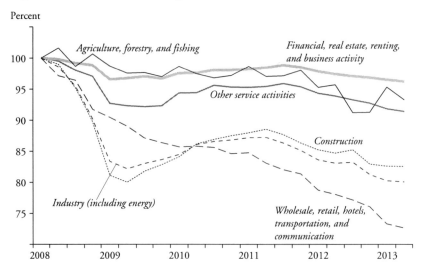

Percent

Source: ISTAT (Istituto Nazionale di Statistica).
a. 2008 Q1 = 100; chained and seasonally adjusted.

OECD member countries. Italy outperforms the OECD average in market size, infrastructure, and health and primary education. But it ranks the worst in labor market efficiency and performs very poorly in financial market development, goods market efficiency, institutions, and the macroeconomic environment.

With growth already stagnating because of deep-seated structural problems, the tax hikes from the austerity measures and the broader systemic uncertainty about the single currency have hurt both firm and consumer confidence. Falling confidence has diminished domestic demand, requiring firms to seek higher levels of export-driven demand. Industries that have been able to improve exports have managed to maintain their production levels.

The value added of all sectors in Italy has declined since 2008 (see figure 4-7). Industry (including energy); construction; and wholesale, retail, transportation, and communication have experienced the biggest decline in value added since the onset of the financial crisis. At the same time, finance, real estate, business activity, and agriculture, forestry, and fishing have been much more successful at maintaining the value of the goods and services they produce.

Similarly, the extent of the exit of firms from the market from 2008 to 2013 has been remarkable. The most innovative and internationalized firms, often larger enterprises, have remained profitable because of export-driven demand. On the other hand, small and medium-sized enterprises (SMEs) have experienced a decline in competitiveness. This is likely due to a lack of capacity to absorb new technologies and an inability to take advantage of significant economies of scale to compete in international markets. These trends have highlighted how the growth of firm size and exports are important factors for efficiency and the ability to remain competitive.

In the face of declining productivity and cost competitiveness, it is remarkable that Italian firms have generally been able to maintain relatively stable export levels. Firms, geographic areas, and manufacturing sectors have been affected differently by external competition. Small enterprises (up to forty-nine employees) have shown less ability to remain profitable during the recession, while medium-sized and large enterprises (fifty or more employees) have assumed a leading role in the first phase of the recovery. Northern Italy has shown remarkable increases in exports, as well as steady growth in total sales in 2011. On the other hand, while central and southern Italy have managed to increase exports, they have not seen the same growth in sales and production as in the north (Centro Studi Unioncamere 2012).

Despite Italy's loss of competitiveness with the emerging economies, the resilience of Italian exports is attributable to "specialized-suppliers," manufacturers of specialized tools and machinery that have few substitutes and are dominated by SMEs in industrial districts (IMF 2013). The IMF indicates that strengths of Italian firms are in their high-quality products and their adaptability. However, in order to maintain the strength of its exports, Italy must implement structural reforms that enhance competition, create incentives for firms to grow, improve innovation, and attract foreign direct investment.

There have been some structural reforms in the product markets and public sector since 2011. Reforms have improved competition in network industries (energy and transport) and professional services (legal/notaries, accounting, medical/pharmacy, engineering), and in the provision of local public services and utilities. Overall, these sectors amount to about one-third of the total value added in the economy; they contribute to about 40 percent of total inputs used (intermediate consumption) by other industries and close to 30 percent of household consumption expenditure. IMF staff estimates suggest that further product and labor market reforms could increase the level of GDP by 6 percent over the medium term and contribute significantly to closing Italy's competitiveness gap (IMF 2012).

Labor Markets

Italy's labor market efficiency ranks lowest among all OECD member countries (WEF 2013). There are many sources of inefficiency: a high rate of long-term and youth unemployment (see appendix figures A-7 and A-8), a low participation rate among women and older workers, the diffusion of unregistered work in the underground economy, and regional disparities in labor market conditions, to name the most important.

The Italian labor market also suffers from significant mismatches between demand for and supply of education and skills. According to the "Excelsior Survey on Occupational Needs" by Unioncamere and the Ministry of Labor (2013), employers stated that they had difficulty finding enough candidates for jobs requiring specific professional skills, such as engineering, medical doctors and nurses, and social workers. Employers also had difficulty finding technicians and legal professionals with adequate professional training. Thus, mismatches in the labor market stem from both the type of skills and the quality of training of the work force. The lack of a highly qualified and adaptive labor force is an obstacle to innovation and the adoption of new technologies by the manufacturing sector, and hence to the improvement of firms' competitive position in international markets.

Moreover, several institutional factors adversely affect the job-matching process. First, employment services, which have been provided at the local level (provincial and regional) since the early 2000s, are unsatisfactory in some regions. Second, government reforms of the pension system will require significant restructuring of the labor market. The labor force participation rate of persons aged 55 to 64—that is, the percentage of the population that is either employed or unemployed and actively seeking work—is expected to rise to 57 percent by 2020, significantly higher than the participation rate of 38 percent in 2010 (Denk 2013). This expansion of the labor supply will have to be absorbed into productive employment, particularly over the next five to ten years. Assuming that the productivity of many older workers is likely to decline between the ages 50 and 65, a key issue is whether the labor market is flexible enough to generate decreases in real wages as people extend their working lives. This problem is particularly salient because both wages and responsibilities increase with seniority (especially in the public sector). In sum, a higher retirement age, with no increase in the flexibility of the current wage system, could lead to the marginal cost of labor rising beyond its marginal product.

Figure 4-8. *Labor Cost Competitiveness: Relative Unit Labor Costs Weighted by Trade*[a]

Index: 2000 = 100

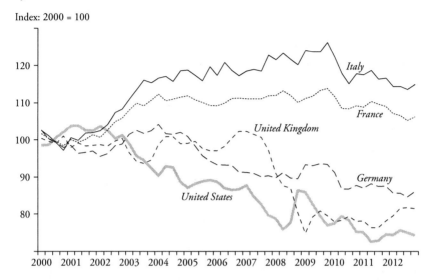

Source: OECD, Economic Survey: Italy (2013a).
a. An increase in the index means that total employee compensation per unit of real output rose relative to that in trading partners. If the index falls by the same amount for, say, both Italy and Germany, this means that their competitiveness position in relation to the rest of the world has improved, but there has been no change in their relation to each other.

Since 2000, labor costs in Italy have become significantly less competitive relative to its European counterparts and the United States, despite the fact that labor compensation per hour has increased by less in Italy than in other advanced economies (see figure 4-8; also see appendix figures A-5 and A-6 for unweighted comparisons of selected European economies). Italy's improvements since 2009, as with the other countries in the sample, are attributable to currency depreciation and some modest decreases in real wages. The key to improving labor cost competitiveness in other advanced economies relies on raising real wages by less than the growth in productivity. However, Italy has been unable to conform to this standard because of the lack of growth in productivity, which we discuss further in the next section.

Making the labor market more dynamic and inclusive was one of the objectives of the reforms adopted by the Monti government. The labor market reform act, which was approved by Parliament in July 2012, addresses a number of the key inefficiencies of the labor market. In general, the reform tackles job insecurity and dualism;[10] it seeks to improve employment protection and the unemployment insurance system and to strengthen active labor market policies. In addition, it aims to increase employment and participation—especially among youth—by encouraging more stable employment relationships and simultaneously lowering termination costs.

Long-Term Strategies: Growth, Innovation, and Productivity

Sluggish growth rates and the declining competitiveness of the Italian economy are related to the stagnant growth of total factor productivity. The dynamics of productivity are associated with the efficiency of public institutions, research and development (R&D), and investment in human capital. Austerity policies, however, have had the consequence of cutting public investment in human capital and the support of private expenditure in R&D. This section addresses the way forward for Italy by identifying areas requiring structural reforms to improve long-term growth prospects.

Productivity and Human Capital

There was no improvement in labor productivity in Italy between 2001 and 2013. On the other hand, Greece, Spain, and Germany saw approximately 15 percent growth in labor productivity over that same period (Eurostat 2013). Growth in total factor productivity has been even worse than growth in labor productivity in Italy. Italy experienced improvements in total factor productivity after the recession in the early 1990s; however, productivity growth was stagnant through much of the late 1990s and began to decline in 2001 (see figure 4-9; also see appendix figure A-4). After the financial crisis, total factor productivity receded to near its 1992 level. At the same time, growth in total factor productivity over the past two decades exceeded 15 percent in other major advanced economies, including Germany, France, the United Kingdom, and the United States. Italy's poor performance in productivity growth, relative to all other EU countries, is associated with

---

10. "Dualism" refers to a divide in the labor market between a primary and a secondary sector. The primary sector is characterized by skilled labor, job security, opportunities for promotion, and worker protection. The secondary sector is often part of the informal economy and is characterized by low skills, little to no worker rights or security, and little opportunity for advancement. Dualism is particularly notable in Italy relative to its advanced economy counterparts.

Figure 4-9. *Growth in Total Factor Productivity*

Index: 1992 = 100

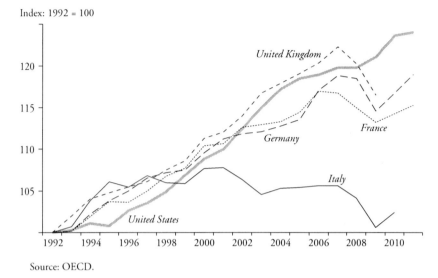

Source: OECD.

the government's attempts to balance fiscal pressures, its inefficient institutions, and slow progress toward innovation.

Productivity must grow in order to improve Italy's long-term growth prospects. Productivity growth may be stimulated through institutional reforms, or through reforms to the product and labor markets, which were discussed in the previous section, because they encourage firm-level expansion and attract foreign direct investment. Other methods to boost productivity include investing in innovation and in human capital.

On the latter, the percentage of the Italian population between the ages of 25 and 34 with at least some higher (tertiary-level) education, which includes both vocational training and university-level education, is approximately 18 percentage points below the average of twenty-three advanced economies (see figure 4-10). In fact, Italy ranks ahead of only one other advanced economy in the sample, Austria. Furthermore, Italy ranks lowest in literacy proficiency among adults and second lowest in numeracy proficiency and problem-solving ability in technology-rich environments, and it has the highest incidence of worker under-qualification among the same sample of advanced economies (OECD 2013b). Italy has, however, made some significant progress toward building a labor force with a tertiary-level education. Among advanced economies, Italy has one of the highest growth rates in the

Figure 4-10. *Population with Tertiary Education, 2012*

Percent, by age group

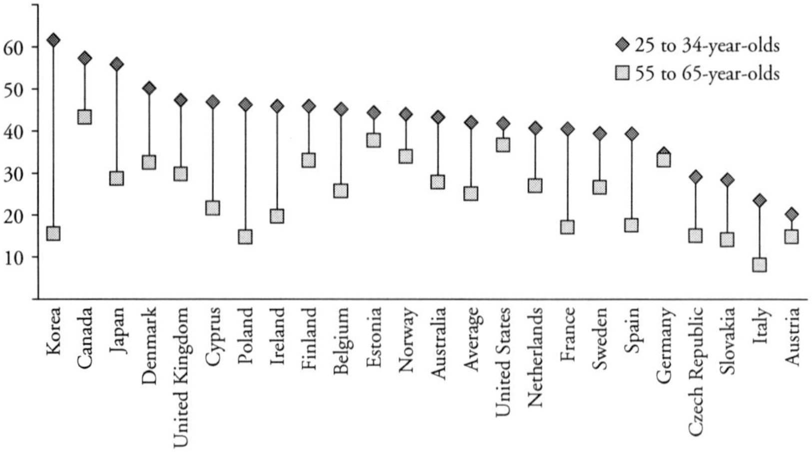

Source: OECD (2009).

attainment of tertiary-level education (that is, the propensity to complete tertiary-level education has increased). Growth in overall attainment levels was 5.2 percent in Italy from 1998 to 2006, significantly higher than the OECD average of 3.5 percent (OECD 2009).

In order for the Italian economy to improve its competitiveness, the restructuring process needs to emphasize investment in human capital, expansion of research capacity, and the creation and diffusion of knowledge. According to the OECD, "if the average time spent in education by a population rises by one year, then economic output per head of population should grow by between 4 percent and 6 percent in the long run" (OECD 2007, p. 34). In many OECD countries, particularly in Europe, the supply of skilled persons is not keeping pace with the demand for knowledge-based economic activity. In fact, Europe lags behind its advanced economy counterparts. In the United States, Canada, Japan, and New Zealand approximately 40 percent of the population between the ages of 25 and 64 have attained tertiary education, while the average in Europe is 24 percent; Italy is lowest among these European countries at 14 percent.

Not only is there a need for higher university and other tertiary-level graduation rates, but the quality of the higher education system must also be improved. Indeed, Italy's public universities attract few researchers and students from abroad because they are too undifferentiated and unspecialized, as well as deeply rooted in the local contexts instead of being connected to international networks. In an attempt to address these concerns, recent university reforms aim to stimulate more internal competition within Italian universities in order to establish higher quality, reward merit, and promote greater differentiation in the supply structure by allowing more administrative independence (Cipollone, Montanaro, and Sestito 2012).

Policies aimed at improving the quality and stock of human capital should especially target youth. Younger people entering the labor force have positive effects on both productivity and growth. On the supply side, youth have greater learning capacity and are more concerned about innovation. These abilities and motivations stimulate labor productivity, which improves potential growth. On the demand side, a younger population has both a more robust demand, according to Modigliani's life-cycle theory, and a higher propensity to follow the most innovative consumption patterns. In order to foster the potential productivity gains from a younger workforce, Italy must implement a set of structural reforms to provide incentives for young people to seek higher education and to establish a career in Italy.

Innovation

Innovation plays a central role in stimulating productivity and growth. R&D intensity increased from 1.1 percent of GDP in 2003 to 1.25 percent of GDP in 2011, which is close to the average increase in R&D in the EU-27 over the same period. However, R&D levels are lower than the EU average and remain very far from the countries at the technology frontier (see figure 4-11).

As has been shown, there is a gap in innovation and productivity growth between Italy and the rest of Europe. But there is also a significant gap in these factors between the United States and Europe. Van Ark, O'Mahony, and Timmer (2008) argue that slower productivity growth in Europe than in the United States is due to the productivity gap between their services sectors. Given the weight of commercial services on business value added (72 percent in the United States and 65 percent in the EU), bridging the productivity gap in the services sector would eliminate approximately 80 percent of the R&D gap between the two and improve productivity growth.

Manufacturing activities have usually been regarded as the main source of innovation and productivity growth. However, the United States has demonstrated that the services sector can also be an important source of productivity growth, particularly in the retail sector, which has undergone substantial transformation linked to the use of information and communication

Figure 4-11. *R&D Intensity and High-Tech and Knowledge Labor Capacity*

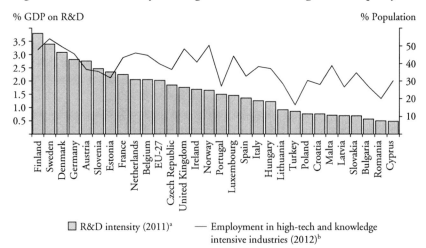

% GDP on R&D   % Population

☐ R&D intensity (2011)[a]   —— Employment in high-tech and knowledge
                                      intensive industries (2012)[b]

Source: Eurostat.
a. In descending order based on R&D expenditure as a percentage of GDP (including expenditures in the business, government, higher education, and private nonprofit sectors).
b. Employment includes high-tech and knowledge-intensive industries and high- and medium-high-technology manufacturing industries.

technologies (ICTs). In contrast, as Van Ark, O'Mahony, and Timmer (2008) point out, Germany, Italy, and Spain show almost zero contribution from market services to productivity growth.

Aside from low rates of innovation in the services sector, innovation in Italy suffers from several other major challenges, including a low level of skills and lower quality higher education systems in many regions, underinvestment in R&D in the private sector because of a lack of financial support, and a large number of SMEs and micro-firms in low-knowledge-intensity sectors.

As highlighted by the ERAWATCH program, one of the main challenges in research is to strike equilibrium in the research system, which includes public and private research centers, as well as firms. Reforms should promote public-private collaboration, improve the efficiency and effectiveness of the public research system (universities and research organizations), and establish appropriate infrastructure to support high-quality research. Most important, reforms should motivate a strong network to ensure that research is relevant to firms and that technology can be effectively transferred from universities and public research organizations to firms.

The quality of research and the effectiveness of the transfer of technology and knowledge to firms tends to be improved by private-public joint research activity, spin-off management, public seed money for innovative start-ups, cooperative research activities like those sponsored by the German Federation of Industrial Research Associations (Arbeitsgemeinschaft industrieller Forschungsvereinigungen, AiF), regional governance of research systems, and the creation of networks of firms and universities for the management of joint laboratories and research infrastructures.

In this regard, Italy has made some progress in improving innovation since the onset of the financial crisis. The technology transfer system initiated by the Italian university system in 2002 has increased the number and quality of personnel working in the technology transfer offices. Moreover, several programs that encourage innovation and technology transfer have been introduced both nationally and regionally. These include technology districts, cooperation between the public and private sectors, and public-private partnerships to carry out large research and innovation projects (for example, the industrial innovation projects of Industria 2015). At the regional level, several clusters have been created in order to take advantage of the existing regional competencies (ERAWATCH 2010).

Corruption

Corruption, broadly defined as government officials designing and implementing public policy for private gain, harms economic growth in several ways. It creates a misallocation of resources by decreasing private investment and inducing inefficient investments by the public sector. It increases expenditures on public sector wages when resources could be devoted to efficiency-enhancing projects and improving the quality of resources. By eroding trust and loyalty, corruption decreases productive efforts in the public sector. In turn, the degradation of institutions indirectly decreases capital formation by reducing investment in both physical and human capital (Gupta, Davoodi, and Alonso-Terme 2002; Wei 2000; Tanzi and Davoodi 1997).

The theory of endogenous growth suggests that the dynamism of an economy can be undermined by negative externalities that may arise from rent-seeking and corruption. Corruption creates a vicious cycle: more corruption decreases the marginal value of honesty, which further encourages corrupt activities. Also, to the extent that corruption entails an arbitrary decisionmaking process that increases the uncertainty of doing business, it may result in the outflow of money or less inflow of foreign direct investment (Wei 2000). It is widely recognized that systemic corruption also undermines government legitimacy and efficiency, thus decreasing consumer and firm confidence and inhibiting long-term investment and growth strategies.

According to the Global Corruption Barometer, the majority of respondents in Italy perceived more widespread economic corruption following the onset of the global financial crisis. Specifically, in both the 2010/11 survey and the 2013 survey, approximately 65 percent of respondents indicated that corruption had increased, while only 5 percent or fewer respondents believed that corruption had decreased (see figure 4-12). Weakened trust in institutions deters entrepreneurial activity, increases tax evasion, and discourages long-term investment in both human and physical capital. Improving transparency and accountability is an important component to reversing the inefficient allocations of resources.

Legislative measures adopted in Italy in 2012 impose tougher penalties on corruption and related crimes in public administration. The new Anti-Corruption Law no. 190/2012, which entered into force in November 2012, aims to improve transparency in the country's public sector,[11] introduces new categories of corruption-related offenses and strengthens enforcement of those already contained in the Italian criminal code. The recent anti-corruption law also provisions for the establishment of a national anti-corruption agency with investigative and remedial powers: the National Anti-Corruption Authority.

Dynamism and Growth

The global financial crisis has revealed the structural problems underlying many advanced economies, and has demonstrated that advanced economies are less resilient and that their longer-term dynamics are more uncertain than was once assumed. This prompts the question of whether the major advanced economies, such as Italy, can maintain their competitive edge.

Economic growth relies on the creation of new ideas. But what lies behind the creation of new ideas? Governments are increasingly devoting strategic resources to developing technology that will lead to changes in markets and production processes. In order to be a leader in innovation, a country must have appropriate infrastructure, such as equipment and advanced technology; supportive institutions, such as an efficient and trusted judicial system;

---

11. Each public administration is required to adopt specific measures to prevent the occurrence of acts of corruption or bribery. These include the adoption of an anti-corruption plan, the appointment of a compliance officer, and the adoption of a code of conduct for employees. In addition, the new Anti-Corruption Law protects public officials who report corrupt behavior. Whistleblowers will not suffer dismissal, sanctions, or discrimination for reporting misconduct (Anti-Corruption Law no. 190/2012).

Figure 4-12. *Perceived Change in the Level of Corruption in Italy, 2010/11–13*

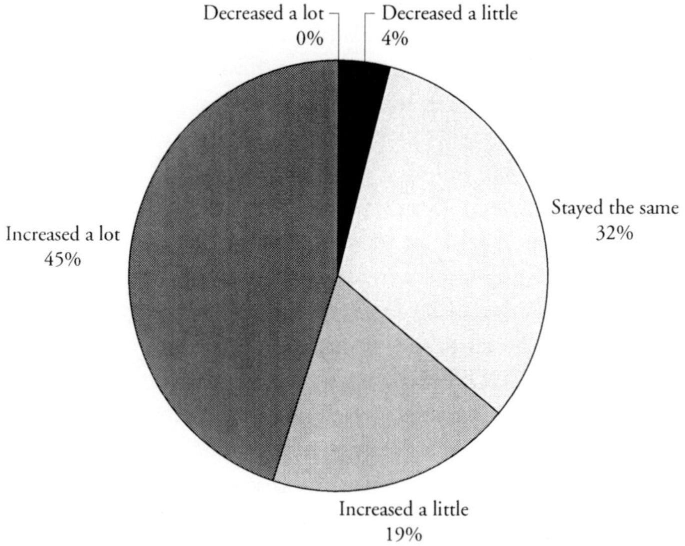

Decreased a lot — 0%

Decreased a little 4%

Stayed the same 32%

Increased a lot 45%

Increased a little 19%

Source: Global Corruption Barometer, 2013.

a strong stock of human capital; and an incentive structure either through grants or clear returns in the product markets. It must also be prepared to take risks, for example by investing in venture capital.

To sum up, the focus should not be on cyclical fluctuations around an economy's potential output, but rather on economic growth and on the corresponding level of well-being. In other words, reforms must look at restoring "good fundamentals," which in the end amounts to restoring a positive growth rate of labor productivity. To overcome the areas of inefficiency and the constraints due to obsolete regulations, backward-looking administration, and the defense of vested interests, action is needed simultaneously on several fronts. The Italian educational and research system must be modernized, with greater emphasis on the scientific and technical disciplines, without neglecting the classical cultural tradition that should be transferred to the younger generation in order to enhance its creativity and human values (Visco 2008).

In fact, the strength and dynamism of an economy do not depend on the short-term approaches so prevalent in current macro- and microeconomic policy—for instance, policies based on the differences in the tax rate or on the strategy of the central bank. The dynamism of an economy depends on much more fundamental elements, such as willingness to take risks, as well as investment in human capital and in new higher-value-added investment projects. A long-term policy view based on a balanced budget, fostering innovation, and investing in human capital is a precondition for improving productivity and long-term growth prospects in Italy.

Conclusion

The current economic crisis in Italy, stemming from stagnating economic growth and little to no progress in total productivity, began a decade before the global financial crisis of 2008. Despite steadily improving its fiscal position since joining the eurozone, it entered the recession with public debt above 100 percent of GDP. High aggregate debt makes a country's financial position particularly vulnerable to variation in growth, inflation, and interest rates. The financial crisis hit Italy particularly hard: unable to sufficiently implement fiscal stimulus policies at the risk of escalating public debt, or to control monetary policy specifically for national interest, Italy suffered a sharp recession in 2008 and 2009 that began escalating its debt burden.

The 2012 austerity measures were supposed to gradually reduce the stock of public debt through large primary surpluses; however, another recession in 2012 and 2013 after the fiscal consolidation further deteriorated Italy's fiscal position. A long-term strategy toward fiscal sustainability must focus on stimulating growth by improving productivity, innovation, and competition.

Deep-rooted structural problems have hindered product market competition, the efficiency of the labor market, productivity, innovation, and technological progress. Structural reforms must be implemented in order for Italy to improve its competitiveness in relation to that of its trading partners and emerging economies.

By eliminating red tape and creating a more efficient regulatory environment, firms can become more competitive and have more incentive to grow and expand into international markets. Further incentives for start-ups will help foster innovation. Such actions will support Italian exports by improving the industrial product mix, fostering international networks, and improving cost competitiveness.

In addition to stimulating domestic demand, improving labor market efficiency may also improve international competitiveness. A more efficient labor market can be achieved by creating more flexibility in the hiring and firing process, as well as more flexibility in the design of employee-employer contracts. Reforms to the labor market should be implemented immediately to thwart hysteresis, a permanent rise in the natural rate of unemployment, and restrain further growth in the informal economy.

Growth in total factor productivity is critical for improving long-term growth potential. Productivity can be stimulated through several dimensions. First, improving the quantity and quality of higher-education graduates will increase the human capital of the labor supply. Second, innovation and knowledge sharing enhances the productivity of current processes and generates new products for which there is a strong demand. Innovation and high-level research can be fostered by increasing competition in the product market, creating a research network composed of public and private research institutions and firms, and implementing incentive-based industrial policies that encourage start-ups with strong innovation capacities. Finally, fighting corruption can encourage integrity in the business community and broader society, allowing for further growth by reducing market failures.

The strength of the Italian economy rests on long-term growth strategies that eliminate inefficiencies embedded in the economic system. Austerity measures that seek short-term debt reduction alone will be unsuccessful at fostering growth and improving productivity. Prudent fiscal policies should be accompanied by structural policies designed to improve the country's innovative capacity and competitiveness.

References

Alesina, Alberto, and Silvia Ardagna. 1998. "Tales of Fiscal Adjustment." *Economic Policy* 13 (27): 487–545.

Alesina, Alberto, and Roberto Perotti. 1997. "The Welfare State and Competitiveness." *American Economic Review* 87 (5): 921–39.

Alesina, Alberto, Carlo Favero, and Francesco Giavazzi. 2012. "The Output Effect of Fiscal Consolidations." Harvard University.

Alesina, Alberto, Roberto Perotti, and José Tavares. 1998. "The Political Economy of Fiscal Adjustments." *Brookings Papers on Economic Activity* 1: 197–266. Washington: Brookings Institution.

Bank of Italy. 2013. "The Governor's Concluding Remarks." Ordinary Meeting of Shareholders. Rome: Banca D'Italia.

Blanchard, Olivier, and Daniel Leigh. 2013. "Growth Forecast Errors and Fiscal Multipliers." Working Paper 13/1. Washington: International Monetary Fund.

Centro Studi Unioncamere. 2012. "Rapporto Unioncamere 2012." Rome: Unioncamere.

Cipollone, Piero, Pasqualino Montanaro, and Paolo Sestito. 2012. "Human Capital for Growth: Possible Steps towards an Upgrade of the Italian Education System." Questioni di Economia e Finanza (Occasional Papers) 122. Rome: Bank of Italy Economic Research and International Relations Area.

Darby, Julia, Anton Muscatelli, and Roy Graeme. 2005. "Fiscal Consolidation and Decentralisation: A Tale of Two Tiers." *Fiscal Studies* 26 (2): 169–95.

Denk, Oliver. 2013. "Italy and the Euro Area Crisis: Securing Fiscal Sustainability and Financial Stability." Economics Department Working Paper 1065. Paris: OECD.

ERAWATCH. 2010. "ERAWATCH Country Reports 2010: Italy." *ERAWATCH Country Reports*. Brussels: European Commission.

Eurostat. 2013. Eurostat Database–Labor productivity per hour worked (http://epp. eurostat.ec.europa.eu/portal/page/portal/statistics/search_database).

Gupta, Sanjeev, Hamid Davoodi, and Rosa Alonso-Terme. 2002. "Does Corruption Affect Inequality and Poverty?" *Economics of Governance* 3 (1): 23–45.

IMF (International Monetary Fund). 2010. *World Economic Outlook, April 2010: Rebalancing Growth*. Washington: International Monetary Fund.

———. 2011. "Italy: 2011 Article IV Consultation—Staff Report." Washington.

———. 2012. "Italy: 2012 Article IV Consultation—Staff Report." Washington.

———. 2013. "Italy 2013 Article IV Consultation: Italian Productivity, Innovation, and Competitiveness." Washington.

OECD (Organization for Economic Cooperation and Development). 2007. "OECD Reviews of Innovation Policy: Luxembourg." Paris.

———. 2009. "Education at a Glance 2009." Paris.

———. 2012. "Economic Outlook Database." Paris.

———. 2013a. "OECD Economic Survey: Italy." Paris.

———. 2013b. "OECD Skills Outlook 2013: First Results from the Survey of Adult Skills." Paris.

Tanzi, Vito, and Davoodi Hamid. 1997. "Corruption, Public Investment and Growth." Working Paper 97/139. Washington: International Monetary Fund.

Unioncamere, Ministry of Labor, and the European Union. 2013. "The Excelsior Survey." Rome.

Van Ark, Bart, Mary O'Mahony, and Marcel P. Timmer. 2008. "The Productivity Gap between Europe and the United States: Trends and Causes." *Journal of Economic Perspectives* 22 (1): 25–44.

Visco, Ignazio. 2008. "Crescita, capitale umano, istruzione." Universita' degli Studi di Genova—Inaugurazione anno accademico 2007/2008.

WEF (World Economic Forum). 2013. "The Global Competitiveness Report 2013–2014." Geneva.

Wei, Shang-Jin. 2000. "How Taxing Is Corruption on International Investors?" *Review of Economics and Statistics* 82 (1): 1–11.

World Bank. 2012. "Doing Business Report 2012." Washington.

———. 2013. "Doing Business Report 2013." Washington.

5

France: Part of the Solution or Part of the Problem?

JACQUES MISTRAL

On November 17, 2012, *The Economist* published a special issue on France. On the cover, baguettes wearing berets were collected in a bucket, like sticks of dynamite, with fuses; the story described France as a "time bomb ticking at the core of the Eurozone." It got a big reaction. "Another British treachery" was the most objective reaction heard in Paris; Minister Arnaud Montebourg used much harsher words. Surprisingly, and contrary to expectations in the City, the story did not result in any trouble on the debt markets. On November 12, the meaningful aspect of French economic policy was to be seen in the recent and widely praised adoption of real measures to improve competitiveness.

Irrespective of this episode, French imbalances in the summer of 2013 raised serious issues that could turn into major policy frictions. In the spring of 2013, the European Commission, in its "In-depth review for France," expressed deep concern and demanded more adjustments. The French government, however, takes comfort in the fact that interest rates on the French debt are extremely low, that economic activity showed a slight improvement in the second quarter, and that a French recession would make the European outlook much worse. Beyond these figures and the institutional European debate about "stability," there lies what will become a major issue in European conversations: the appropriate balance between austerity and growth, which dominated the spring meetings of the IMF. The French government welcomed the IMF view that too speedy an effort to rebalance the budget in a weak economic situation could prove counterproductive. This view, however, is not widely shared in Berlin; Germany still expects its French partner to be more decisive in applying the rules agreed upon.

The purpose of this chapter is to assess France's role in the management of the eurozone crisis: will it be part of the solution or part of the problem? The present French imbalances have deep roots. This is why I place them in a longer-term context that I summarize as "a lost decade." I then report on and assess the decisions made by the government after François Hollande's election in May 2012. Finally, I explore the challenges and the opportunities for the government if it wants to escape the present dilemma and in particular improve the Franco-German relationship.

A Lost Decade

Given the present condition of the French and German economies, it is difficult to remember how different the situation was in the early 2000s: France had been surprisingly successful during the 1990s, and Germany, tangled up in the difficulties of reunification, was the sick man of Europe. *The Economist,* in 1999, expressed open stupefaction: "The most perplexing question about contemporary France is this. If, as champions of economic liberalism argue, France embodies all the vices of an over-sheltered, welfare-cushioned, state-stifled, centralized, quaint and archaic European model, then how does it manage to be such a vibrant and prosperous place?" As I write in 2013, the situation is exactly the reverse. Much has been written to explain the German miracle; but how could France have managed its own affairs so poorly as to fall so quickly from that elevated and celebrated position to the tumble-down and debilitated place it today occupies in European affairs?

Days of Glory

The 1990s were dominated in Europe by two events, the reunification of Germany and the establishment of the European Monetary Union (EMU). While Germany was struggling to unify two very different economies under a single currency, France was mobilizing to successfully manage the coming adoption of the European currency. The policy was defined by a simple motto, "competitive disinflation," introduced by Jean-Claude Trichet (1992) at the beginning of the decade; and it worked! Jacques Delors, finance minister under François Mitterrand, had already stopped a vicious wage-price spiral by ending the indexing of wages; thus France in the 1980s had broken with its traditionally high inflation rates. But Trichet (against strong opposition from a vast majority of the left) went further, organizing what would later be known as "internal devaluation" within a fixed exchange-rate area: moderate wage increases would gradually improve competitiveness, exports, jobs, and tax resources. That plan, plus structural reforms such as the reduction of social contributions imposed on unskilled labor, incentives to direct additional financial resources to innovative firms, and an ambitious bipartisan reform of budgetary procedures, resulted in success for the French economy. These achievements are reflected in the IMF Article IV report for 2001:

> France has enjoyed impressive rates of growth with low inflation in recent years, sustained by the virtuous interaction of sound macroeconomic policies and a favorable economic environment. In particular, several years of gradual structural reforms have significantly improved labor market performance, contributing to the unprecedented job-richness of growth. At the same time, taxes have been reduced, while the fiscal deficit has narrowed. No doubt the economy is now structurally sounder. (IMF 2001)

Intervening events have so tarnished these phrases that one cannot read them in 2013 without a sigh of nostalgia.

Retreat

Upon entering the twenty-first century, France was under the strange rule of political *"cohabitation,"* with a conservative president, Jacques Chirac (right wing Union pour un movement populaire, UMP), and a leftist prime minister, Lionel Jospin (Socialist). Divided government is a recipe for deadlock: the team could only coexist and survive in the eyes of the voters by making mutually reinforcing promises and actions to maintain the protection offered by the state against the widely feared harm of "globalization." The fruits planted at that time are still flourishing on the political scene. This decade thus was a time of increased minimum wages, improved pensions, extended health care, and more generous policies for the disadvantaged; economic and financial conditions were viewed with benign neglect; competitiveness, more or less the pivotal word of French economic policy since Georges Pompidou in the early 1970s, completely disappeared from the public discourse; economic elites lost interest in France as a site of production and focused on the global development of the French "national champions." These results are in sharp contrast with the previous decade: here lie the roots of the grave difficulties now facing

France. In this chapter I focus on three main aspects: public finance, the balance of payments, and competitiveness.

Lax Management of Public Finance

France has not had a budget surplus since 1974. The best result was a deficit of 1.5 percent of GDP in 2000 and 2001, under the aforementioned propitious conditions of the late 1990s. After that, things went from bad to worse; but Germany had deficits equal to or higher than those of France until 2006: why should Paris worry if Berlin is doing worse? At that time, France and Germany even teamed up to destroy the discipline of the Stability Pact (designed to enforce budget discipline) that they were unable to comply with.

Diverging trends between the two countries started to develop in 2007 with the election of Nicolas Sarkozy to the French presidency; he had campaigned on the need for French reform, but he proved to be a most negligent president for public finance. While, under Chancellor Gerhard Schröder, Germany finally decided to restore fiscal discipline (from a 3 percent deficit in 2005 to a balance in 2007), France continued on its easygoing path, with the result that there was a difference as high as 4 percent of GDP between the deficits of the two countries in 2007 and 2008; this difference remained unchanged during the whole of Sarkozy's presidency (see appendix tables A-1 and A-2).

Trade Surplus Plunging into Deficit

Managing the balance of payments has been a constant problem for French policymakers since the end of World War II, and even as far back as the 1920s. Devaluation was the unavoidable solution to serious external deficits in 1958, 1969, 1981, 1983, and 1994. Thereafter, during the golden decade previously mentioned, external trade disappeared from radar screens. There was even a significant current balance surplus in 1999 (3 percent of GDP). That was not destined to last, however, and the current account turned into a deficit in 2005 that reached −2.2 percent in 2011 (see appendix tables A-3 and A-4). This persistent deterioration indicates a major weakness.

In France, these poor results are frequently linked to energy imports or to competition from emerging economies. However, such explanations are deceptive: owing to its nuclear program, France is relatively less dependent on oil and gas imports than many other countries; and the emerging economies argument would be correct if France did not have catastrophic export market share losses, among the highest of the euro area countries—higher than Italy's and much higher than Spain's. They indicate a serious problem of competitiveness.

Long-Term Loss of Competitiveness

For fifty years the word "competitiveness" was used in France, first as a catch-word for willingness to quickly rebuild and modernize after the war, then to successfully join the "common market," and finally to lead in the creation of the European currency. After the turn of the new century, the word came to be used as a synonym for an "anti-social/pro-globalization" bias. Nicolas Sarkozy, who campaigned as a modernist candidate desiring to reform France, did not espouse competitiveness; rather, he introduced himself to the voters by saying, "I am the candidate for your purchasing power," not a good stance to take to prepare his fellow citizens to accept international discipline. The expected happened: competitiveness declined steadily; it was duly and regularly reported, but no action ever followed. As a result, France has suffered an increasing cost handicap in relation to other eurozone countries such as Germany and Spain (which means on both sides of the competition: goods with high value added from Germany, and more basic goods from Spain). The cost handicap in relation to Germany grew during this decade and is most frequently estimated at around 10 percent. Now competitiveness has two dimensions, price and non-price, concepts that are frequently difficult to disentangle; this is particularly true in the recent French experience.

For years, economists have tried to explain the evolution of market shares by the price factor, with only limited success. Most export equations tend to minimize the influence of price competitiveness. Statistical measures by Eurostat, the European Statistical Office, show that "non-price competitiveness" seems to be much more important than price competitiveness; it is a strongly negative factor in France and a positive one in Germany. A frequent argument heard in France is thus, "Don't try to compete on a price basis, the end result of such a strategy would be Chinese wages; rather, try to emulate Germany and build a non-price advantage." This argument, however, too facilely assumes the independence of price and non-price factors. Non-price factors have been extensively documented: they include such elements as research and development costs, the number of export firms, and the average size of export firms, all factors that take time to have a measurable impact (the strength of the German *Mittelstand,* for example, has its origins in the late nineteenth century and has never been duplicated anywhere). Many of these factors do not favor France in the long term, but that does not explain the break between the 1990s and the following decade.

Non-price competitiveness also relates to a different set of factors that are indirectly linked to price. Consider the success of Audi compared with that of Renault: it can be said that Renault is a "price-taker" and Audi a "price-maker"; true enough, but how did Audi, which was a second-tier producer in the 1960s, achieve its present extraordinary reputation? Non-price competitiveness is the outcome of a gradual accumulation of improvements in all aspects of a product's life: innovation, quality supervision, design, marketing, sales networks, advertising, customer service, and others. All of that takes time and continuity, and it is costly; it requires expenses and investment from origin (development of the product) to maturity (customer service). In short, non-price competitiveness is nothing more than patiently accumulated and wisely invested price advantage. This argument cuts both ways: when a price-taker is losing its price advantage, it needs to fight back to preserve existing market share by reducing prices; but this results in an erosion of profit margins, making illusory any hope of improvement in non-price competitiveness. This is why econometricians fail to assess the proper role of prices; rather than price indexes, they should use profit measures. This is confirmed by a direct examination of costs and prices, distinguishing between tradable and non-tradable sectors. A comparison between France and Germany of the real effective exchange rate (REER) is illustrative: if the comparison is based on export prices, France is seen to be accumulating a non-negligible but limited loss of competitiveness—that is, 1 percent a year over ten years, in line with the estimate previously mentioned.

But that is not the end of the story. If the comparison is based on labor costs, it shows a bigger advantage for Germany: since the German REER advantage based on unit labor costs (ULC) is larger than that based on price, German export margins have continuously and significantly improved. The result was a winning strategy, relying more and more on non-price parameters. France took the opposite course, with excessive ULC being partially counterbalanced by limited price increases that ultimately brought double-edged losses to French exporters: prices remained excessive, and reduced margins gradually foiled every attempt at counterattack (see appendix figure A-6).

Illusory Relief

After brilliantly entering the twenty-first century, France lost its way and retreated on a path of slow growth and increasing unemployment (see appendix figure A-7). "Globalization" was an easy scapegoat: the voters demanded protection, and the country took the easy path and improved its social system. No one—no government, no statesman—offered a vision of how the country could maintain its place in a changing world, told the truth to the voters, and made the economic and financial decisions that were more and more clearly necessary. This was a time of illusions. The contrast between France and Germany is fascinating in this respect. Chancellor Schröder assumed the role of effective economic statesman, and in a couple of years he transformed a struggling country into the economic powerhouse that his successor, Angela Merkel, would inherit.

From the very beginning, German elites decided to organize Germany's competitive comeback ("Model-Deutschland"). It started early in the decade and was patiently organized. It was completed by sound fiscal decisions. The timing was perfect, taking advantage of the previous period of global expansion in 2005–07, before the financial crisis. By contrast, French voters and politicians agreed to "kick the can down the road" as long as they could. In comparison with most other eurozone countries, the French economy weathered the "great recession" in 2008–09 relatively well; the strength of public and private expenditures alleviated the consequences of the contraction in international trade that severely harmed more open economies. But that proved to be yet another dash of illusory relief.

After his election, Nicolas Sarkozy, rather than immediately adopting badly needed reforms, reveled in his ability to successfully defend the "French model" against the dramatic consequences of a financial crisis imported from the countries of "casino capitalism." In the summer of 2011, anxious that the deepening eurozone crisis could spread to France, the French government adopted a more restrictive stance, but it was too little too late: France lost its AAA credit rating in January 2012. The French primary deficit was (and remains) among the highest in the eurozone and has not started to recede. The public debt stood at 90 percent. The time to face the situation had arrived: the resilience of the country to external conditions had diminished, and those long-standing imbalances hampered its prospects.

A New Presidency

The most recent presidential campaign (in the first half of 2012) thus took place in a gloomy economic and financial environment. As a late convert to austerity, Nicolas Sarkozy campaigned this time as the candidate of competitiveness. François Hollande adopted a more cautious tone, promising little and declaring the need to restore a better-balanced budget in the medium term.

A New Fiscal Stance

Restoring better-balanced budgets turned out to be one of the clearest priorities of the new presidency. First, government policy was immediately dominated by the goal of reducing the deficit to zero in 2017; second, the government took immediate revenue actions amounting to 0.6 percent of GDP to meet the 2012 target; third, the 2013 budget was prepared with a view to quickly reducing the deficit to 3 percent, including actions equivalent to 1.2 percent of GDP; fourth, the "golden rule" of future eurozone tax policy included in the "European compact"—that is, that annual budgets be balanced—was adopted in September. All of this met with the obvious displeasure of the newly elected socialist and environmentalist majority, not to mention the extreme left whose support had been vital in Hollande's victory. "*Austerité*" is a harsh word, but the government immediately committed to a sort of "rigorous management" with the same nuance. This was also not lost on the financial markets, which rewarded this policy by reducing interest rates on the French debt and making them closer (as compared with the Sarkozy era) to German rates.

These decisions raise two questions. First, was this the right rate of progress in balancing the budget? My answer is yes. The weakness of the French financial position was such that decisive action was required to dispel the very real fear that France would join the southern camp of countries, with their huge financing difficulties. The financial world has multiple equilibria, and the Italian experience in July 2011—when suddenly the financial markets became very apprehensive about the Italian debt—is a reminder that very little is needed to tip an economy over the edge (a declaration by former prime minister Berlusconi in this case). Any hint of a return to Mitterrand's policy in 1981 would have immediately had negative consequences with a very dramatic impact on the country and the eurozone. The government decided to act preventively precisely to avoid having to take the extreme steps necessary when a country is under immediate pressure from the markets; this is why the government constantly rejected the idea of "*austerité,*" claiming that its policy was to seek to restore the budget without causing a recession.

Second question: Was the mix of tax increases and spending cuts the appropriate one? The answer is no. The level of public spending in France has reached 57 percent, which is 5 percent higher than, for example, that of Sweden and ranks at the top of the eurozone. To be sure, these expenditures produce value: a generous social network, a renowned health system, esteemed universities (the *grandes écoles*), excellent infrastructure, and so forth. But spending on other items is less convincing; a large part of these expenses is not financed, and a deterioration of services is visible; the costs of a multilevel administration are extremely high; it is frequently said that

France has 90 civil servants for every 1,000 inhabitants as compared with 50 in Germany. As stated by Michel Pébereau as early as 2005, in his report on the dangerous path of public debt: "[F]or a quarter of a century, each time a new problem arose, the country responded with more spending." And not much reform (see appendix figure A-9 for a comparison between France and Germany of general government expenditures by function). In 2013, the government decided on spending cuts to reduce the deficit, but these constituted only one-third of the actions taken; and that (relatively) modest portion proved difficult to implement. It is a particularly challenging task with so many vested interests close to the state (and the present political majority), made even more difficult by new spending (for example, on reducing poverty and on military action in Mali) after the adoption of the budget. In short, the budget package relied too heavily on increasing taxes, which rose by 5.8 percent between May 2012 and May 2013; more discouragingly, in the same period, spending increased by 6.2 percent, and the result was an increase in the deficit of 3 billion euros. Not exactly the hoped-for path.

Adapting to a Less Favorable Macroeconomic Outlook

In 2012, the European Commission expected France to reduce its structural deficit by 4 percent between 2010 and 2013, and to be under the 3 percent ceiling in 2013. Relying on a fast resolution of the eurozone crisis, the authorities expected growth to bounce back to 0.8 percent in 2013. This forecast quickly proved overly optimistic and was revised to 0.4 percent and then to +/− 0. It was then publicly acknowledged in the spring that France would miss its target of a 3 percent budget deficit this year. It is now recognized in Brussels and in Paris that the 2013 budget deficit will be close to 3.7 percent (after reaching 4.5 percent in 2012). The discussion between Brussels and Paris comes from two different standpoints.

In the French view, the country had reduced its structural deficit by 2.4 percent between 2010 and 2012; in 2013, as the figures above show, the reduction would be −0.7/−0.8 percent; if one takes into account the slowdown of growth (0 in 2013) as compared with a potential growth rate of 1.3 percent, the cyclical component of the 2013 deficit would be some 0.65 percent; add this to the existing reduction, and the 2010–13 total structural deficit reduction amounts to 3.9 percent (2.4 percent + 0.75 percent + 0.65 percent), not far from the 4 percent target. The government's position is thus that "the deficit reduction is under way and it is fully legitimate to delay reaching the target." It is interesting to observe that the government's position was supported by the IMF in its Article IV report in December 2012: "Staff took the view that the medium-term balanced budget target was appropriate but that if growth in 2013 were to fall short of the authorities' assumption, maintaining the 2013 target unchanged at 3 percent of GDP would move fiscal policy into an overly pro-cyclical stance, notwithstanding the importance of coordination at the European level."

How is this argument seen in Brussels? There was no question but that a delay would be granted. but additional conditions were attached to a green light, which were only reluctantly agreed to by Berlin. How will the French government try to follow the path that was agreed upon? The answer will be expressed in the 2014 budget.

Two things, however, have already been made clear: First, the government will maintain its line; second, the government immediately launched a new wave of pension reforms to prepare for the post-2020 period (this project, however, is already deemed, unofficially, as inappropriate by Brussels). Interestingly, a brief debate emerged in early March regarding the need for a "stimulus." Different ministers have started to be more vocal in expressing their views to the prime minister that austerity is bad and that the government would be well advised to adopt a new economic strategy based on "investment." But all this has not resulted in a new economic strategy, no one so far has tried to demonstrate how the resources could be better used, and no one has mentioned a rupture with Brussels (even though some socialists have harshly criticized Chancellor Merkel). All this should thus be seen as political maneuvering for the future. For now, the government is designing the measures that will define the 2014 budget. Experts have for the most part agreed on the following figures:

—The previous estimate for the 2014 annual effort to restore a balanced budget in 2017: €10 billion

—Additional expenses in 2014: €10 billion for competitiveness measures; €3.5 billion for other measures already announced (poverty; war and more generally the military will be a hot topic)

—One-shot tax resources in 2013 (absent in 2014): €6 billion

—Efforts from the negotiation with Brussels to be "significantly" below a 3 percent deficit: €10 billion

—New tax measures already resolved: €6 billion (VAT/competitiveness plan)

—Total: €30 billion

These figures speak volumes about the size of the difficulties still to be overcome by the government.

Microeconomic Issues and Competitiveness

France is a land of economic contrasts. On the positive side, there are successful, world-class multinationals in a wide range of industries (not just in luxury goods): Accor (hotels and resorts), Airbus, Air France, Air Liquide (sophisticated chemicals), Alstom (transportation equipment), Arianespace (rockets), AXA (financial services); the same for B: BNP-Paribas . . . , C: Carrefour . . . , and so on through the alphabet. There are more French companies in the Global Fortune 500 than there are, for example, British companies. These French companies are highly competitive and offer job opportunities for well-educated and highly motivated French young people everywhere in the world; for example, Citroen, the car manufacturer, is building a new plant in Shenzen, China.

The new plant in Shenzen presents a contrast to the Citroen plant in Aulnay sous bois near Paris, which is due to close in 2014; the two plants illustrate the French paradox. It is considered promising for young people graduating from the *grandes écoles* to start a career in Shenzen, while popular frustration is growing in Aulnay. As a production site, France has suffered a dramatic decade-long loss of competitiveness. Deindustrialization is the major result of what is seen, in retrospect, as a lost decade; despite the oft-expressed French disdain for British policies, which supposedly sacrificed industry to the interests of the City, the manufacturing share of GDP is now lower in France than in Britain. The world-class multinationals just mentioned are expanding worldwide; according to a study by INSEE (2013), 2,500 French groups have 31,000 subsidiaries outside France with a staff of 4.7 million, as compared with 4.2 million employed in France. The sixty-seven most important of these are in some fifty countries where they realize 55 percent of their business (employment and turnover); employment outside France grew by 5 percent in recent years while falling by 4 percent in France. Plant closures in France (in Florange and Aulnay; by Petroplus, Goodyear, and others) regularly make the news and contribute to the ingrained pessimism of the populace. Unemployment is rising, above 10 percent at this writing in 2013, and there is an even greater division between young people struggling to find a place in society and insiders defending "*les avantages acquis.*"

Nobody expected the new government to be able to restore competitiveness in the blink of an eye. François Hollande was very much aware of the terrible situation of public finances, and he made a radical choice on this issue, but not about competitiveness. Referring again to the aforementioned non-price factor of competitiveness, there is always in France, on both sides of the aisle, the idea that the target should be *"une sortie par le haut"* (escaping by taking the high road), specialization based on higher value added, higher skills, higher wages. There is also the widely held conviction that the state can better drive such high-end specialization than a weak private sector can. This was the industrial policy under De Gaulle, Pompidou, and Mitterrand, and it is still thriving. Now, despite the absence of decisions like the nationalizations in 1981, both the rhetoric of Arnaud Montebourg, the leftist minister for "industrial renewal," and the tax measures adopted in the name of justice (with a 75 percent marginal tax rate as the banner) gave the impression of an anti-business government. Flashy declarations about the need to avoid plant closures, but not followed by decisive actions, fuel the pessimism of the French and increasing distrust of the political class but also produce a lose-lose business context: the deindustrialization process is marginally slowed at best, and new projects and investments are postponed or canceled.

The end of the year 2012 nonetheless brought two pieces of good news from and for the president and the economy.

First, the previously mentioned Gallois report on competitiveness proposed significant supply side measures that were included in an important fiscal rebate that should reduce labor costs by 6 to 8 percent in 2014. In fact, the report recommended more rapid and direct action in the form of a reduction in employers' social security contributions equal to roughly 7 percent of GDP. The adopted measure is not ideal. It is not a simple, clear-cut tax reduction; it is a complex redistributive scheme, not directly affecting individual costs, with the result that it could have only limited or even perverse effects. After receiving this subsidy, firms not desiring to hire additional staff could very well decide to share this "windfall profit" with insiders rather than create jobs. In any event, in the difficult relationship between the government and the private sector, the measure was ultimately well received as a measured answer to the challenge of excessive costs, but even more as the start of a new attitude toward business. The success of the measure over the course of 2013 proved to be limited at best: it is difficult to implement, it is not sufficiently focused on improving the competitiveness of the tradable sector, and it benefits mainly protected industries.

Second, industrial relations are historically very rough in France; room for collective negotiation and decentralized agreements is very limited, in comparison with Germany, for example. In France, state action and the uniformity of the law are most frequently considered the main vehicles of "social progress." François Hollande has been convinced for years that this mix was improper and had to be changed and that the "social partners," not the government, had to find a new equilibrium regarding the trade-off between flexibility and protection. It is no surprise that this turned out to be a difficult negotiation, but it was finally successfully concluded in January, and this is renewing the social playing field in a way potentially not seen since the end of World War II. The agreement is thus widely recognized as a step in the right direction, but much remains to be done for the extremely rigid labor market to function better. The introduction of pension reform in the autumn will be another deciding moment.

These reforms have not ushered in a completely new season. The effectiveness of the first remains unclear, and the second still must be widely implemented; but there is at least the hope that some of France's more entrenched rigidities have yielded and that the time is ripe for exploring—cautiously, to be sure—some unconventional avenues, and that is good news.

France and the Management of the Eurozone Debt Crisis

"*Le changement, c'est maintenant*" was the motto of François Hollande as a candidate. French leftist voters took this message as a promise of a more generous government, and their disappointment when faced with tax increases and spending cuts is regularly seen in the polls. But let us assume that the major ambition of the new president, for economic policy, was to change the economic policy in Europe from one based on austerity for all, a policy illustrated by Europe's "odd couple," Angela Merkel and Nicolas Sarkozy, to policies that avoid pushing the eurozone into recession. Hollande has many reasons to think that there is no solution to the debt problem if tax revenues are continuously declining and that the future of European youth cannot be one of eternal unemployment, except in Germany (see the chapter on social conditions). Hollande has good reason to think that the populace will not tolerate years of austerity without reward and that only extremist movements would benefit from this political slide. Hollande is right to think of global interdependencies that make a prosperous Europe a desirable goal for its partners, principally the United States. It was no surprise to see President Obama so concerned by the threat of a recession in Europe and welcoming of his French counterpart at their first G-20 meeting in 2012. President Hollande has many reasons to cling to his vision when facing a crisis that has not been seen since the 1930s. Designing a good policy mix for the future of Europe, not a narrowly partisan "tax and spend" policy, is a great ambition. According to the IMF (2012), the main challenge of French fiscal policy is "to pursue consolidation at a pace that balances cyclical considerations with the need to preserve market confidence in French policies and in the euro area crisis resolution strategy."

Owing to the weakness of the French economy and the threats to its external financing, France under Sarkozy lost most of its influence in the eurozone, specifically in its dialogue with Germany. A necessary condition for restoring the voice of France was to put its house in order; this is why the rebalancing of public finance has been the overarching goal of Hollande's five-year presidential term. So far this has proved not to be a sufficient condition, and the "Franco-German engine" is not delivering much. There are signs that the Franco-German partnership is not going well. The celebration of the 1963 Elysée treaty lacked ambition and warmth; this was not good. The German perception is clear. There is an ancient and widespread uneasiness about French economic policies. In German eyes, things are simple: France is in a weak financial position, a situation demanding resolute action and clear communications about public finance and competitiveness. Period.

Without denigrating what is being done to better balance the budget, the Germans see a tortured course of contradictory decisions, two-edged language about industrial policy, and incomprehensible governmental communication. Echoing the comments of many other German officials, the president of the Bundesbank has repeatedly expressed these concerns. French officials react negatively to these criticisms. They place a high value on the sort of confidence that is visible in the markets, permitting extraordinarily low interest rates, and they saw a positive comment from Goldman Sachs as testimony that their policy reflects an "appropriate balance." Their view seems to be: "Imagine what the European economic outlook would be if France were following extreme austerity measures, beyond what has already been decided." Among French officials, the hope that Hollande's election would permit a new compromise between austerity and recovery is in abeyance. For the Socialist government, this hope has now been deferred until after the German elections, even if it is unlikely that they can produce any dramatic change in German strategy.

How serious is the Franco-German misunderstanding? It certainly does not help "European" momentum (unlike the compromise on the European budget between Angela Merkel and Britain's David Cameron), but it also should not be exaggerated. There is also the traditional left-right discord that has regularly produced tensions in the past between Berlin and socialist governments in Paris. French imbalances are the biggest hurdle in the relationship. I previously mentioned that the European Commission expected

France to reduce its structural deficit by 4 percent between 2010 and 2013 with a view to being under the 3 percent ceiling in 2013. This is a significant source of misunderstanding. French officials see two different, possibly conflicting, goals; they emphasize the 4 percent reduction and call for an adjustment of the target. Their German counterparts consider the 3 percent target to be the cornerstone and the 4 percent reduction only a tool to reach that target. The German position thus remains ambivalent: on the one hand, there is widespread belief that, as always, France is tempted to maneuver on the wrong side of budget discipline; on the other hand, there is deep conviction that if France is a ticking time bomb it could be extremely dangerous for the future of the eurozone. Berlin's political position could thus be: as much severity as possible without pushing the French government toward unmanageability.

The answer to the question raised in the introduction is relatively clear. France is certainly not the ticking time bomb that *The Economist* depicted in early 2013: the government inherited long-term imbalances that no one expected to be resolved in a short time. On the contrary, the president's commitment to sounder public finance has so far proven to be credible; the determination of the government is unyielding; the fine-tuning of a budget that is strict, but avoids pushing the economy into recession, is appreciated both by the financial markets and by the international financial institutions; and competitiveness has been recognized by the government as a primary challenge. But the situation remains very fragile. The resilience of the country to any adverse shock is diminishing; its external financial position remains extremely weak; and policy relies too heavily on tax increases, rather than on spending cuts. A deterioration of the social environment could abruptly derail these efforts. Beyond the macroeconomic figures, France remains a problem within the eurozone because François Hollande's France did not succeed in bringing a new momentum to the management of the crisis. The French "model" today remains incomprehensible and unconvincing outside of France, and the German government has not demonstrated any warmth toward the French proposals.

Broadly speaking, 2012 marked a turning point in the eurozone crisis, but brought no end to it. The political willingness to build a "more perfect monetary union" was reaffirmed by the June European Council, and the markets have been smoothed by European Central Bank president Mario Draghi's subsequent commitment to do "whatever it takes" to ensure the future of the euro. The financial markets are calm, but social tensions are on the rise. The Italian vote could be a warning bell: Italy's turning ungovernable would be a bad sign for other democracies. France is not in a similar situation, since the political institutions of the Fifth Republic are resilient; but the two major parties, the Socialist Party and the center-right UMP, are divided and uncertain, while the extreme left and the extreme right are making gains. According to Gérard Grunberg (2013), a sharp observer of the French political scene, this could herald a coming political crisis.

At the European level, 2012 could be seen in the future as a welcome digression in the resolution of the debt crisis. The eurozone as a whole remains fragile; Germany may have to face more quickly than expected the consequences of the economic policies that it desires its European neighbors to implement. By just waiting for unexpected good news from austerity programs everywhere, the period of calm the eurozone enjoyed in 2012 and 2013 could come to an end without decisive governmental action. In addition to the present sterile national disputes, the May 2014 European elections could be an opportunity for the expression of all sorts of frustrations and disappointments. And this could be the real time bomb ticking in Europe. Without popular support, the consequences of future economic policies could be grim, whatever their political color or their national flag. The solution to the austerity-versus-growth dilemma needs to be clarified and explained to the public. But first it needs to be clarified between governments. In this regard, there is nothing more urgent than a better Franco-German understanding, an understanding that is sorely lacking at present.

References

Cour des Comptes. 2011. "Les prélèvements fiscaux et sociaux en France et en Allemagne." Paris.

The Economist. 1999. "A Wiser, Weaker State." June 3.

———. 2012a. "France in Denial." March 31.

———. 2012b. "A Time-Bomb at the Heart of Europe." November 17.

European Commission. 2012a. "Macroeconomic Imbalances—France." Occasional Paper 105 (July). Brussels.

———. 2012b. *Special Eurobarometer* 378 (January). Brussels.

———. 2013. "In-depth review for France, in accordance with Article V of Regulation 1176/2011 on the prevention and correction of macroeconomic imbalances." Staff Working Document. Brussels (http://ec.europa.eu/europe2020/pdf/nd/idr2013_france_en.pdf).

Grunberg, Gérard. 2013. "La crise politique française." *Telos* (April 23).

IMF. 2001. "France 2001 Article IV Consultation, Concluding Statement of the Mission." Washington.

———. 2012. France 2012 Article IV Consultation. December. Washington.

INSEE (National Institute for Statistics and Economic Studies). 2013. "Les groupes français à l'étranger." INSEE Première 1439 (March).

Mistral, Jacques. 2010. "La France en faillite, le miroir allemand." *Le Débat* 162 (November–December).

OECD. 2012. "Society at a Glance—2011." Paris.

Pébereau, Michel. 2005. "Des finances publiques au service de notre avenir, rompre avec la facilité de la dette." *La Documentation Française.* December 16.

Trichet, Jean-Claude. 1992. "Dix ans de désinflation compétitive." *Les notes bleues de Bercy* (October).

———. 2011. "Competitiveness and the Smooth Functioning of the EMU." Brussels: European Central Bank. February.

6

Germany: Constraints in the Crisis

FRIEDRICH HEINEMANN

Whether German politicians and voters like it or not, their country today carries a particular responsibility for the future of Europe. Since a deep and self-intensifying crisis of confidence shattered the euro area in the year 2010, the overall good state of the German economy has become one of the important assets in the European aspiration for new credibility. It is inevitable and completely natural that this constellation results in conflicting views and interests. On the one hand, the countries in crisis want solidarity and support from Germany and the smaller stable countries, such as Finland and the Netherlands; on the other hand, German voters and their representatives fear excessive costs and tend to stress the crucial role of economic responsibility.

Given this natural antagonism, this chapter has one key objective: to identify the actual constraints that the German government faces in the European debt crisis. The economic literature has been highly creative in coming up with solutions to the crisis—for example, joint euro area government bond issues ("eurobonds"). Some of these creative solutions, however, may be ignoring the constraints that Germany faces. In this context, the personalization of German positions in the debt crisis (such as the "Angela Merkel position") may be misleading and could result in unrealistic expectations about the freedom of future German governments, which is determined by voter preferences, constitutional constraints, and dominant economic perceptions. In this chapter I seek to clarify the boundaries for the evolution of German euro policies.

The Constitution and the Constitutional Court

A primary constraint on German policy is to be found in the country's constitution, the "Basic Law" (*Grundgesetz*) and the court responsible therefor, the Federal Constitutional Court (hereafter "the Court"). It is now an almost empirical fact that any significant step toward deeper European integration will be challenged in numerous complaints brought to the Court. The case brought against the European Stability Mechanism (ESM) and the European Fiscal Compact (EFC), had 37,000 plaintiffs, the largest number of parties ever to raise a constitutional complaint, indicating the intensity of the conflict (Schmidt 2013).

The Court traditionally defends the autonomy of German constitutional law against claims of the dominance of the European Court of Justice (ECJ) and of European law over national constitutions (Vranes 2013). The Court regularly defines "red lines" for the evolution of European policies that would still be consistent with the German constitution: in its ruling on the Maastricht Treaty, for example, it paved the way for Germany's participation in monetary union as a "stability community." If monetary union developed in a way inconsistent with this characteristic of stability, the contractual basis for German participation would be breached, resulting in a German exit as a possible ultima ratio (Herrmann 2012). The Court also asserts the right of an "ultra vires" review of EU secondary law—that is, an examination of whether new legal acts are within the limits of the authority transferred to the European level. The ruling on the Lisbon Treaty also established an "identity review," an examination of whether the exercise of EU authority endangers the inviolable core of the German constitution (Vranes 2013).

As long as these red lines are very abstract and general, they may have few practical consequences. However, the recent rulings on the financial aid package for Greece (2011), the European Financial Stability Fund (EFSF) (2012) and ESM/Fiscal Compact (2012) include not only general principles, but also some very specific conditions for the constitutionality of the new European institutions and procedures. At the same time, the EFSF/Fiscal Compact preliminary ruling also indicates a certain openness to the future development of the European Monetary Union (EMU) and demonstrates judicial restraint on specific risk assessments and policy decisions.

A leitmotif of all of the recent rulings is the priority of the rights of the Bundestag, the lower house of the German legislature (Wendel 2013). The principle is that the German parliament must have a continuous and decisive say in all credit and guaranty decisions in all circumstances. The Court stresses that the Bundestag may not relinquish its "parliamentary budget responsibility" by means of any kind of vague budgetary authorization. In the Greece and EFSF cases, the Court states that the Bundestag "may not . . . deliver itself up to any mechanisms with financial effect which . . . may result in incalculable burdens with budget relevance without prior mandatory consent" (Wendel 2013, p. 35). Any automatic mechanism that would make Germany liable for the financial consequences of the actions of other EU member countries would be unconstitutional: each new guaranty must be precisely quantifiable and subject to parliamentary consent (Herrmann 2012). A consequence of this thinking was the condition imposed in the ESM ruling that the government had to seek a clarification that the guaranty cap in the ESM Treaty would apply under all circumstances.

But even parliamentary consent cannot legitimize any amount of a guaranty. In its ruling, the Court refuses to quantify a maximum limit and defers to the responsibility of the legislature to assess the risks involved. Still, it makes clear that such a constitutional maximum does exist in principle: the budgetary responsibility of the (future) Bundestag, and hence the principle of democracy, would be violated if budgetary autonomy as a consequence of German losses in a guaranty scheme could cease to exist for a considerable period of time (Wendel 2013). The level of a constitutional maximum for liability was not reached with the initial German guaranty amounts for the ESM (170 billion euros), and the Court does not provide any precise indication of a critical level. The Court also emphasizes that the principle of a constitutional limit would only become relevant where there was a "manifest overstepping of extreme limits" so that "budget autonomy, at least for an appreciable period of time, was not merely restricted but effectively failed" (Bundesverfassungsgericht 2012, no. 216). A judge on the Court hinted that the size of one annual federal German budget (about 300 billion euros) could serve as a benchmark for a critical upper limit (Mayer and Heidfeld 2012), but this should be seen as a personal opinion. Thus a quantitative upper limit for possible future guaranties is vague, but it does exist. Joint and several guaranties for eurobonds as a general refinancing tool for euro area governments would be a likely case of unconstitutional "manifest overstepping," given that the combined Italian and Spanish government debt exceeds the German GDP.

The Court also draws some red lines for the involvement of the European Central Bank (ECB) in a crisis strategy: It denies the ESM access to ECB financing (Herrmann 2012). This would violate the prohibition of any central bank credit facilities in favor of government institutions (art. 123 of the Treaty on the Functioning of the European Union (TFEU)). At the turn of the year 2013–14, the Outright Monetary Transaction (OMT) program was under consideration by the Court. The decisive question for the Court is whether the OMT is still within the limits and powers conferred on the EU. If the OMT program cannot be seen as an instrument serving monetary policy objectives, it would have to be deemed a violation of TFEU art. 123 (prohibition of ECB loans to sovereign entities) and may also violate TFEU art. 130 (independence of the ECB). If the Court concludes that there is a violation of EU law, it could, in theory, prohibit the German Bundesbank from further participation in any actions not covered by EU treaties and thus in effect stop the OMT program. However, the more likely outcome also with respect to this case is a "yes, but" decision, in which the Court limits only the future implementation of the program (Siekmann and Wieland 2013).

While all these examples seem to indicate that the Court is interfering intensely in specific strategy decisions, there is a strong countervailing tendency in recent decisions, one of judicial restraint (Wendel 2013). The Court is limited to assessing whether there are "manifest violations" of important principles such as budgetary autonomy, whether Parliament carries out its responsibility to make a proper assessment, and whether Parliament has access to comprehensive information.

The Court's principled refusal to surrender to the ECJ its authority to review EU law has specific consequences for any future German government's room for maneuver in any crisis strategy. Far-reaching eurobond solutions such as the idea of generally replacing national bonds in the euro area with jointly and severally guaranteed EU issues are clearly incompatible with the Court's ruling. For Germany to assume liability for billions of euros would doubtlessly constitute a "manifest violation" of the principle of budgetary autonomy. It is disputed whether certain, more limited variants of eurobonds might be constitutional (Mayer and Heidfeld 2012). The clear rejection of any automatic procedure and the hints of critical upper limits of guaranties, however, stand in the way of many of the ideas that are being debated. Even if a certain eurobond variant could pass constitutional muster, each new tranche of the issue would require renewed consent by the Bundestag. Hence, the credibility of this financing scheme for the future of the bond markets would not be too different from today's capped and limited guaranty EFSF/ESM schemes.

Thus the bottom line is that Karlsruhe has significantly reduced the likelihood that a European pooling of government debt issues may someday offer a way out of the credibility crisis.[1]

1. Whether the Court also defines narrower limits to the ECB intervening in government bond markets was uncertain at the time of writing, since the case on the OMT program was still pending.

Voter Preferences

Voter acceptance can be a further constraint on Germany's room for maneuver in the crisis. The European debt crisis was the dominant political and economic issue in public debate and media coverage in Germany between 2010 and 2013. In spite of all the dramatic developments in the crisis, Germany continues to be a country where the principle of support for a single currency is strong, and above the EU average; it is equal to levels of support by French or Belgian voters (see figure 6-1). A series of surveys by the Allensbach Institute shows consistently over time that nostalgia for the DM has been on the decline continuously since the introduction of the euro (see figure 6-2). It seems surprising that even the dramatic years of the debt crisis have not stopped this trend. On the contrary, the speed of the decline has accelerated recently. One interpretation is that the years of crisis may have demonstrated the merits of a large currency area; in a comparable crisis situation, the deutsche mark (DM) would have fallen victim to the shock of significant appreciation, to the detriment of German exports and jobs.

In spite of these fairly favorable results for support of monetary union, detailed surveys indicate significant concerns on the part of German voters: [2]

—A significant minority is opposed to the single European currency.

—Even if German citizens may not see an advantage in a return to the DM, more than two-thirds indicate a lack of trust in the euro.

—German voters state their solidarity with the citizens of the countries in crisis, and most think that many of the victims do not have personal responsibility for the crisis. Nevertheless, voters think that aid must be limited. Eurobonds are particularly unpopular according to a July 2012 survey, in which 73 percent were against this instrument.

—Chancellor Merkel's actions in the crisis were supported by a majority in the spring and summer of 2013.

Given the prominence of eurobonds in the debate on possible strategies for a resolution of the crisis, it is useful to take a closer look at German voter preferences. Figure 6-3 shows the correlation of support for eurobonds with the rating grade of all euro area member countries. Theory would predict a negative correlation between rating quality and voter support for eurobonds.

2. Bertelsmann Stiftung (2012); *Deutsche Mittelstands Nachrichten* (2012); EurActiv (2013); Focus online (2011); *Handelsblatt* (2012); *Handelsblatt* (2013); Ich will Europa (2012); Köcher (2013); Kunz (2013); *manager magazin online* (2010); *merkur-online* (2013); *RP online* (2012); *Spiegel Online* (2010); *Spiegel Online* (2011); *Spiegel Online* (2012); *Stern.de* (2012a); *Stern.de* (2012b).

Figure 6-1. *European Attitudes toward the Economic and Monetary Union*

Q: What is your position toward the Economic and Monetary Union with a single currency?
Percent share of all responses

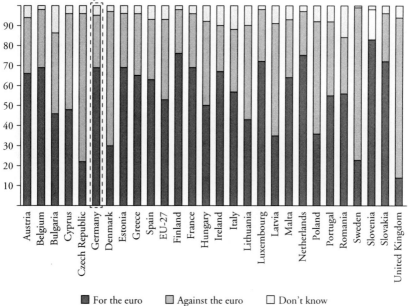

■ For the euro   ▨ Against the euro   ☐ Don't know

Source: European Commission (2012, table 69).

Figure 6-2. *German Citizens' Preference for the Deutsche Mark*

Q: Would you prefer returning to a system with the Deutsche Mark?
Percent share of "yes" responses

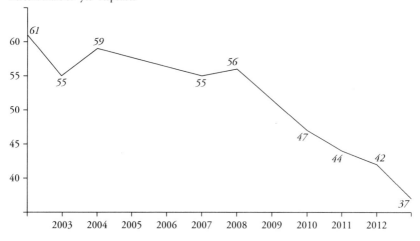

Source: Köcher (2013).

Figure 6-3. *European Support for Eurobonds and Sovereign Rating*

Q: Are in favor of or against the introduction of Eurobonds?
Percent share in favor of eurobonds

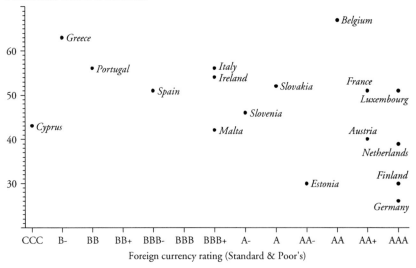

Foreign currency rating (Standard & Poor's)

Source: European Commission (2012, table 145); Standard & Poor's (2013).

Eurobonds, with their interest rate equalization as a consequence of complete mutual guaranties, involve implicit transfers from countries with a low credit risk toward the high-risk countries. Hence one would think that this option would be popular in fiscally weak countries and less attractive to voters in countries that are (relatively) fiscally sound.

This expected correlation can be seen in the data. It is, however, interesting to compare countries within a single rating category: among the four triple-A countries, German voters (followed closely by Finnish voters) indeed show the fiercest opposition. It is striking that voters in Luxembourg and France have majorities in favor, even though they have an equal or similar rating. French voters may expect a further weakening of the country's creditworthiness, which makes a mutual guaranty scheme more attractive in the future. Conversely, voters in Estonia, a country with very low debt levels, do not see any future advantage from credit-risk pooling, and thus they demonstrate a resistance similar to that of voters in Finland and Germany. Whatever the precise explanation, it is a fact that more extensive guaranties are more unpopular among German voters in Germany than among voters in other euro countries.

In general, an examination of the attitudes of German voters in the debt crisis demonstrates that the euro project as such still enjoys support. Fundamental euro-skeptics are an ever shrinking minority in Germany. This minority is, however, much larger than the complete absence of euro-skeptic parties in the German Bundestag would suggest.

The Debate in the Economics Profession

Public opinion and political debate in Germany are influenced by controversies about the euro within the German economics profession. These opinions are an additional constraint, since they have an effect on the understanding of the crisis by politicians.

There is a pronounced tradition of euro-skepticism in the academic debate dating back to the early 1990s, when the monetary union was being debated and decisions made. German economists reacted to the signing of the Maastricht Treaty in February 1992 with a widely publicized manifesto advising against a premature start of the European Monetary Union (Ohr and Schäfer 1992). While euro-skeptical German economists never have been particularly anti-integrationist, they have been critical of early and far-reaching monetary union. But the pro-euro camp of economists also received academic support and public attention at the time. In their view: the euro had the chance to become a stable currency, fears of a transfer union (which would be based on fiscal equalization transfers between members) were exaggerated, and EMU should start on a timely basis in order to reap the advantages of a common currency (Bofinger and others 1997).

This old debate is an important point of reference for today's controversies. Clearly, events since the spring of 2010 tend to confirm the fears of the euro-skeptics and to dash some of the expectations of the defenders of the euro: It has not been possible to punish fiscal irresponsibility by means of a strict application of the convergence criteria and the Stability Pact. Nor was market discipline effective before 2010: before the crisis, yields on government bonds had largely converged and did not reflect the different credit quality of euro member countries. The euro area has clearly demonstrated that it is anything but an optimum currency area. Furthermore, fears that, with the introduction of the euro, Germany would become part of a "transfer union" have proven to be well founded.

Since the actual experience in the crisis strongly indicates the empirical truth of many anti-euro arguments, it should not be surprising that German academic debate on the future of the single currency is once again highly skeptical and that these views are influential in the public debate. For the critics, the Hamburg economist Bernd Lucke established a communique from the "plenum of economists" in February 2011 (Plenum der Ökonomen 2011), which strongly criticized the rescue policies and the establishment of the "euro umbrella". Later, 277 economics professors signed an open letter against the "European banking union" (Krämer 2012). A prominent economist on the side of the critics of rescue and one with a particularly strong presence in public debate is the Munich economics professor Hans-Werner Sinn, who stresses the high risks involved in the euro system's TARGET imbalances (Sinn 2012a, 2012b).

The banking union manifesto provoked a reaction in the form of an open letter by economists with expertise in financial markets and macroeconomics who support an active stabilization policy and an expansion of European instruments (Heinemann, Burda, and others 2012). Similarly, the German Council of Economic Experts is not only a prominent supporter of an active rescue policy but also has gained much attention in Europe as a result of its initiative for a far-reaching European financing mechanism, the "European Redemption Fund," which would imply that countries like Germany accept much larger financial liabilities for mutual debt issuance than they do today (German Council of Economic Experts 2012).

Although this debate among German economists may be typical, to some extent, of the debate in Europe as a whole, some common aspects are striking from a European perspective: most German economists regard moral hazard-problems as highly relevant problems demanding a lot of attention (with differing evaluations of the possibility of coping with them).[3] And even the supporters of broader German engagement, such as the German Council of Economic Experts, demand that any financial aid be strictly conditional and limited in time. In addition, the council rejects the idea of a transfer union and regards its debt redemption fund as a transitory instrument with the objective of autonomous debt financing after the transitory period of debt redemption.

In the international debate on the crisis and its economic causes, there is one more market difference between the debate among German economists

3. "Moral hazard" describes a standard incentive problem involved in any insurance contract. Insurance creates incentive for the insured party to act less cautiously, since the risk is shifted to the insurance provider. The analogy to the euro area debt crisis is that any credits or guaranties in favor of the crisis countries might lower these countries' incentives to make structural reforms and undertake consolidation.

and the international economics profession: in Germany, the origins of the crisis are predominantly interpreted as structural, by both the supporters and the critics of the rescue policy. As a consequence, demand management aspects do not play a major role in the debate on appropriate policy responses. Nor is the German current account surplus—currently at about 6 percent of GDP—viewed as a cause of great concern for economic policy.

Of course, German economists take account of the criticism that the country's current account surpluses are part of the European imbalances and need to be addressed by means of active fiscal policy or wage increases.[4] The Council of Economic Advisors, which is strongly in favor of an active EU rescue approach, in its 2010 report (German Council of Economic Advisors 2010), takes a comprehensive position on that criticism, which represents the thinking of mainstream economics in Germany[5] and can be summarized as follows:

The Council stresses the intertemporal dimension of current account developments. With an intertemporal perspective, it can be seen as optimal for a highly developed economy with an aging population to have a significant current account surplus. By means of such a surplus, this economy accumulates assets needed to cushion the impact of declining growth on future consumption. Furthermore, it is efficient and contributes to global convergence for a highly developed economy, by means of its current account surplus, to export capital to developing countries and assist them in catching up. Thus,

4. Paul De Grauwe and Yuemei Ji have forcefully made this point: "The responsibility of Germany is key here. This is the leading eurozone country that has accumulated the largest current account surpluses during more than a decade. These surpluses also made it possible for the periphery countries to accumulate large current account deficits. Thus, the responsibility of the unsustainable imbalances in the eurozone is shared between debtor and creditor countries. For every reckless debtor there must have been a reckless creditor" (De Grauwe and Ji 2013, p. 10).

5. In the council's reports, minority statements indicate that a single member does not agree to the majority view. Such a minority statement by one of the five members has also been given with respect to this section with a plea for a more active wage policy. The typical majority in the council (4:1) is probably not too distant from the dominance of different economics schools in the German economics profession in general. According to a survey of the members of the leading association of German-speaking economists (Verein für Socialpolitik), only 12 percent of respondents would classify themselves as Keynesians. The dominant self-classifications are "Neoclassical" (42 percent), "Public Choice/Institutional Economics" (37 percent), and "Ordo-Liberalism" (24 percent) (multiple self-classifications were allowed in this survey: Frey, Humbert, and Schneider (2007).

an economy such as Germany most likely should run a current account surplus in an intertemporal equilibrium situation.[6]

The council also rejects the beggar-thy-neighbor criticisms of German wage policies. It argues that German wage and current account developments must be interpreted in a long-run perspective starting from German unification. The shock of unification and the subsequent high unemployment resulted in intensive adjustment pressure, which for a long time led to wage settlements improving competitiveness and more labor-intensive production, both in the export and the domestic sectors. The resulting wage moderation, together with structural reforms, was successful in substantially increasing employment, although there still is not full employment. The Council also questions whether higher wages would necessarily help shrink the current account surplus, since the net impact of higher wages is ambiguous. As higher wages decrease employment, the net effect on the aggregate of wages, consumption, and imports is unclear. In addition, setting wages is not subject to German governmental policy, so that any demand for a more active wage policy in Germany ignores the institutional constraints.

In the same manner, deficit spending is, in the view of the council, not a sustainable way to stimulate import demand since it would only be a flash in the pan. The best way for Germany to stimulate growth and import demand is through a continuation of structural reforms that generate sustainable growth. For a real and sustainable German contribution to higher growth in Europe, the council recommends higher investment in long-run growth factors such as education, research and transportation infrastructure, further deregulation of product markets, and further reforms of labor markets and social security.

These mainstream positions in the German economic debate do not imply that the exact current level of the German surplus is appropriate. However, the dominant view is that government policy should not manipulate the current account and would also hardly be able to do so successfully. A (modest) fall in the current account surplus will be rather the endogenous and market-led outcome of higher German employment and growth (as a consequence of the country's successful structural reforms).

6. Sinn (2012a) points out that Germany's net foreign assets had been almost fully depleted since the 1990s as a consequence of financing German unification through current account deficits. Only since the early 2000s has Germany again started to rebuild net foreign claims. In this sense, the high current surpluses could be seen as an intertemporal rebalancing of the costs of German unification.

Figure 6-4. *Recorded Votes in the Bundestag on Art. 136 of the TFEU Law, June 29, 2012*

Number of votes

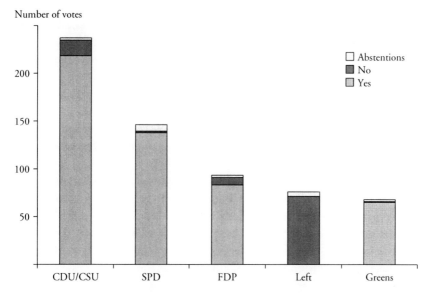

Source: Bundestag (www.bundestag.de/bundestag/plenum/abstimmung).

Established and New Parties

The euro area debt crisis was the key issue in German political debates during the years 2010–13. Given the pro-European position of the established parties, the crisis offered room for new parties to enter the political discussion. Hence, a comprehensive survey of party programs must include both established parties and the most important new party.

Positions of the Parties in the 2009–13 Bundestag

So far there is a large measure of agreement among Bundestag parties for the major stabilization measures. Figure 6-4 shows the voting behavior of all Bundestag parties on the law agreeing to amended art. 136 TFEU (the legal basis for the establishment of the ESM) at the end of June 2012. With the exception of the Left Party (Die Linke), all other parties supported the law with overwhelming majorities, resulting in a favorable vote of 81 percent by all members of parliament. This is indicative of parliamentary support for the rescue policy in the federal German Parliament so far: the general pro-

European stance has resulted, as in all major integration decisions in the past, in consensus votes of government and opposition parties alike. Even the opposition of the Left cannot be regarded as anti-European: rather, it is based on the view that instruments like the ESM with its conditionality impose damaging constraints on macro-policies and hence are ineffective tools for dealing with the crisis. The Left demands even greater solidarity between member countries (Höhn 2012).

Despite this consensus in principle, there are different perspectives across the parties on both the origins of the crisis and the best tools to fight it. Naturally, party documents do normally not reveal consistent analyses of complex economic developments and are not free of inconsistencies. Nevertheless, the emphasis clearly differs, as can be seen in table 6-1.

While the coalition parties of the 2009–13 Merkel administration stressed the role of weak fiscal rules and unsound budgetary policies, the opposition parties pointed instead to the underlying macro-imbalances and the financial market exuberance that favored these imbalances. For example, the Greens criticize Chancellor Merkel for referring to the euro crisis mainly as a debt crisis, since this definition improperly undervalues the impact of the financial crisis (Bündnis 90/Die GRÜNEN 2012). In addition, there is the usual difference in emphasis on either supply-side arguments (government parties) or demand-side problems (opposition), with the Left Party echoing the strongest southern European criticisms of austerity in the Merkel administration.

There are also significant differences as to a quantitative and qualitative extension of guaranties. It can already be inferred from the number of dissenters in the ESM vote (see figure 6-4) that Christian Democrats and the Liberals have greater reservations against German guaranties for other euro area countries than do the Social Democrats or the Greens. For the coalition parties, the current guaranties are only an emergency measure to permit the countries in crisis to regain market access as soon as possible. Both the Christian Democratic Union (CDU)/Christian Social Union (CSU) and the Free Democratic Party (FDP) firmly reject all eurobond variants. The opposition parties are rather supportive of more extensive and longer-term collective European issuance of debt, at least within the scheme of the European redemption fund (SPD 2012; SPD 2013), as developed by the German Council of Economic Experts (German Council of Economic Experts 2012). The SPD regards the common approach to liabilities in Germany and Europe as a long-term requirement (Wiemken 2012), even though the SPD candidate, Peer Steinbrück, has carefully avoided any commitment. The Greens argue that a European rescue fund, financed by banks, should be implemented along with

Table 6-1. *Views of the European Financial Crisis according to Statements of Parties in the Bundestag and Election Results*

	CDU/CSU	FDP	SPD	GREENS	LEFT
Origin of the crisis	High level of debt	Deregulation of financial markets, softening of Stability and Growth Pact	Ideology of market radicalism	High debt caused by consumption exceeding production, problematic trade deficits	Trade imbalances, financial capitalism
Position on further reaching guarantees	Rejection of a transfer union	German Bundestag should maintain its budgetary rights, German liabilities must be strictly limited	The establishment of a redemption fund could be acceptable	There is a need for a European rescue fund paid for by the banks	Capital controls and strict financial market regulation contribute to stabilization
Position on eurobonds	Clear rejection, eurobonds violate the principle of conditional aid, undermine the stability of Europe	Clear rejection, due to incentive effects, constitutional and political reasons	Open to a redemption fund and a partial pooling of debt issuance within such a scheme	Open to eurobonds, in line with a strategy fostering solidarity and trust	Eurobonds are an effective instrument, among others, in solving the crisis
Share of vote received in 2009 general election (%)	33.8	14.6	23.0	10.7	11.9
Share of vote received in 2013 general election (%)	41.5	4.8	25.7	8.4	8.6

Source: Bündnis 90/Die GRÜNEN (2011); Bündnis 90/Die GRÜNEN (2012); Bündnis 90/Die GRÜNEN (2013); CDU (2013); Die LINKE (2013); FDP (2013); Lötzsch (2011); SPD (2012); SPD (2013); Troost (2012a); Troost (2012b); Vogt (2012); Wiemken (2012); Wissing (2012). The euro-skeptical new party AfD received 4.7 percent of the vote in the 2013 election.

stricter regulation of the European financial markets and an introduction of eurobonds (Bündnis 90/Die GRÜNEN 2011; Bündnis 90/Die GRÜNEN 2013). The Left voted against implementation of the European Fiscal Compact, although they support eurobonds.

The New Anti-Euro Party

It is notable that the significant anti-EU and anti-euro minority among German voters is not yet represented at all in the German Bundestag. Thus it is not surprising that new parties are trying to enter the political market. In the past, these parties failed to establish themselves in German legislatures.[7]

Currently, there is one main new entrant with an anti-euro program in the national political field: the "Alternative für Deutschland" (AfD, "Alternatives for Germany"). Among its initiators and more prominent supporters are economics professors, journalists, and businesspeople. According to its electoral program, the party takes a differentiated position toward Europe. It claims to be pro-Europe and explicitly supports the internal market project. However, it stresses the sovereignty of national states and the need for shifting policy responsibility back to the member states, and it is highly critical of the bureaucracy in Brussels. The programmatic focus that forms the identity of the party is determined by a program relating to the euro. The AfD demands an orderly dismemberment of the euro area and the reintroduction of national currencies or, alternatively, a division of the euro area into smaller and more stable monetary unions. It says that the European treaties should be amended to permit a member state to withdraw from the euro area. Consequently, Germany should cease to accept any new ESM aids, and the problem of unsustainable debt levels should be addressed through debt restructuring, shifting a major part of the costs to banks, hedge funds, and institutional investors (Alternative für Deutschland 2013). This new party cannot simply be categorized as right-wing populists. Its program on the future of the euro echoes positions with great support from the influential euro-skeptic camp of German economists.

The Outcome of the General Election in September 2013

The results of the general election of September 2013 confirm the view that Angela Merkel's crisis strategy has broad support within Germany (see table 6-1): With 41.5 percent of the vote, her Christian Democrats finished

---

7. In 1998 "Initiative Pro-DM" ran in the general election lobbying against the introduction of the euro but only won 0.9 percent of the vote.

just five seats short of an absolute majority in the Bundestag and earned substantial gains over the 2009 election.[8] Merkel also effectively contained the anti-euro movement: The AfD received 4.7 percent of the vote, thus failing to reach the 5 percent threshold. The Social Democrats and Greens who showed support for a more comprehensive guaranty scheme like a European redemption fund failed in their objective to form a government coalition by a large margin (together they only reached 34.1%), and the Green Party made a particularly poor showing. Other topics like taxation were significant in the failure of Merkel's challengers, but the more lenient European crisis strategies of these parties might have contributed to their disappointing election results.

After three months of negotiations a "grand coalition" of Christian Democrats and Social Democrats was formed and in December 2013 elected Angela Merkel to a third term as chancellor (2013–17). In the coalition agreement, Merkel's course in the euro crisis based on the principle of conditional support was confirmed and the idea of any European debt collectivization rejected.[9] This continuity of the German strategy was also stressed by the reappointment of Wolfgang Schäuble as minister of finance. In comparison with the former coalition of Christian Democrats and Liberals, the new coalition could, however, have slightly more open views on some limited European growth initiatives. Even then, however, there will be a consensus that any growth initiative must not endanger Germany's own balanced budget objectives enshrined in the constitution's "debt brake." Thus no significant change in German macroeconomic policy stance is to be realistically expected for the coming years.

Conclusion

Support for the progress of European integration has been part of the core consensus of German policy for decades. Even the years of crisis have so far not been able to shatter this consensus. This is true both for the major political parties and a large majority of voters.

8. In Germany, a party must receive 5 percent of the vote in order to gain seats in the Parliament. Since several parties failed to reach that threshold (such as the market-liberal FDP, which used to be Merkel's coalition partner), the Christian Democrats thus came close to an absolute majority of seats.

9. Arithmetically, a coalition of Social Democrats, Greens, and the Left Party would have had a thin absolute majority. However, this type of coalition was firmly excluded by the Greens and Social Democrats during the election campaign and would be met with both heavy ideological disputes and voter resistance.

However, this stable pro-Europe stance does not imply that Germany can be expected to accept any burden in its commitment to Europe in general and for the defense of the euro in particular. Any future German government will face the same constraints that tied the hands of Chancellor Merkel and Finance Minister Schäuble from 2009 to 2013: the German constitution (in the decisive interpretation of the Court) sets narrow limits on the types of fiscal union that are feasible. In addition, German voters regard very critically any development that could be interpreted as a move toward a transfer union.

In this context, there is a striking difference between the non-German and the German perceptions of Merkel's engagement for an active policy to rescue the euro. From the perspective of France or the countries in crisis, the German government seems to be guided by a narrow national self-interest and an obvious lack of European solidarity. The perception of large parts of the German population is exactly the opposite: in their view, Angela Merkel has gone to the maximum justifiable extent (or even beyond) in her acceptance of financial risk for Germany and in her compromises with the European partners. The new party, Alternative für Deutschland, alludes to a highly disputed statement by Merkel (one that is incorporated into the name of the party) that the package of measures to rescue the euro was "without alternatives" ("*alternativlos*"). With each additional rescue package, the government has had increasing difficulties in selling this argument even to its traditional voters.

Economic arguments that Germany's economic strength may be partially a consequence of the crisis or that Germany is benefiting at least in some way from the crisis (for example, through lower interest rates for government bonds and through massive capital inflows) do not get any significant public attention.

The one clear bottom line of this analysis relates to the notion that Germany could be ready to accept larger fiscal liabilities after the general election or even open the door to solutions such as that of eurobonds. In light of the constitutional obstacles described and the clear position voters expressed in the 2013 general elections, this is a highly unrealistic idea. Any future German government would face an uphill battle if it tried to push for joint and several guaranties and would have to spend all its political capital on that project with a highly uncertain outcome.

References

Alternative für Deutschland. 2013. Die Alternative für Deutschland setzt sich ein."
    Wahlprogramm 2013 (www.alternativefuer.de).

Bertelsmann Stiftung. 2012. "Deutsche zunehmend skeptisch über die Vorteile der Europäischen Union." Press Release, September 17 (www.bertelsmann-stiftung.de/cps/rde/xchg/SID-76443594-5CFD0E57/bst/hs.xsl/nachrichten_113500.htm/).

Bofinger, Peter, Lutz Hoffmann, Claus Köhler, and Gerold Krause-Jung. 1997. "Ein Manifest für den Euro," *manager magazin,* September, pp. 8–11.

Bündnis 90/Die GRÜNEN. 2011. "Europa hängt am seidenen Faden." Interview with Claudia Roth, December 5 (www.gruene.de/partei/europa-haengt-am-seidenen-faden.html).

————. 2012. "Der Weg aus der Euro-Krise, Uns geht's ums Ganze," August 17 (www.gruene-bundestag.de/medien/publikationen_ID_2000006/publikation/flyer-europa/seite/12.html).

————. 2013. "Zeit für den Grünen Wandel, Teilhaben. Einmischen, Zukunft schaffen." Antrag für das Bundestagswahlprogramm 2013, April 26–28. Berlin (www.bundestagswahl-bw.de/wahlprogramm_die_gruenen.html).

Bundesverfassungsgericht. 2012. BVerfG, 2 BvR 1390/12 vom 12.9.2012 (www.bverfg.de/entscheidungen/rs20120912_2bvr139012en.html.

CDU (Christian Democratic Union). 2013. "Gemeinsam erfolgreich für Deutschland." Regierungsprogramm 2013–2017 (www.cdu.de/artikel/regierungsprogramm-zum-herunterladen).

De Grauwe, Paul, and Yuemei Ji. 2013. "From Panic-Driven Austerity to Symmetric Macroeconomic Policies in the Eurozone." *Journal of Common Market Studies* 51: 31–41.

Deutsche Mittelstands Nachrichten. 2012. "Umfrage: Deutsche wollen Euro nicht mehr." September 17 (www.deutsche-mittelstands-nachrichten.de/2012/09/46877/).

Die LINKE (Left Party). 2013. "100% sozial, Entwurf des Wahlprogramms." Bundestagswahl 2013, March 5 (www.bundestagswahl-bw.de/wahlprogramm_die_linke.html).

EurActiv. 2013. "Die Deutschen wollen nicht zur D-Mark zurück." *Forsa-Umfrage,* April 9 (www.euractiv.de/finanzen-und-wachstum/artikel/die-deutschen-wollen-nicht-zurueck-zur-d-mark-007398?newsletter).

European Commission. 2012. *Standard Eurobarometer* 78, Tables of Results, Public opinion in the European Union, Fieldwork: November 2012 (ec.europa.eu/public_opinion/archives/eb/eb78/eb78_en.htm).

FDP (Free Democratic Party). 2013. "Wahlprogramm zur Bundestagswahl 2013." Arbeitsdokument, February 1 (www.bundestagswahl-bw.de/wahlprogramm_fdp.html).

Focus online. 2011. "Krise lässt Deutsche am Euro zweifeln." Umfrage, June 25 (www.focus.de/politik/deutschland/umfrage-krise-laesst-deutsche-am-euro-zweifeln_aid_640255.html).

Frey, Bruno S., Silke Humbert, and Friedrich Schneider. 2007. "Was denken deutsche Ökonomen? Eine empirische Auswertung einer Internetbefragung unter Mitgliedern des Vereins für Socialpolitik." *Perspektiven der Wirtschaftspolitik* 8 (4): 359–77.

German Council of Economic Advisors. 2010. "Chancen für einen stabilen Aufschwung." *Jahresgutachten* 2010/11. Wiesbaden.

German Council of Economic Experts. 2012. "After the Euro Area Summit, Time to Implement Long-term Solutions." Special Report, July 30. Wiesbaden.

Handelsblatt. 2012. "Deutsche in Sachen Euro gespalten." Umfrage, August 18 (www.handelsblatt.com/politik/deutschland/umfrage-deutsche-in-sachen-euro-gespalten/7016972.html).

———. 2013. "Deutsche finden den Euro gut." *Exklusivumfrage,* April 9 (www.handels blatt.com/politik/deutschland/exklusivumfrage-deutsche-finden-den-euro-gut/8037270.html).

Heinemann, Frank, Michael C. Burda, and 14 additional signatories. 2012. "Stellungnahme zur Europäischen Bankenunion." *Ökonomenstimme,* July 9.

Herrmann, Christoph. 2012. "Die Bewältigung der Euro-Staatschulden-Krise an den Grenzen des deutschen und europäischen Währungsverfassungsrechts." *Europäische Zeitschrift für Wirtschaftsrecht* 21 (2012): 805–12.

Höhn, Matthias. 2012. "Merkels Sicht auf die Krise ist eng begrenzt." Statement des Bundesgeschäftsführers der Partei DIE LINKE, Matthias Höhn, auf der Pressekonferenz im Berliner Karl-Liebknecht-Haus, July 16 (www.die-linke.de/).

Ich will Europa. 2012. "Umfrage: Deutsche zunehmend skeptisch über die Vorteile der Europäischen Union" (www.ich-will-europa.de/project/umfrage-deutsche-zunehmend-skeptisch-ueber-die-vorteile-der-europaeischen-union).

Köcher, Renate. 2013. "Alternative für Deutschland?" Allensbach-Analyse, *Frankfurter Allgemeine,* April 17 (www.faz.net/aktuell/politik/inland/allensbach-analyse-alternative-fuer-deutschland-12151120.html).

Krämer, Walter, ed. 2012. "Bankenkrise." Aufruf von 277 deutschsprachigen Wirtschaftsprofessoren (www.statistik.tu-dortmund.de/kraemer.html).

Kunz, Anne. 2013. "Deutscher Mittelstand zweifelt am Euro." Commerzbank-Studie. *Die Welt,* April 18 (www.welt.de/wirtschaft/article115406060/Deutscher-Mittelstand-zweifelt-am-euro.html).

Lötzsch, Gesine. 2011. "Eurobonds werden kommen." August 15 (www.die-linke.de/).

manager magazin online. 2010. "Streit um den Euro, Neue Umfrage zeigt Mehrheit für D-Mark." December 12 (www.manager-magazin.de/politik/deutschland/0,2828,734183-2,00.html).

Mayer, Franz C., and Christian Heidfeld. 2012. "Verfassungs- und europarechtliche Aspekte der Einführung von Eurobonds." *Neue Juristische Wochenschrift* 7 (2012): 422–28.

merkur-online. 2013. "Weniger Deutsche wollen die D-Mark zurück, Fast 70 Prozent vertrauen dem Euro." April 9 (www.merkur-online.de/aktuelles/wirtschaft/forsa-umfrage-mehr-deutsche-befuerworten-euro-waehrung-zr-2842121.html).

Ohr, Renate, and Wolf Schäfer. 1992. "Die währungspolitischen Beschlüsse von Maastricht: Eine Gefahr für Europa." *Frankfurter Allgemeine Zeitung,* June 11.

Plenum der Ökonomen. 2011. "Stellungnahme zur EU-Schuldenkrise." February 17 (www.wiso.uni-hamburg.de/lucke/?p=581).

RP online. 2012. "Griechenland soll die Eurozone verlassen, Neue Umfrage in Deutschland." June 13 (www.rp-online.de/politik/deutschland/griechenland-soll-die-eurozone-verlassen-1.2868635).

Schmidt, Susanne K. 2013. "A Sense of Déjà Vu? The FCC's Preliminary European Stability Mechanism Verdict." *German Law Journal* 14 (1): 1–20.

Siekmann, Helmut, and Volker Wieland. 2013. "The European Central Bank's Outright Monetary Transactions and the Federal Constitutional Court of Germany." Working Paper 71. Frankfurt: Institute for Monetary and Financial Stability.

Sinn, Hans-Werner. 2012a. "Die Europäische Fiskalunion, Gedanken zur Entwicklung der Eurozone." *Perspektiven der Wirtschaftspolitik* 13 (3): 137–78.

————. 2012b. "Kurzvortrag zur Eurokrise vor dem Verfassungsgericht." *Ifo Schnelldienst* 65 (15): 22–26.

SPD (Social Democratic Party). 2012. "Krise in der Eurozone, Was wir wollen." June 5 (www.spd.de/aktuelles/72902/20120605_eurokrise_was_wir_wollen_spd.html).

————. 2013. "Das Wir entscheidet, Das Regierungsprogramm 2013–2017" (www.bundestagswahl-bw.de/wahlprogramm_spd.html).

Spiegel Online. 2010. "Umfrage: Deutsche wollen Euro behalten." Wirtschaft, December 10 (www.spiegel.de/wirtschaft/umfrage-deutsche-wollen-euro-behalten-a-733874.html).

————. 2011. "Umfrage: Deutsche misstrauen dem Euro massiv." June 26 (www.spiegel.de/wirtschaft/soziales/umfrage-deutsche-misstrauen-dem-euro-massiv-a-770587.html).

————. 2012. "Umfrage zur Euro-Krise: Mehrheit der Deutschen hält weitere Rettungspakete für sinnlos." July 5 (www.spiegel.de/politik/deutschland/umfrage-deutsche-resignieren-im-kampf-um-euro-rettung-a-842785.html).

Standard & Poor's. 2013. "Sovereigns Rating List" (www.standardandpoors.com).

Stern.de. 2012a. "Deutsche für Euro-Austritt Griechenlands." stern-Umfrage, June 5 (www.stern.de/wirtschaft/news/stern-umfrage-deutsche-fuer-euro-austritt-griechenlands-1836506.html).

————. 2012b. "Deutsche sind europafreundlich—unter Vorbehalt." stern-Umfrage, July 4 (www.stern.de/wirtschaft/news/stern-umfrage-deutsche-sind-europafreundlich-unter-vorbehalt-1850777.html).

Troost, Axel. 2012a. "Keine Einigung zum EU-Haushalt—2013 das "Jahr des Schreckens" in der Euro-Zone?" November 12 (www.die-linke.de).

————. 2012b. "Nach dem ESM-Urteil, Unkonventionelle Maßnahmen zur Rettung der Euro-Zone sind nötig!" September 17 (www.die-linke.de).

Vogt, Rainer. 2012. "Urteil zum Euro-Rettungsschirm, Karlsruhe stimmt ESM unter Auflagen zu." September 12 (www.spd.de/aktuelles/76056/20120912_esm_urteil_karlsruhe.html).

Vranes, Erich. 2013. "German Constitutional Foundations of, and Limitation to, EU integration: A Systematic Analysis." *German Law Journal* 14 (1): 75–112.

Wendel, Mattias. 2013. "Judicial Restraint and the Return to Openness: The Decision of the German Federal Constitutional Court on the ESM and the Fiscal Treaty of 12 September 2012." *German Law Journal* 14 (1): 21–52.

Wiemken, Jochen. 2012. "SPD-Fraktionschef Steinmeier fordert von Regierung Ehrlichkeit, 'Gemeinsame Haftung findet längst statt.'" August 9 (www.spd.de/aktuelles/74806/20120809_steinmeier_zu_schuldenhaftung_europa.html).

Wissing, Volker. 2012. "Peer Steinbrück stellt sich in der Finanzmarktregulierung ein Armutszeugnis aus." Press Release 731, September 20 (www.fdp.de).

Cross-Cutting Issues

7

The Financial Sector: Key Issues for the European Banking Union

DOUGLAS J. ELLIOTT

E uropean leaders have committed to the creation of a "banking union," in which there will be an integration of (1) bank regulation, (2) bank supervision, (3) deposit guaranties, (4) and dealing with troubled banks (known as "resolution"). Geographically, the banking union will encompass the euro area with the addition, on a voluntary basis, of most of the other members of the European Union (EU).

The advent of a banking union is positive for two major reasons. Most immediately, it helps solve the euro crisis by weakening the link between debt-burdened governments and troubled banks, where each side has added to the woes of the other. In the longer run, it will make the "single market" in European financial services substantially more effective. In one sense, the EU has had a banking union for years, given the legal flexibility for a group in one EU nation to conduct financial services across the EU that has resulted in a considerable volume of cross-border activity within the union. It just lacked the necessary regulatory and legal apparatus to effectively manage the risks to the economy from that banking union.

Unfortunately, it is much easier to endorse the concept of a banking union than it is to design and implement one. Banks are central to the European financial system, supplying about three-quarters of all credit and are therefore critical to the functioning of the wider economy in Europe. Supervision of banks is not merely a technical issue; it requires many subjective judgments with significant implications for the provision of credit, economic growth, and jobs. Choices about how much credit banks provide, and to whom, strongly affect the relative performance of national economies and individual businesses and families. Not surprisingly, national governments have been extremely reluctant to give up control over more than 30 trillion in bank assets and are doing so now only because of the severity of the euro crisis. Implementing the integration that comes with banking union will result in additional disputes over the division of power among various European institutions and national authorities.

Nor is it the case that we have the right answers and merely need to summon the political will to push them through. Financial regulation is a balancing act, requiring judgments about the relative importance of many things, including

—dealing with the short-term euro crisis versus long-term improvement of the single market for financial services in the EU;

—the trade-off between economic growth and financial safety. It is well established that many safety margins in banking carry with them an economic cost;[1]

—the efficiency of centralized supervision versus the benefits of local knowledge;

—the efficiency of a single regulator versus the benefits of multiple specialized regulators, such as for consumer protection or specialized financial institutions such as savings banks;

—supervisory independence from political interference versus political and legal accountability; and

—the allocation of losses when a troubled bank must be resolved or deposit guaranties honored.

These choices are inherently subjective, since they require trading off one set of policy benefits for another. (In most cases, we do not even have sufficiently developed theory to know the magnitude of the trade-offs.) Adding to the political difficulties, some aspects of a banking union directly involve the allocation of costs of significant magnitude and the risk of future costs that could be even higher. This is particularly true for the establishment of integrated deposit guaranty funds and the creation of new rules and funding sources for

---

1. For a detailed analysis of the cost of higher safety margins in finance, see Elliott, Salloy, and Santos (2012).

resolving banks on the edge of insolvency. Naturally, sharing the pain and the risk will be very complicated, with all sides arguing cogently for minimizing their own share.

All that said, European leaders have already answered some of the most critical policy questions:

Which countries should be in the banking union? Given the crucial inter-relationships between monetary policy and the financial system that have been underlined by the euro crisis, it was essential to include at least the entire euro area in the banking union. It would have been highly desirable to include all of the other EU member states as well, so that the banking union and the EU's single market in financial services would have been coterminous and the EU-level financial regulatory institutions could have played a full role. The United Kingdom vetoed this, however, and some of the other non-euro member states were nervous as well. Instead, the entire euro area will be included, plus volunteers from the remainder of the EU. In practice, the large majority of the EU member states will be part of the banking union. Unfortunately, the self-exclusion of the United Kingdom, which dominates European wholesale banking, creates significant complications, described below. Sweden has also indicated that it will remain outside the banking union initially, and this appears likely to be the decision of the Czech Republic and Denmark as well. Unlike the United Kingdom, however, it is easy to envision the others joining in the medium term if banking union proceeds effectively.

Who should be the principal supervisory authority? The European Central Bank (ECB) has been designated as the principal supervisory authority. Here, too, politics and practical considerations prevented the best long-term option, which would be a much-enhanced and improved European Banking Authority (EBA) as the supervisory authority, working closely with the ECB. In the long run, the EBA's role as guardian of the EU-wide single market and its pure focus on bank supervision make it the right focal point for European supervision, the role for which it was designed. However, the ECB is central to the euro-zone and is crucially important in the management of the euro crisis, which was more pressing than the long-term future of the single market. This made it nearly inevitable that the ECB would play the main role, especially once the UK vetoed an EU-wide banking union.

Further, the ECB could be given this authority on the basis of article 127(6) of the Treaty on the Functioning of the European Union (TFEU), one of the two fundamental treaties governing the EU. This article permits the euro system of central banks run by the ECB[2] to assume supervisory powers over banks.[3] Some of the other choices, such as setting up a new independent authority, would have required treaty changes that could have taken years and might not have received the necessary ratification, particularly in countries where a referendum would be required.

Meshing the single market in financial services, which is EU-wide, with the less-inclusive banking union entails some additional complexity. The EBA retains its role as the coordinator of bank supervision within the entire EU, with the ECB acting as a supervisor. As part of this, there will be a "single supervisory handbook" created by the EBA. Further, the EBA could find that it has to arbitrate disputes between the ECB and other national supervisors in the EU that are not in the banking union, just as it has the authority now to arbitrate disputes between national supervisors.

A central role for the ECB does bring a number of advantages. It would have been better, however, to have had a new authority allied with the ECB, but not directly part of that organization. There will be a council within the ECB overseeing supervision, but the ultimate power will reside with the ECB's governing council, partly for constitutional reasons based on the fundamental EU treaties. This gives the ECB an uncomfortably large accumulation of power in a Europe with no effective counterweight, and it raises the risk of tainting the ECB's monetary policy with too close an association with supervisory concerns and vice versa.

When will the ECB assume supervision? The expectation is that the ECB will assume supervisory responsibilities in October 2014, approximately a year from the date at which their powers are authorized. The ECB will have the ability to defer assuming the role, if it needs more time after the twelve months have elapsed, but this would likely be quite embarrassing unless it can point

---

2. Monetary union, and the creation of the ECB, did not eliminate the national central banks. Instead, the ECB is placed at the peak, as the ultimate authority and supervisor of the "euro system" of central banks (known more formally as the European System of Central Banks). This can lead to situations where different national central banks operate differently, to the extent permitted by the ECB, such as with certain bank lending programs, where national central banks, at their own risk, are allowed to set collateral requirements somewhat more loosely than the overall ECB rules.

3. The Treaty on the Functioning of the European Union states in article 127(6) in its entirety: "The Council, acting by means of regulations in accordance with a special legislative procedure, may unanimously, and after consulting the European Parliament and the European Central Bank, confer specific tasks upon the European Central Bank concerning policies relating to the prudential supervision of credit institutions and other financial institutions with the exception of insurance undertakings." See EU (2010).

to clear causes outside of its control, so it is most probable that they will begin supervision in the fall of 2014.

Which banks should be covered by the banking union? All banks in the member states of the banking union will be under the authority of the ECB, despite various suggestions for the exclusion, for example, of smaller banks or public, cooperative, and savings banks. This is the right choice, and one hopes that it will not be undercut in practice by pressures to leave the actual supervision completely in the hands of the national authorities that will be part of the ECB's supervisory apparatus, as discussed below.

Should any other financial institutions be covered by the banking union? The ECB has not been given any authority over non-bank financial institutions, and there has been little discussion of the issue. The European Systemic Risk Board (ESRB), an EU-wide institution, is responsible for analyzing and flagging potential systemic risks, which include those that could be created by non-banks. However, it has essentially no direct authority and must operate by alerting the appropriate EU-wide institutions and national regulatory authorities. Unfortunately, the EU-wide institutions themselves have little direct power over non-banks, with national authorities still in full charge.

Should banks pass a financial test before the ECB takes over? The ECB insists that it will not assume supervision of any bank unless that bank is capitalized to acceptable standards. Europe's leaders are in agreement on this approach, although some of them are doubtlessly nervous about the potential implications for their banks. The ECB will conduct an extensive review process over the months before it starts as a supervisory authority. This review will examine whether the asset values in the loan book and other parts of the balance sheet are appropriate based on their credit risks. There is concern among many observers that some banks may be systematically understating their loan losses, so this will be a key area of focus for the ECB. It is critical that the ECB design credible stress tests and apply them rigorously, avoiding the problems of the previous national and European stress tests. Further, it needs to be clear how authorities will handle any banks that fail the stress tests. This could involve providing capital or winding down or otherwise resolving such banks.

There remain a host of important but unresolved policy choices, as well as detailed questions about the design of the banking union. These include:

How should responsibilities be allocated between the ECB and national supervisors? It has been established that the ECB is ultimately in charge. At the same time, it will clearly rely on the existing national supervisors for a long time for much of the detailed work and may choose to retain this structure permanently. National supervisors have the key advantages of existing infrastructure, accumulated expertise, and local knowledge, including language skills and relationships. At the other extreme, almost everyone agrees that ECB teams in Frankfurt will need to directly oversee the cross-border banks and the largest of the national banks, with some assistance from national authorities, but with detailed central control.

Therefore, the practical answer is that the ECB will directly oversee the most important banks, will cooperate with national supervisors on the mid-sized banks, and will largely leave day-to-day supervision of small banks to the existing national supervisors, with the option for more direct intervention from Frankfurt if systematic problems seem to be developing with the small banks. This overall approach is the right one, although it will take some time to find the optimal balance in practice. In that sense, it is like the prescription for being a good manager: provide clear direction but do not micromanage. This is much easier to say than to do.

A particular concern in this regard is the relationship of the ECB and the German banking authorities in regard to the public, cooperative, and savings banks that form a key part of its national financial system. German officials had argued strongly that these should be left out of the ECB's supervisory authority and continue to be supervised directly by German authorities. They argued that these banks have safer business models and that their small size means they are not of systemic importance, despite linkages between them. That battle was lost, but there are some indications that a de facto political agreement was reached that would keep the ECB away from these banks unless the central ECB headquarters in Frankfurt sees clear problems developing. Any such agreement would be worrisome, since it would provide a quasi-immunity from European oversight that could lead to trouble, given that these banks have strong local political ties and could be tempted to make non-economic decisions in the future. That might not matter if the ECB saw compelling evidence in time to stop the problems before they became systemic. However, as we saw in the bubble that led to the financial crisis, there are always arguments over why a perceived problem is not real or not important, resulting in excessively slow reactions—a problem that already plagues Europe in most of its decisionmaking.

Should a European-level body act as a single resolution authority? There is strong agreement on the concept of a single resolution mechanism, in the sense of a common approach to dealing with failing banks. However, there remains some resistance, particularly from the Germans, to having the actual decisions made by an authority at the level of the banking union or the EU. The alternative is to have national authorities continue to be in charge of bank resolution, but to apply common rules across the banking union.

It is important to have a single resolution authority, and not just common rules and approaches, in order to help break the damaging linkage that has existed between the financial strength of a sovereign and of its banks. In theory, this could be achieved by enabling national resolution authorities to draw on a common fund to cover losses, but this would create a very risky incentive structure. Both resolution decisions and their funding should be at the level of the banking union. Politics may render it impossible to get to this point soon, but this is the right goal and leaders should get as close as possible as soon as possible to this outcome.

What European-level body should handle the resolution of troubled banks? There is a range of options for a resolution authority: (1) the ECB, (2) the European Stability Mechanism (ESM), (3) the European Banking Authority, (4) a new deposit guaranty fund, (5) a new resolution authority, or (6) an arm of the European Commission.

The best option seems to be a new authority, possibly with combined responsibility for resolution and deposit guarantees. Resolution activities can require committing taxpayer funds, especially in a severe crisis. They also entail allocating losses among various parties. Neither activity correlates well with the political independence and technical nature of central banking activity, which is why the ECB would be a bad choice. On the other hand, the ESM does have fiscal and allocational responsibilities, but is probably too closely tied to the national governments and has too cumbersome a decision structure. The EBA both lacks the clout to enforce the necessary tough decisions and is too closely tied to its supervisory role, which might taint its ability to take resolution actions that put previous supervision in a bad light. A new authority would not have any of these disadvantages. The deposit guaranty function is closely related to resolution, which might make a combination in the same authority natural, although this would not be free of conflicts.

To the surprise of many, the initial proposal of the European Commission in July 2013 was for the sixth option, to give the ultimate powers to itself. There would be a new Resolution Board, based in Brussels, which would issue non-binding recommendations for consideration by the Commission. In practice, the Commission would be unlikely to overrule the board, but it could. This creates a major political hurdle to the proposed structure, since many, particularly in Germany, are reluctant to hand such power over to the Commission. However, it appears to resolve the constitutional issue that makes it hard to find another body that can take on this role without amending the EU's basic laws, which would be time-consuming and face a real danger of failure. The political obstacle is worsened by a voting structure in the board that would effectively allow the Brussels-based representatives to overrule the representatives of the national authorities.

There will almost certainly be major changes to the proposal before it is accepted, and there is some risk that legislation will not be passed before the European Parliament elections in May of 2014, after which the proposal would have to be reconsidered by a new Parliament and a new European Commission.

Who should operate the European deposit guaranty fund? A new authority is almost certainly the best answer, for essentially the same reasons as just discussed for a resolution authority. However, such a fund, whether operated by a new authority or an existing one, appears to have been tabled for at least a few years. There are a number of difficult political issues involved in using premiums on banks in one country to support depositor losses in another country. Some of these relate to the existence in Germany of several different deposit guaranty schemes, such as one for the savings banks; also, constituent banks want to stay separate from each other, and even more from funds in other countries. It is simply unclear whether, when, and how a European-level deposit guaranty fund might come into existence. This is unfortunate, since Europe, following the imposition of losses on depositors in the major Cypriot banks in 2013, is now in a world in which depositors know they can lose money under certain circumstances.

How should the losses from insolvent or restructured banks be allocated? This breaks down into two questions. Who pays for existing losses, whether recognized or not, and how will the cost of future losses be allocated? The right answer on past losses is fairly clear: they should be evaluated transparently and then explicitly allocated. In particular, the troubled countries of the banking union should not expect to slip the losses from their banks onto the books of the new European deposit guaranty or resolution funds as a backdoor subsidy for their national governments. Explicit aid may be appropriate; implicit aid in this manner is not. Future losses are best dealt with through a system of prefunding, in which premiums are charged to the covered banks. Ideally, the premiums would be risk-adjusted so that banks that present a higher risk of needing future rescue must pay more.

All of the preceding is focused on the losses that taxpayers end up bearing. One key to an effective resolution regime, however, is to maximize the extent to which any losses are borne by shareholders and debt holders. This excludes unsophisticated depositors, who should be protected both for their own sake and to avoid damaging bank runs. In June of 2013, the European Commission and the European Council agreed on a proposal that would create a standard approach across all nations in the EU on how losses would be shared under their national laws. This would carry over to any resolution procedures at the level of the banking union when they are agreed. The European Parliament still needs to agree, which has still not occurred as of early 2014.

Goals of a Bank Resolution Framework

The most important goal of any approach to bank resolution must be to contribute to the avoidance or minimization of severe financial crises such as we just experienced in the global financial crisis and subsequent euro crisis. Banks are crucial to the European economy, and the damage that a financial crisis can cause is quite evident in light of the pain from the most recent one. There is a limit to what a good resolution framework can do in this regard, because the more important factors will relate to private sector decisions and the quality of bank regulation and supervision. However, the right framework gives all of the key players in the financial sector, including regulators, the incentives to avoid financial crises. In addition, a good approach to resolution will ensure that critical financial services remain available, even in crises, and will minimize the financial contagion of losses from the failure of one institution, or fear that such losses will afflict others. All of this must, of course, be done in a way that does not foster an excessive conservatism that chokes off lending or makes it too expensive.

A second critical goal is to minimize the cost to taxpayers if a bank does encounter trouble. In part, this can be accomplished by encouraging early intervention, before too much economic value has been destroyed. Perhaps more important, the right regime will place the economic burden on those who have voluntarily funded the banks, by buying their equity or debt, rather than on the taxpayer or ordinary depositors. That said, taxpayers will ultimately need to stand behind any resolution mechanism, since a widespread financial crisis may exhaust the funds available to ensure the effective working of the financial system. In such a case, there needs to be a mechanism to recoup over time any such losses for the taxpayer through levies on the banks and perhaps on other participants in the financial system.

A third key goal is fairness, which is particularly important in the allocation of any losses among the member states of the banking union. It does not arise to the same extent at the national level, since there is usually an acceptance by the public that losses in one part of a country may need to be borne by the entirety of the nation.

How should the resolution authority be funded? The European Commission has urged that resolution funds be aggregated in advance. There are excellent policy arguments for ex ante funding. First, funding in advance is the best way to ensure that taxpayers do not bear the cost, since ex post funding requires the political will to charge levies on banks that may well already have been battered by a financial crisis. Second, ex post funding intensifies a pro-cyclical bias that should rather be counteracted. Charging high insurance premiums to banks in the wake of a financial crisis could easily exacerbate a credit crunch, especially as they will almost certainly attempt to pass the cost on to borrowers and other customers. Funding in advance spreads the burden over time. Third, ex ante funding does a better job of encouraging loan pricing that reflects the true risks. Funding in advance effectively means that the price of loans and other bank services will generally reflect the insurance premium. Finally, ex ante premium charges are likely to be easier to agree upon. Allocating resolution costs will always create difficult political arguments, especially across borders. However, it is likely to be less painful to agree on the level of a relatively modest annual charge and how it is to be allocated among the banks than it is to agree in the face of large known losses.

The most convincing argument against ex ante funding is that establishing a precautionary fund might encourage its use. If the resolution fund already has substantial resources, it may be easier to make decisions that cost money. However, the other arguments fairly clearly outweigh this one.

How does a banking union relate to moves toward a fiscal union? The eurozone is making major strides toward coordination of national fiscal policies, with the real possibility of further steps toward fiscal union. These steps include eventual mutual debt guarantees, for at least a portion of national liabilities, and/or the creation of a central European Treasury with the ability to deploy significant resources. These moves toward a greater degree of fiscal union to complement the existing monetary union interact in significant ways with a banking union.

Most obviously, governments may need to provide fiscal support for deposit guaranty funds or to assist in the resolution process for banks. As a practical matter, this would represent yet another aspect of fiscal union and one of real significance. Ireland and Spain, among others, have found bank resolution a very expensive process when done at a national level, one that contributes significantly to their sovereign debt burdens. Moving this to the European level would provide a much larger and more stable base of support but also effectively spread the costs across all the governments involved. One implication is that a strong country such as Germany could find itself contributing significantly to bank rescues in more troubled countries as the result of a relatively automatic mechanism in situations in which it would not have voluntarily provided that same level of support to the sovereign states had they remained responsible for their own banks. Of course, the flow could be in the other direction as well. Some German banks have experienced major losses, and there are persistent concerns about still more losses to come. Conceivably, a poorer nation with a relatively strong banking system might end up as a net contributor to a German bank rescue.

There are also moral hazard issues that arise if banking union is more complete than fiscal union. Banks are already major holders of the government bonds of their home countries, partly out of choice, partly out of explicit regulatory pressure to own highly liquid assets, and sometimes in response to covert pressure from their home governments. There is, however, some limit to how far this can be pushed, since loading up local banks with a country's debt can make the banks riskier, with attendant problems for the state. If, though, much of the pain from those bank problems is shifted to a European guaranty fund, then it will be all the more tempting for national governments to push their debt onto the balance sheets of their banks, to the extent that European authorities will let them.

A banking union also affects fiscal union in the other direction, making national fiscal conditions more stable and thereby easing the difficulties of creating more fiscal coordination. Removing the potential for major increases in national debt burdens as a result of the collapse of the national banking systems should help significantly.

How would a banking union affect monetary and "macroprudential" policies? Monetary policy could be quite significantly affected by a banking union, at least while the euro crisis remains an active problem. Monetary policy achieves its principal effects by altering the availability and price of credit. Therefore, central banks rely on financial institutions to transmit moves on interest rate policy to the broader economy. Under normal conditions, the direct impact of central bank moves is considerably amplified by reactions from banks. In the current euro crisis, it appears that a number of banks are hoarding any liquidity they can find, in order to have greater capacity to deal with potential runs on their deposits and bonds and to deter such runs by showing that they can do so.

If European banks were perceived as safer as the result of a banking union, then they would be more prepared to redeploy the reserves they hold at the central bank by lending them out. Thus the monetary transmission channels would be unclogged, and monetary policy would again work in more predictable and effective ways.

In recent years, a consensus has developed that there has been a gap in the regulation of the financial system, falling between monetary policy and other macroeconomic policies that operate at the level of the economy as a whole, and traditional prudential (or "safety and soundness") regulation of individual financial institutions. New "macroprudential" policies are being developed that operate at the level of the financial system as a whole, with the intent of reducing the frequency and level of damage to the wider economy from financial crises. (Traditional prudential regulation of individual institutions has been renamed "microprudential" policy to distinguish it.) Such policies would include system-wide increases or decreases in capital or liquidity requirements for banks or the tightening or relaxation of credit standards for mortgages or other debt, such as by altering the maximum loan-to-value ratio.[4]

Creating a banking union would have advantages and disadvantages for macroprudential policy. It would make it distinctly easier to deal with credit bubbles or crunches broader than those in a single country but might make it somewhat more difficult for national authorities to tackle homegrown problems, if too little flexibility is provided for national responses. In addition, choices about the structure of the banking union would also tend to strengthen or weaken the role of various institutions in setting macroprudential policy, with the ECB potentially the biggest winner from this change, simply because its role in overseeing the banks will almost certainly expand greatly.

A full discussion of macroprudential policy in Europe is beyond the scope of this chapter, but decisions in this area could be quite important, as they have the potential to lower the risk of damaging bubbles in housing or other areas in the future or to reduce the impact of their bursting. Avoiding such bubbles, and their very painful bursting, would make it substantially easier to operate a monetary union going forward.

How do decisions about different pillars of banking union affect each other? Supervision, resolution, and deposit guaranty arrangements all affect one another. Ideally the key pillars of banking union would have been designed simultaneously, with clear consideration of these interactions. Instead, political considerations led to the design of the supervisory approach before a thorough consideration of the other pillars. Similarly, the resolution process is being designed before key agreements about the shape of the deposit guaranty mechanisms at the European level.

The pillars interact in multiple important ways. Supervision can have a major effect on the conservatism with which a bank operates, increasing or decreasing the risk that a resolution will be necessary and deposit guaranties be called upon. For this reason, some national regulatory systems, including that of the

---

4. For a deeper explanation of macroprudential policy, see Elliott (2011a).

United States, give the deposit guaranty authority at least some supervisory powers in order to protect its own interests. Coming from the other direction, resolution and deposit guaranty approaches provide incentives and disincentives that affect the direct willingness of bank managements to take risks and of their owners and funders to accept the taking of risk. For instance, complete deposit guaranties can make depositors entirely indifferent to the level of risk being taken at the various banks, since all of their deposits are effectively guaranteed by the state. This makes supervision more important and more difficult, because it will benefit less from effective market discipline.

Similarly, resolution mechanisms are affected by deposit guaranties and vice versa. On the one hand, if deposits are not guaranteed beyond a certain limit, or certain types of deposits are not guaranteed at all, then the risk aversion of depositors, and their actions in a crisis, will be affected by how well protected they are in a resolution process. On the other hand, the degree of protection that depositors enjoy will have a major impact on the allocation of losses among non-guaranteed parties and therefore on their behavior in anticipation of such losses.

What will be the impact of the United Kingdom's remaining outside of the banking union? Leaving the City of London, Europe's dominant financial center, outside of the European banking union raises serious concerns. There is a real risk that two somewhat differing supervisory regimes will develop in practice, one in London and the other on the continent. This could encourage regulatory arbitrage, where activities shift to whichever locale provides the lighter regulation for that activity. Moreover, there is also a risk that a single regime develops and that the ECB's supervision effectively annexes the rest of the EU. A single supervisory regime for Europe would be good, but only if it has the right governance structure, so that all concerned can defend their viewpoints and their interests. Having a eurozone entity effectively dictate overall EU policy is not appropriate and would ratchet up tensions with the United Kingdom sharply, especially given the often divergent views of the United Kingdom and the continent on finance and its regulation. In the worst case, tensions of this nature could help push the United Kingdom to exit the entire EU.

The European Commission's proposal in the summer of 2012 attempts to ameliorate this issue by cementing the EBA's legal position as the overseer of the supervisory framework for banking in Europe (particularly by making it the author of a "single supervisory handbook" that would bind the ECB and all other supervisory authorities in the EU) and by offering a new voting structure in the EBA to protect non-members of the banking union. These intentions are laudable, but it is not clear that either step will be very effective. Unfortunately, there is no good answer, given the United Kingdom's unwillingness to join the banking union or the eurozone. There will simply be a major potential for conflict that will have to be managed carefully over time. With good will on the part of all concerned, it should be workable, but that premise may not always be fulfilled.

Can London remain the principal European financial center without being in the banking union? In theory, the City of London could certainly remain the heart of Europe's financial system, even if it were outside the banking union. New York and London are the dominant global financial centers for a great variety of reasons, and it would be a difficult and long-term process for another center to shove either one aside.[5] They have the specialized infrastructure, including human talent, to effectively and efficiently perform a wide range of services needed by the financial industry and its customers. They also benefit from economies of scale and scope that would be hard to duplicate.

That said, there is real fear in the City about the long-term effects of a banking union in which the United Kingdom does not participate. The biggest danger is probably that barriers would be created to the functioning of the single market in financial services by differentiating between activities that take place in euros, or in the eurozone, from other activities. For example, if certain services were required to be provided in the monetary union itself or by legal entities headquartered and regulated in the zone, this could make U.K. financial institutions uncompetitive for those activities and perhaps for related activities as well. This is not an idle concern. A policy paper issued by the ECB in the summer of 2011 called for a requirement that derivatives clearinghouses that handled more than 5 percent of the volume in a euro-denominated financial instrument be located in the euro area.[6]

Similarly, regulation or supervision in the euro area could develop differently from that for the EU as a whole, despite safeguards intended to preserve uniformity on key issues. This could either make it difficult for U.K. banks to compete or force them to choose between retaining their current approaches and moving to a less profitable model in order to retain their share of European business. A gradual disengagement of City institutions from financial activities in the eurozone could ensue, with a greater focus on emerging markets or other growth areas.

Thus the question of the role of London in a banking union that does not include the United Kingdom is likely to turn on regulatory and political issues

5. For an analysis in the context of Shanghai of the various global financial centers and the characteristics necessary to achieve that status, see Elliott (2011b).

6. See *Financial Times* (2011).

more than on purely economic ones. This is perhaps the core of the City's fear, since the British model of finance is not popular with many of its European partners.

Conclusion

Barring a big surprise, Europe will have major parts of a banking union in place by 2015 or even a bit earlier, with the ECB as the single supervisor and some approach in place for the single resolution mechanism. Integration of the deposit guaranty systems is, unfortunately, likely to be pushed off years beyond that, if it ever happens. There are problems with the construction of this banking union, and many important implementation details need to be worked out, but it will almost certainly be a better and safer approach than the current system of loosely linked national banking authorities. This improvement will make it easier to deal with the euro crisis and will be even more useful in helping to prevent future financial crises.

References

Elliott, Douglas. 2011a. "An Overview of Macroprudential Policy and Countercyclical Capital Requirements." Washington: Brookings Institution (March) (www.brookings.edu/research/papers/2011/03/11-capital-elliott).

———. 2011b. "Building a Global Financial Center in Shanghai: Observations from Other Centers." Washington: Brookings Institution (June) (www.brookings.edu/research/papers/2011/06/10-shanghai-financial-center-elliott).

Elliott, Douglas, Suzanne Salloy, and André Oliviera Santos. 2012. "Assessing the Cost of Financial Regulation." IMF Working Paper 233. Washington: International Monetary Fund (www.imf.org/external/pubs/ft/wp/2012/wp12233.pdf).

European Union (EU). 2010. "Consolidated Version of the Treaty on the Functioning of the European Union." *Official Journal of the European Union.* Luxembourg (http://eur-lex.europa.eu/LexUriServ/LexUriServ.do?uri=OJ:C:2010:083:0047:0200:en:PDF).

Financial Times. 2011. "Britain to Sue ECB over Threat to City." September 14.

8

Building a Stronger Union: Social Policies in Europe and the Management of the Debt Crisis

JACQUES MISTRAL

The European integration project has been built on a broad concept of convergence, common regulation of markets and promotion of competition, shared prosperity, and a common standard of democracy. This multidimensional convergence has progressed quite well since the Rome Treaty in 1957, followed by the Single European Act in 1986–87, the creation of the European Union in 1992, the introduction of the single currency in 1999–2002, and, most recently, the "Eastern enlargement" in 2004.

For the first time since the late 1950s, however, this process of economic convergence has been seriously challenged by the worldwide financial crisis and its impact on Europe and the eurozone. The effects of this crisis have varied significantly among the countries of Europe. Some countries, such as Germany and others in Northern Europe, managed to weather the storm rather well despite a tough shock in 2009. Other European countries had a severe debt crisis: Greece and Ireland followed by Portugal, Spain, and Italy suffered serious losses in GDP, rising unemployment, and a surge in poverty that Europe had not experienced since the war years. In Greece and Spain, the recession became a depression comparable to that of the 1930s. Much of

This chapter was prepared following suggestions by Kemal Derviş, whom I thank for his continuous support and useful comments. I also thank Edith Joachimpillai, who provided excellent research assistance; she skillfully prepared the statistical materials and the methodology appendix.

Europe, except Germany and a few other northern countries, is in economic and fiscal stress. At the center of the debate are the nature, quality, and sustainability of the fiscal and social policies of individual countries, as well as the European convergence process.

In addition to the economic aspect of convergence, the European Union's integration project has also always had an inherently political nature. The launch of the single currency was conceived as both a further step in the consolidation of the single market and a further step toward the long-term goal of political union. The fact that the United Kingdom and Denmark, latecomers to the union, then decided to stay outside the eurozone shows that there has never been complete unanimity inside the European Union on the nature of the multidimensional convergence process. The members of the eurozone, however, shared the objective of further economic and political convergence, including, implicitly, the convergence of social conditions. Indeed a lot of "social" convergence was achieved by 2008. The mechanics of social policy were national, but there was a common philosophy and intent on social issues in the eurozone, setting it apart from other parts of the world. The outcomes of social policies, such as the degree of income inequality, life expectancy, and poverty rates, were surprisingly similar.

The crisis put pressure, however, on social policies in the southern countries. The austerity and adjustment measures that the countries in crisis had to pursue have started to create a new gap between them and the rest of Europe in social outcome indicators, particularly unemployment and poverty rates (see Heise and Lierse 2011). If this gap becomes permanent, it could undermine the dynamics of the single market, including free mobility of labor. It would also be a serious setback for the entire European convergence process. The key question in this regard is if, beyond what is hoped are shorter-term macro-economic problems created by the crisis, ongoing policy reforms can be made consistent with a social policy system and social outcomes common to the eurozone countries (similar retirement conditions, comparable unemployment insurance, equivalent access to health care, and so forth, as well as similar outcomes), or if these policies are creating a dual Europe, where citizens in the North have access to social benefits denied to citizens in the South.

At the end of the chapter I outline the way to restore confidence in a "Social Europe" and a process for doing so. Present macro-economic conditions are dictated by the need to restore sustainable fiscal situations; but they create different social outcomes in the northern and southern countries. If these divergences were to become structural, they would undermine the political basis of the European project. If the eurozone is no longer seen as bringing the people and the living standards of the European countries closer together, the political basis on which the functioning of the eurozone relies will erode, threatening the future of the euro itself. This is why the time is ripe for the formulation of new social objectives that would complement the "four unions" described by the June 2012 European Council as the basis of a better functioning European Monetary Union (EMU).

"Social Europe" Matters

Since 1957 the European integration project has been based on the creation of a single market. The basic principle underlying the common market is "competition," and enforcing the rules of competition is one of the two major tasks of the European Commission. The European Monetary Union was conceived in the 1970s and 1980s to consolidate the common market during a period of international monetary instability and to give further impetus to political cohesion in Europe. By contrast, a "Social Europe" never appeared explicitly as a component of the integration project. Social policies were not part of the European architecture; explicit and mandatory harmonization of social policies was explicitly rejected. In the meantime, social policies and outcomes developed everywhere, reflecting distinct national characteristics. The strands of history, culture, and politics in each nation were inevitably woven into different social institutions and specific policies. As a result, common wisdom has it that Europe is an extremely diverse patchwork of national institutions and policies. But is it really?

It is easy to describe the diversity of principles and institutions that govern social policies in Europe (as distinct from the social safety net in the United States); a vast literature documents these differences and analyzes and explains them (a major source of this abundant literature is Esping Andersen 1990). This section focuses on the outcomes and social conditions: the degree of inequality, life expectancy, employment protection and poverty. Table 8-1 summarizes a set of major social indicators for core European countries in 2008. These figures show strikingly that European countries as diverse as France, Germany, Greece, Italy, Spain, and Sweden—which constitute the sample in this research— have had very similar social situations, ones that have been significantly different from those in the United States, with the United Kingdom frequently somewhere in the middle. In 2008, life expectancy at birth was 80.9 years in continental Europe (unweighted average between 80.0 and 81.8), 79.9 in the United Kingdom, and a low 76.1 in the United States. Another example is the poverty rate, which is 17.1 percent in the sample (unweighted average between

Table 8-1. *Social Convergence within Continental Europe, 2008*

	Gini coefficient	Life expectancy at birth	Employment Protection Index[a]	Poverty rate (%)[b]	Poverty rate 65+ (%)
Germany	0.30	80.2	2.6	14.8	8.4
France	0.29	81.0	3.0	13.5	8.8
Italy	0.34	81.8	2.6	19.9	12.8
Spain	0.32	81.4	3.1	20.6	22.8
Greece	0.31	80.0	3.0	17.8	22.7
Sweden	0.26	81.2	2.1	16.4	6.2
United Kingdom	0.34	79.9	1.1	18.4	10.3
United States	0.38	78.1	0.9	24.4	22.4

Source: OECD (2013); Venn (2009).

a. The Employment Protection Index is an aggregate based on the following three elements: (1) protection of regular workers against individual dismissal, (2) additional costs for collective dismissals, and (3) regulation of temporary contracts. It uses a scale from 0 to 6: 0 indicates least restriction and 6 indicates the most restriction.

b. The poverty rate (percent of the total population where the poverty threshold is 60 percent of the median income) and Gini coefficient are calculated after taxes and transfers.

13.5 and 20.6), 18.4 percent in the United Kingdom, and a high 24.4 percent in the United States. Inequality is frequently considered the single most important indicator of social conditions and merits closer investigation. From the work of Atkinson, Piketty, and Saez (2011), it is well known that a "great convergence" of income distribution occurred in industrialized countries from 1930 to 1980; it then came to an end and indeed was reversed in the United Kingdom and the United States. In the 1990s, inequality also increased in most European countries in the sample, but in a comparatively gradual and modest way. The period between 1990 and 2010 can be more significantly described as one of further convergence among the continental European countries. Everywhere on the continent, policies were implemented to lessen the widening of market income disparities so as not to replicate what happened in the United Kingdom and the United States.

The oft-mentioned "generosity" of European-style social policies is frequently criticized as unsustainable and underfinanced. A comparison of the financing of social protection before the financial crisis is instructive. There are in fact two conceptions of social protection: (1) "social insurance," the historically Bismarckian schemes prevailing in the eurozone, and (2) "taxation and redistribution," the Beveridgean schemes dominant in the Anglo-American tradition. A major difference is that the Beveridgean schemes have their place in the budget framework of Social Security, Medicare, and Medicaid in the United States; such spending is on a par with other government expenditures such as defense and national parks, and like them, they are financed by the government's resources (taxes on incomes, profits, capital gains).

"Social insurance" schemes by contrast are administered by a distinct part of public institutions. They collect specific resources, called "contributions," and the benefits they distribute are the result of previous contributions. In short, despite being public institutions, they work like insurance companies. These data are summarized in table 8-2 for the sample countries, comparing the years 2000 and 2008 according to harmonized data published by the OECD. The high, and increasing, level of social benefits is immediately apparent for continental Europe, where they amounted to 15.7 percent of GDP in 2000 and 16.2 percent in 2008; by comparison, the same ratios are 12.6 percent and 13.2 percent in the United Kingdom and 10.6 percent and 13.1 percent in the United States. It is surprising that the increase was greatest in the United States, at 2.5 percent, as compared with 0.6 percent and 0.5 percent in the United Kingdom and other European countries. Between 2000 and 2008, social benefits expanded everywhere in relatively similar proportions except Greece (where the expansion was much greater) and Germany (much smaller).

A final major difference between continental Europe and the Anglo-American nations appears in the financial dimension of the social state equation: the (unweighted) average of social deficits in the former was −0.8 percent in 2000 and −1.3 percent in 2008; the same ratios being −5.0 percent and −4.8 percent in the United Kingdom and −3.4 percent and −6.1 percent in the United States. The conclusion is obvious: before the financial crisis, social protection was better financed in the eurozone countries than in the United Kingdom or the United States, even though, in the eurozone, Italy and Greece were already facing severe financial imbalances. Continental European nations designed a social protection network that delivered value for money, and citizens were willing to pay for these benefits. Nowhere on the continent has there been the equivalent of a "taxpayer revolt" that has been a major political trend in the United Kingdom and the United States for a quarter of a century. This suggests a stronger resilience of the "social insurance" schemes in the eurozone than of the "taxation and redistribution" schemes of the Anglo-American tradition.

This chapter does not dissect the infinite diversity of idiosyncratic national experiences. It presents a broad view of social conditions in continental European nations in a time of globalization and emphasizes the singularity of the European evolution toward a distinctive social model. Despite a variety of national institutions and social conditions, the countries of the EMU have, for

Table 8-2. *Financing Social Protection*

	Social security benefits paid by general government[a] (% GDP)			Social security contribution received by general government (% GDP)			Social surplus (+) or deficit (−)		
	2000	*2008*	*Change*	*2000*	*2008*	*Change*	*2000*	*2008*	*Change*
Germany	18.0	16.3	−1.7	18.6	16.5	−2.1	0.6	0.2	−0.43
France	17.2	17.8	0.6	17.9	18.1	0.2	0.7	0.3	−0.41
Italy	16.3	17.6	1.3	12.3	13.7	1.4	−4.0	−3.9	0.13
Spain	12.0	12.5	0.5	12.9	13.2	0.3	0.9	0.6	−0.27
Greece	14.9	16.7	1.8	12.6	13.2	0.6	−2.3	−3.5	−1.2
Sweden	15.6	14.4	−1.1	13.1	9.0	−4.1	−2.4	−5.4	−3.0
United Kingdom	12.6	13.2	0.6	7.6	8.4	0.8	−5.0	−4.8	0.25
United States	10.6	13.1	2.5	7.2	7.0	−0.2	−3.4	−6.1	−2.66

Source: OECD (2013).

a. For definitions of social security and general government, please see the methodology appendix to this chapter.

decades, progressively evolved with astonishingly converging goals and results (Mistral [2006], investigates the various reasons for this surprising convergence by comparison with the U.S. model): we can call this aggregation "Social Europe." Social benefits expanded to face the consequences of innovation or globalization; resources increased to pay for this preferred form of social state. Without common policies designed in Brussels, Social Europe has been a reality, as clearly identifiable as the common market rules or the common external trade policy. This convergence of social situations in the eurozone is a fascinating by-product of a supposedly market-driven integration story.

Politically speaking, the European integration project has been supported by hundreds of millions of voters for fifty years. During all those years, it is not likely that the popular support for the European integration project has been predominantly driven by the strict enforcement of the competition rules by the Commission and the Court of Justice. More likely it has resulted from the fact that the prosperity created by the single market was shared by fair social frameworks. This is why Social Europe, even if it was never the predominant goal of common policies, constitutes a foundation of the eurozone. The sovereign debt crisis in the eurozone today weakens this construction.

Social Europe at Risk

Convergence of social outcomes in Europe was a reality; as suggested by Busch and others (2013), it is now threatened as a result of austerity policies adopted in Southern Europe. At this writing in early 2014, Europe appears to be a polarized region. There is clear evidence of the deterioration of social conditions in Greece and Spain and other countries affected by the crisis. Eurostat social indicators precisely illustrate the gulf on the continent between Germany, which is doing well on practically every front, and the southern countries, where deterioration is evident. From 2007 to 2013, unemployment fell from 9 percent to about 6 percent in Germany, while it increased from 7 percent to 16.5 percent in the Southern European countries; youth unemployment is even worse (see appendix to this book for detailed country reports). France is in the middle with a moderate increase in unemployment. The poverty rate is declining in Germany and surging in the South, where the proportion of poor in the population is now double that of Germany.

The Eurobarometer results come as a crude confirmation of anecdotal evidence; they reveal that the proportion of Greeks living "day-to-day" is as high as 70 percent and is close to 50 percent in Spain. A precarious lifestyle is now common in many countries: only 30 to 40 percent of Spanish and Italian households, and a mere 5 percent of Greek households, expect their circumstances to be stable for the next six months. Compare this with German and Swedish households, which broadly expect "1 to 2 years of stability." A result of increasing unemployment and poverty is the deterioration of every single social parameter. Access to health care services, for example, is more and more difficult in many countries owing to excessive costs. In Greece, bad health indicators and suicide rates are increasing steeply. It is thus no surprise that deep pessimism is common on the continent, except in Germany: from 2007 to 2013, the proportion of Germans with a positive economic outlook increased from 63 to 73 percent, while the proportion of "optimists" fell to 19 percent in France, 6 percent in Italy and Spain, and 2 percent in Greece (Pew Research 2013).

The deterioration of social conditions, the contraction of GDP, the reduction of resources, austerity policies, and the recession have put a lot of stress on the financing of social protection everywhere in the South (see table 8-3). Despite budgetary cuts, social expenditures as a proportion of the often declining GDP have surged in the sample countries (except Germany); the increases vary from 1.9 percent in France to 2.3 percent in Italy, 3.9 percent in Spain, and 3.3 percent in Greece. But despite tax increases, social contributions remain fairly flat (except in France where they show a large increase). Despite three years of austerity, social deficits in Southern Europe in 2012 were still at unsustainable levels: −6.3 percent in Greece, −6.1 percent in Italy, and −3.3 percent in Spain. France has only a moderate social deficit (−0.8 percent) and Germany a modest surplus (0.7 percent) (OECD 2013). Social convergence now seems financially unsustainable. The fifty-year path to convergence of social conditions among continental European countries is certainly fading. Even ignoring the cyclical aspects of the crisis, one must wonder whether there is a future for Europe with such diverging social conditions.

Social Security Financing in Europe

The OECD data cited in the previous section are infrequently used; often the figures differ from those most usually reproduced and discussed. This is due to the complexity of social financial accounts that mix social contributions and benefits with policy decisions related to the general budget. It is difficult to abstract the financing mechanisms behind the social security and welfare programs of one country, let alone create a cross-country comparison. Still, many government budgets provide the surplus or deficit of their social security program in a given year as part of their budget analysis. France, for instance, makes this information available through its Commission des Comptes de la

Table 8-3. *Unsustainable Social Convergence*

	Social security benefit paid by general government (% GDP)			Social security contribution received by general government (% GDP)			Social surplus (+) or deficit (−)		
	2008	2012	Change	2008	2012	Change	2008	2012	Change
Germany	16.3	16.1	-0.2	16.5	16.8	0.3	0.2	0.7	0.52
France	17.8	19.9	1.9	18.1	19.0	0.9	0.3	-0.8	-1.08
Italy	17.6	19.9	2.3	13.7	13.8	0.1	-3.9	-6.1	-2.15
Spain	12.5	16.4	3.9	13.2	13.1	0.0	0.6	-3.3	-3.88
Greece	16.7	20.0	3.3	13.2	13.7	0.5	-3.5	-6.3	-2.78
Sweden	14.4	14.4	0.0	9.0	7.7	-1.3	-5.4	-6.7	-1.28
United Kingdom	13.2	15.7	2.5	8.4	8.5	0.1	-4.8	-7.2	-2.40

Source: OECD (2013)

Figure 8-1. *French Social Security Deficit*

Billions of current euros

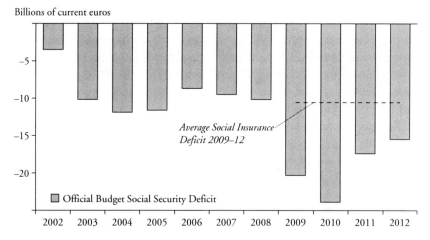

Source: Commission des Comptes de la Sécurité Sociale.

Sécurité Sociale (CCSS), the social security accounts commission. Figure 8-1 shows the French social security deficit from 2002 to 2012; note that the numbers are different from the data presented above.

The OECD national accounts data on social security are limited to contributions and benefits; they provide an iconic example of the financing of national insurance schemes. But each country aggregates these data differently based on their social service institutions; the accounts of the various countries, however, are conceptually the same and are the basis for the OECD figures. Contributions consist of employee and employer contributions to the social security account of a given employee. Benefits paid out are traditionally related to the contributions paid in. While the specific institutions may vary, the difference between the contributions and benefits provides a measure of the surplus or deficit specific to a country's insurance program. The French social accounts, however, aggregate the expenses and resources of the insurance and assistance programs. Assistance programs—which provide benefits to the neediest who do not contribute enough—do not respect the insurance principle of benefits being financed by pre-existing contributions. Assistance programs are fiscal decisions by nature (benefits without pre-existing contributions); they are made by the central government; and they should be but are not adequately financed by the central government. This is why the OECD accounts (which are limited to insurance programs) exhibit a smaller deficit than the French accounts.

Figure 8-1 more precisely shows two things. First, deficits before 2008 may reflect the government's willingness to extend social benefits beyond the credit available from social contributions paid in. In France, for example, health care coverage has been progressively extended to the whole population (*couverture medicale universelle* [CMU]), including social groups that do not pay social contributions. These policies are "social" in nature but should be considered in financial terms, as fiscal measures. They are implemented by social institutions but have to be financed by taxes, rather than by social contributions.

Second, the financial crisis has had an extraordinary effect on the social security deficit in France. Although there was a deficit before the crisis, it has more than doubled since 2008. Social assistance and social insurance programs each have had higher expenditures than the modest increases in revenues.

The social security deficits of the Southern European countries have been severely intensified in the same way by the crisis. Italy, Spain, and Greece each carry a large social security deficit. Most of this can be ascribed to the effect of the eurozone crisis on households and the resulting reliance on government social programs and a reduction in contributions. Social benefits paid by the government have significantly increased. Reform is certainly needed in some categories of social security, such as old-age expenditures, which will rise to an unsustainable level without reform in the coming decades, but it is clear that much of present high expenditures are immediately necessary to counter further deterioration of social conditions.

The weaknesses of the European-style social state were known long before the sovereign debt crisis; intense academic scrutiny and numerous official reports have dealt with economic inefficiencies, financial stress, the need to adapt to new social challenges, and declining political legitimacy. While there is a conservative ideological component to this criticism of the European social state, it is clear that too often inaction has been the default option in the South; fragile and indecisive governments have too easily resorted to increasing deficits and debt in the period of extraordinarily low interest rates following the introduction of the euro. By contrast, German chancellor Gerhard Schröder undertook a decisive and wide-ranging series of reforms, placing the German economy, its finances, and its social protection network on a much stronger foundation than in the rest of the eurozone. Now, in the sovereign debt crisis, Social Europe confronts a huge challenge.

Enforcing sound fiscal policies as defined by the "fiscal compact" is now an absolute condition for successfully implementing the decision of the European Council in June 2012 to build a more sustainable monetary union. On the other hand, social conditions are so severely affected in the South by the austerity policies and the resulting recession that the Monetary Union now threatens to become a polarized and fragmented economic and social grouping, a "union" in name only. In late 2013, the acute phase of the financial crisis seems to have ended, but 2014, the year of European elections, could see a very different threat—a popular revolt against unending austerity policies and distrust of the European integration project. Social Europe so far has been a very important component of convergence; its destruction would likely threaten the future of the single currency. In brief, reforms of national social systems are badly needed; such reforms must result in financial sustainability and overcome the inevitable resistance, but they should also include a reassertion of social convergence within the eurozone and not a perpetuation of present divergences.

Reforming Social Policies in Europe

The European integration project still does not include any ambitious or explicit plan to harmonize social rules and benefits or to pool individual nations' resources to pay for those benefits. Following the disaster of unsustainable public and private debt in southern countries, the idea of a broad and generalized social solidarity funded at the eurozone level does not appear realistic; German voters will not let that happen. European "solidarity" and "convergence" must thus be achieved through the convergence of national policies. The social benefits in any nation will have to be paid, at least for the foreseeable future, from the resources of that nation.

There is no future for any kind of Social Europe without a rebalancing of public finance in every country. But austerity policies have dramatic social consequences. The question is not whether such policies are costly: they are. The question is whether the measures adopted in the name of austerity promote convergence. Practically speaking, will the prevailing divergence among European countries translate to a future where the northern countries will enjoy social conditions from which the southern nations are excluded? Will early retirement or extensive unemployment protection be a privilege of the North that is unavailable for the South? Or will the reforms, as harsh as they are, prove to be a process that corrects previous unsustainable differences, putting the main parameters of social policy on a more similar footing, thus ensuring a more sustainable social European model? It is difficult to respond to these questions with empirical evidence, not only because it is speculative by nature, but also because there is such a complex and diverse patchwork of social institutions and policies among the European countries. How, for example, can one simply compare "equality of access" to health care among countries with widely varying rules governing the medical professions, hospital organization, the distribution of medication, sharing of costs, and so forth?

I shall, however, attempt to do this by focusing on three major issues for which imperfect but consistent evidence is available: pensions, unemployment benefits, and health care.

Pensions

Greater longevity makes pensions a ticking time-bomb in most of the world, not only in the European countries, but in the United States, China, and Japan as well (see Clements and others 2011). It has been properly addressed in only a few countries. Until 2008, generous social expenditures were paid for by German savings in the European southern countries (and by Chinese savings in the United States). The music is still playing in Washington, but the sovereign debt crisis in Europe put an end to the previous temptation of simply "kicking the can down the road." Despite the immense variety of pension schemes (wage earners/independents, public/private, male/female), pensions are the easiest social phenomenon for international comparison, because they involve only three parameters (see OECD 2011): the retirement age, the number of years of contribution, and the net theoretical replacement rate (TRR), which measures the extent to which a pension system enables typical workers to preserve their previous living standard when moving from employment to retirement (see European Commission 2012a, 2012b, and 2012c for a detailed examination of these issues).

The old-age dependency ratio will substantially increase in all eurozone countries in the coming decades (see table 8-4). In 2050 the ratio will range from 64 percent in Germany and Greece to 73 percent in Spain, which is the most problematic country in this regard. France is a special case due to a still high fertility rate, and the ratio will stay at a (relatively) low level of 50 percent. Clearly, "one size fits all" policies will not work; uniformity would not be an appropriate goal. Nonetheless, it is crucial to examine whether recent reforms have had a tendency toward more converging parameters or have introduced politically unacceptable divergences. The data clearly indicate that pre-crisis pension rules (prevailing in 2007) were too different for a sustainable monetary union. First, the official retirement age ranged from a low of 58 years in Greece to 65 in Germany, Italy, and Spain, which had already adapted to the new demographic context. Second, the net theoretical replacement rate (the TRR as measured in 2012 for the year 2010) reveals even greater differences, ranging from 59.1 percent in Germany to an astonishing 121.3 percent in Greece. Measures adopted as a consequence of the crisis are hard to accept

Table 8-4. *Pension Reforms*

	Old-age dependency ratio[a]		Official retirement age			2012 contribution to receive full benefit[b]	2006 projected net theoretical replacement rates		2012 calculated and projected net theoretical replacement rate	
			2007	2012	2012					
	2010	2050	Male	Men	Women	Reform	2010	2050	2010	2050
Germany	34.0	64.4	65	65	65	**40**	67.0	67.0	59.1	63.7
France	28.7	50.9	60	65	65	41	75.9	62.6	77.6	58.8
Italy	33.3	68.1	65	66	66	42	88.5	92.0	89.5	69.1
Spain	26.8	73.2	65	65	65	37	97.2	91.6	94.5	86.5
Greece	31.1	64.0	58	67	67	40	117.0	106.0	121.3	87.0
Sweden	31.3	43.8	65	65	65	**30**	67.8	56.7	60.3	53.0

Source: OECD (2013); OECD (2012).

a. The old-age dependency ratio is defined as the ratio of the population aged 65 and over to the population aged 15 to 64.

b. Bold contribution years indicate that the country did not adopt any increases to the contributory period necessary to receive full benefits over the 2010–12 period.

in a period of depressed activity, but this, unfortunately, is the price for having delayed the necessary structural reforms.

After three years of reforms (2010–13) of the pension systems in the different countries, the parameters are converging toward a more similar and sustainable model. The normal retirement age and the number of years of contribution have been raised and now range between 65 and 67 for the former, 40 and 41 for the latter. The net theoretical replacement rate projected by the European Commission for 2050 on the basis of present legislation exhibits a much greater level of convergence, ranging from 87 percent in Greece to 63.7 percent in Germany and 58.8 percent in France—compared with extremes of 59 to 121 percent when projected in 2010. This clearly demonstrates the magnitude of the reforms adopted under the pressure of the debt crisis, even if additional efforts are still demanded from countries facing continuous financial difficulties. In brief, correcting unjustifiable differences in pension parameters has a price, but that does not mean that Germany, for example, is relying on a model from which southern countries are excluded. On the contrary, it seems that costly reforms have been implemented in the South in order to prepare a more sustainable future within the monetary union. Can similar conclusions be drawn from other social reforms?

Unemployment Benefits

The labor market is the major casualty of the debt crisis in Southern European nations. Unemployment has reached extremely high levels in Greece and Spain (25 percent). Based on its 2003 "Hartz" reforms and owing to its export success, Germany is doing much better; the unemployment rate has fallen to a low 5.5 percent. Italy and France are in an intermediate situation, with high, but not desperate, levels of unemployment. As noted, unemployment is a major source of financial pressure for social finance. Interestingly, public unemployment expenditures do not necessarily reflect the situation in the labor market (see table 8-5): as a share of GDP, they reach a high of 3.5 percent of GDP in Spain and 2.2 percent in France; the same expenditure items in Germany and Greece (1.7 percent) suggest very different policies; and in Italy finally, a surprisingly low ratio of GDP to unemployment (0.8 percent).

Dividing the expenditures ratio by the unemployment rate allows us to statistically determine an "average replacement rate" of professional incomes with unemployment benefits:

$$\frac{Unemployment\ Benefits}{GDP} : \frac{Unemployed}{Labor\ Force} = \frac{Unemployed\ Benefits}{Unemployed} : \frac{GDP}{Labor\ Force}$$

Table 8-5. *Unemployment Expenditures and Unemployment Replacement Rates*

	Total unemployment expenditures (% GDP)	Unemployment rate (%)		Average replacement rate (%)	Net replacement rate year 1 (%)[a]	Net replacement rate years 2–5 (%)
	2010	2011	2012	2011	2011	2011
Germany	1.7	5.9	5.5	40.9	66.8	56.9
France	2.2	9.6	10.2	19.1	70.0	55.2
Italy	0.8	8.4	10.7	10.1	68.3	0.0
Spain	3.5	21.7	25.0	16.2[b]	71.3	41.1
Greece	1.7	17.7	24.3	6.3	48.0	5.4
Sweden	1.4	7.8	8.0	17.9	66.8	64.1
United Kingdom	0.7	8.0	7.9	4.7	61.9	61.8

Source: Eurostat; OECD (2013).
a. See notes on methodology for more information.
b. 2010 data.

It is striking to see that, according to this particular measure, Germany is the most generous, with an average replacement rate of 40.9 percent, while all other countries are under 20 percent. Changing the legislation governing the labor market was a major component of the Hartz reforms in Germany, consisting of both a liberalization of short-time, low-paid jobs and social income benefits to support low-income families. The low level of unemployment did not produce any incentive to change these rules after the debt crisis.

Comparing the "generosity" of unemployment benefits in policy terms should in principle rely on a comparison of the official replacement rate and the length of public support. This is a very difficult statistical task since unemployment benefit rules and conditions are very country-specific—even more than for pensions. We can, however, refer to the Eurostat aggregate measures of the net replacement rate (NRR), which permit a crude comparison (see methodology appendix to this chapter). Two conclusions can be drawn from table 8-5: for the first year of unemployment, the NRR is close to 70 percent in all major economies, higher in Spain and France, lower in Italy and Germany; Greece is a case of its own with a low NRR of 48 percent. The rules are more differentiated in the second year; benefits are practically interrupted after one year in Italy and Greece, Spain maintains a NRR of 41 percent, and France and Germany 57 percent.

A more sophisticated approach has been developed by Klara Stovicek and Alessandro Turrini (2012) to compare the generosity of social systems.

Their approach distinguishes between insurance and benefits (or assistance) as another way of indicating the diversity of national policies. "Generosity" is defined as the difference between the country's figure and the EU-27 average. France and Spain are among the more generous; Italy, Greece, and the United Kingdom are less generous. National idiosyncrasies thus seem to be confirmed, when focusing on generosity rather than on a differentiated use of the two instruments, insurance and assistance. The interesting point here is that German policies sharply differentiate between the insurance and assistance, with the former being less generous and the latter more so than the European average.

Health Care

International comparisons are much more complex for health care than for other social policies; health care is not a matter of transfers or redistribution (between workers and pensioners, between workers and unemployed); the issue is the organization of a whole industrial sector involving the supply of complex goods and services, innovation, investment, and a wide diversity of payment arrangements: nationalized systems, social insurance, private insurance. The organization of the systems is always deeply rooted in the interests of various constituencies; reforming the health care system is one of the most difficult policy issues, as the epic battle surrounding "Obamacare" (officially, the Patient Protection and Affordable Care Act) in the United States demonstrates. It is thus no surprise that there are substantial differences in health care expenditures among European countries.

In continental Europe, public expenditures on health care are approximately 75 percent of total health care expenditures. According to OECD data, France and Germany are the most generous countries in this regard, spending close to 9 percent of GDP; southern countries spend significantly less, 7 to 7.5 percent in Italy and Spain, less than 6 percent in Greece. Out-of-pocket payments are similar in Italy and Spain, significantly lower in France, and higher in Germany. In brief, there is no evidence of wasted social resources in southern countries. As is to be expected, countries with higher average income spend more on a "superior good" such as health care. Material indicators are also frequently used to indicate the organizational aspect of the health care industry. Employment in the health care industry does not suggest highly visible divergences: as a share of total population, the health care sector is relatively more developed in Germany and Spain than in France, Greece, and Italy. Hospital bed availability is high in Germany and France, but also in Greece, while it is lower in Italy and Spain. The interesting lesson in this comparison is that,

Table 8-6. *Health Care Expenditures*

	2010 calculated public health care expenditure (% GDP)	2050 projected public health care expenditure (% GDP)	Out-of-pocket payment (US$PPP)[a]
Germany	8.0	9.5	571.1
France	8.0	9.4	289.8
Italy	6.6	7.2	527.9
Spain	6.5	7.7	601.1
Greece	6.5	7.3	1118.3
Sweden	7.5	8.1	632.2
United Kingdom	7.2	8.3	305.7

Source: Eurostat; European Commission (2012).
a. PPP = purchasing power parity.

despite significant differences in the level of expenditures, the results of these policies are, as noted in the first part of this chapter, extremely similar as measured by synthetic indicators such as mortality at birth and life expectancy.

Facing drastic obligations to restore their budget balance, southern countries have enacted structural reforms, including the reorganization of fragmented administrative frameworks and changes in the provision of services and reimbursement methods (see de la Maisonneuve and Oliveira Martins 2013). Will these reforms produce more efficiency? Because they may well eliminate some of the serendipitously odd results of history and politics in these countries, the answer is probably yes. Hard times can also offer an opportunity to increase preventive care, which is a small proportion of health care expenditures but has the greatest potential return on investment. Looking at the results of these policies, it is interesting to refer to the latest forecast from the European Commission published in 2012 (see table 8-6). It shows the progression of health care expenditures, which are now higher in Germany and France (from 8 to 9.5 percent of GDP) than in the southern countries (from 6.5 to an average of 7.5 percent). If countries are willing to organize a convergence process within the eurozone, there seems finally not much more to gain from reducing health expenditures.

The latest International Monetary Fund (IMF 2013) fiscal monitor has a slightly different message. Focusing specifically on age-related spending projections for 2030, it shows significant increases in France, Spain, and more importantly in Greece. Greece should consequently continue to reduce age-related spending by 1.5 percent of GDP in the coming twenty years in order to be in line with what is expected in the rest of the eurozone. This

IMF forecast confirms the resiliency of welfare state financing in continental Europe: spending on health care, and age-related spending generally, is a bigger problem for the United States (and to a lesser degree the United Kingdom) than for the eurozone. As for eurozone policy issues, it appears that cutting health care expenditures will yield modest marginal results in solving sovereign debt problems, but at a very high social cost. Only Greece seems to need a special effort; but reducing spending by 1.5 percent over fifteen years, which means 0.10 percent every year, is a goal that seems attainable. Beyond specific national circumstances, the general message from this survey is that reforms are under way and are more or less what is needed. Low growth in health care expenditures and increasing out-of-pocket payments already make affordable health care less accessible to all and inaccessible to many. Restricting health care expenditures would now be "penny wise and pound foolish."

One major issue when trying to analyze ongoing social reforms in the eurozone is to determine if different social conditions developing between European countries since the beginning of the debt crisis are a new European structural reality or the product of temporary adjustments. Two preliminary conclusions are clear. First, there is no evidence that Germany is selfishly offering its citizens new social benefits that contrast unfairly with the belt-tightening efforts of the southern countries. In short, Germany is reaping the fruits of early structural reforms while other countries are paying the price of financial exuberance during the period of excessively low interest rates. Also, there is a tendency toward harmonization, not toward divergence, in the area of pensions, the most sensitive social issue. The initial situations were wildly different, with pension parameters having been decided on in many countries with no consideration of changing demographics. Under the pressure of the debt crisis there has been a convergence of pension parameters, promoting a better sustainability of this central element of the European social state: not a threat, but rather a guaranty of the survival of Social Europe.

Two other social policies, unemployment benefits and health care, are both areas for which comparisons are much more complex. Two important conclusions are possible, however. First, there is no evidence of any extravagance (at the macro level) in the policies presently implemented in the southern countries; second, preparation for an aging society is relatively homogeneous, with Greece being the notable exception. These observations may seem to lack precision; but the reality is that it is difficult to find a good balance between two contradictory requirements: ensuring precision in the analysis of complex data and providing an intelligible macro-interpretation of those data that could inform the policy debate. If this position is wrong, then it is by conscious choice in favor of the latter requirement, because it is politically urgent to clearly debate the future of social conditions in the eurozone. Clearly, all necessary actions have not been completed (though France, for example, adopted another, limited, set of pension reforms in the autumn of 2013), but the eurozone nations are on a reasonable track toward convergence. Whatever fiscal adjustments remain to be made, it is time to make sense of this convergence and to offer to the people of the countries of Europe a vision of what Social Europe could be in the future.

Social Europe and the Future of the Euro

For sixty years, social policy has been absent from the European integration project for very understandable reasons. Historically, each country has made different choices, and the resulting policies may not be easily integrated with those of the others. The United Kingdom, for example, desires to preserve more sovereignty and more autonomy than many other countries on the continent, and it is not the only one. These differences explain the divide, in the 1990s, between those who decided on the creation of the Economic and Monetary Union and those, such as the United Kingdom, that did not accept it. As expected, the single currency proved a huge success in the further integration of the single market. But, it was not perfect, and as a result of its imperfections, the EMU proved unable to prevent a catastrophic debt crisis. The resolution of the debt crisis now calls for more integration. But integration in what form? Finance and tax policies are obvious parts of this process, but they are by no means sufficient. Further integration can only move forward with popular consent, which has been brutally battered by the results of austerity policies. Social disruptions could become the next major threat to the survival of the euro. As has been powerfully argued by Tony Judt (2010), too much has been ceded to a free-market vision of the economy. Developing a new social vision could be the next and presently unexplored frontier of the monetary union (see European Commission 2013 as testimony to this trend).

Polls indicate that, in fact, people in the eurozone are ambivalent about Europe. According to a Pew Research poll that received wide attention in the spring of 2013, it is striking that people remain highly in favor of the euro, with two-thirds practically everywhere willing to retain the euro (69 percent in Greece, 67 percent in Spain, 66 percent in Germany, 64 percent in France) and only one-third favoring a return to their former national currencies. The European Council was right in June 2012 to confirm the shared willingness of the eurozone countries to form a better economic and monetary union through the implementation of what they called the "four unions": public finance, banking, business, and politics. Thus European Central Bank (ECB) president Mario Draghi was able to state in July 2012 that the ECB would do "whatever it takes" to maintain the euro. And that proved to be a turning point in the debt crisis. Since then financial tensions have eased, and the disintegration of the single currency is no longer a daily topic of discussion.

But another threat is lurking. The mood of the people in most European countries has been severely affected by the consequences of the crisis: years of effort, few rewards. According to the same Pew Research poll, the European project is a clear casualty of these policies. People are disappointed with the performance of the union and support for the European project is now lower in France than in Britain (22 percent vs. 26 percent!) and even lower in Italy and Greece (11 percent). According to the Pew Research Institute, the European Union is the latest casualty of the euro crisis. And bear in mind that 2014 is a European election year. The temptation to fall back into nationalism is stronger than at any time since the end of World War II. The disparity between the positive perception of the currency and the negative evaluation of economic conditions cannot continue. Dealing with employment and social conditions will have to be at the center of any reconciliation of this discordance. Social Europe is absent from the four unions identified by the European Council, but Europe can no longer afford to remain silent on social conditions. Another chapter of the integration project has now to be written. What are we able to say in this context about Social Europe in 2025?

Most of the social protection networks will likely still reflect national policies implemented by national institutions within a stronger European framework. These policies will confirm the converging trends, the initial phases of which I described earlier. Stronger institutions and procedures will exist to regularly evaluate national policies as precisely as the fiscal compact does for national budgets. A "social semester" would allow an in-depth examination of past results, future trends, and the need for reforms in every country. That would offer guidance for gradual changes to pension rules, control of health care costs, assistance to immigrants, and so forth. An important part of this program would be European policy guidelines regarding working time. These would clearly remain under national sovereignty because they directly reflect different national income levels and social choices. According to the OECD (2013), average annual working hours range from 1,397 hours in Germany to 1,479 in France, 1,686 in Spain, 1,752 in Italy, and 2,034 in Greece (the numbers are 1,654 in the United Kingdom and 1,790 in the United States). In 2025 the working week as well as the yearly periods of activity will probably be shorter and much more flexible everywhere; this is a perfect example of where the eurozone social framework would help in the achievement of different, but coherent, evolutions. In this process, the European Economic and Social Committee will have a strong voice, and the Parliament will work with national legislative bodies to place the indispensable convergence of policies under democratic control. Note that this framework would be applied to countries with different income levels, different age structures, and different perceptions of equality. Convergence means that these different situations would be made coherent, not identical. And this would cover roughly 80 percent of social expenditures. But Social Europe can no longer be limited by national boundaries. There is a need to develop the sense of a community that is united, but not only by rigorous budgets and well-regulated finance. The "single market" is the basis of a competitive economy, and rightly so. It needs to become, in line with a vision shared within the eurozone, a "social-market economy."

Twenty percent or so of social expenditures would thus be designed and implemented in 2025 as policies for the eurozone as a community (it is not expected that the United Kingdom will be willing to join in this initiative, just as it rejected the single currency). Financing these expenditures would come from eurozone resources that would be allocated within the budget procedure. These policies would complement, not replace, national policies; they could serve as a common minimum for social conditions, but they would preferably be oriented toward a common future rather than toward correcting the troubles of the past. The most meaningful and realistic example of a social floor could be an unemployment scheme for the entire eurozone (see Ciccarone 2011 and Dullien and Fitchner 2013). This makes a lot of sense from an economic point of view because countercyclical effects between regions diversely affected by changing conditions on the continent can be dealt with most effectively at the eurozone level (see Gago and Serrano 2011 and Ginest 2011). The most important contribution of social policies to a well-functioning EMU would be a strong policy to increase labor mobility. Interestingly, such a policy would not be developed from scratch but by learning from, and expanding on, many small-scale existing initiatives. These measures would cover the whole lifecycle, from school to professional or higher education and then to the workforce, facilitating mobility within Europe-wide groups and making it easier to practice a profession in a "foreign" country.

There is also a huge area of potential relating to older people in Europe: seniors, who may have worked hard for forty or forty-five years, have a lot of experience to share with younger people and to use to serve the public good. If we are creative enough, eurozone senior citizens will not be a threat weighing down an aging society; they will be an increasingly important part of a vibrant social-market economy. Another part of this policy would be to encourage the sense of a European identity within European-wide companies. For those companies that have taken the lead in this policy, a European-wide social committee is a recognized forum for exchanging information, building support for the company's projects, and more generally developing a positive social dialogue. Extending this experience, it appears that overcoming national rigidities by deriving useful lessons from other countries could open a wealth of possibilities; this will require flexibility and imagination in developing appropriate public-private partnerships.

Confronted with increasing competition from both the United States and emerging countries, Europe urgently needs to continue to increase its innovation level, and its policies must encourage innovative activities for those with talent in business and research. Compared with the United States, European business is notoriously weak at nurturing start-ups. This is not an industrial policy issue, and it has an important social component: successful start-ups are based on vibrant skills, creativity, and drive as much as they are on appropriate finance schemes and tax incentives. In short, success is based on extracting the potential of the transition between education and mature activity. New policies should be introduced to stimulate innovation and risk-taking for young professionals and university graduates, making it easier to launch businesses, develop ideas, innovate, and find appropriate support from society to contribute to a vibrant economy.

With a willingness to open more creative avenues and establish the social state of the twenty-first century, one can finally envision the introduction of a version of a generalized minimum income as proposed by Philippe van Parijs (2013). It would commence as a limited instrument specifically earmarked, for example, for the young (18–25), many of whom are suffering today from adverse labor market conditions. After a modest start-up, a eurozone-wide minimum income could prove to be a powerful tool that, after 2025, would have an effect comparable to old-age and health care protections: those were unthinkable a century ago but turned out to be central strands of the contemporary social fabric.

Conclusion

The preceding arguments bring me to four major conclusions:

1. The convergence of social conditions between most eurozone countries before the debt crisis was surprisingly strong but was based on weak foundations.

First, financing was fragile; insurance schemes were better financed in continental Europe than in the United States, but thanks to extremely low interest rates, many governments had indulged in easy budget policies, including more social spending as part of general government expenditures and not financed by social contributions. Second, this easy-going policy translated into significantly divergent trends in major policy parameters, the clearest example being pension rules with unjustifiable and unsustainable differences between countries belonging to the same monetary union. This could not last, and the debt crisis was a moment of truth.

2. Social policy reforms introduced since 2010 can be evaluated according to two metrics: some of them contribute primarily in cyclical terms to the general policy of budget consolidation; others seek to correct in structural terms the aforementioned divergences and set the stage for a better functioning monetary union. We have seen that pension reforms were clearly directed toward the second goal and in this regard make the eurozone today more homogeneous than it was. The situation seems different for unemployment benefits and health care; here the southern countries showed no clear, macro-social sign of excessive generosity; spending cuts in these areas thus mostly contribute to fiscal consolidation. These measures could have future undesired consequences by increasing social differences among European countries. This possible outcome raises questions about decisions made by national governments under the pressure of various constituencies and lobbies; reducing social spending could be a last resort when facing too much opposition on other fronts (public employment, military expenditures, subsidies of state companies, and so on).

3. It appears that the excesses that made the social protection network unsustainable in the South have essentially been corrected. Presently diverging social conditions in different countries could mostly reflect differences in macroeconomic policies and outlook. A return to more convergent social conditions thus will require a proper solution to the austerity-versus-growth debate. In this context, it would be wrong to enforce further consolidation of the social network; that would undermine confidence in the euro rather than contribute to a better functioning monetary union. Consolidating the single currency from now on requires rebuilding a sense of social progress in the eurozone.

4. Regarding the future of Social Europe, it is tempting to use, in a broad sense, a term introduced by Philippe van Parijs (2013). I have imagined what the eurozone could look like in 2025 from a social aspect, and it is tempting to qualify this future as a "euro-dividend." Why? Because solving the debt crisis

could end the contradiction between a European project driven by the ideal of convergence and the intransigence of specific national realities that have produced divergent social trajectories. Jean Monnet and others were bold enough to think that the economy could be the engine of economic and political convergence; no one was daring enough to imagine that social specificities could be tackled in a similar way. The peoples of the European countries were the ones who, within their national boundaries, had a clear idea of what they wanted the social conditions of Europe to be. And in 2008 they were able to think they had achieved their goal. This achievement is now imperiled by the harsh consequences of austerity policies. But these costly adjustments also create the conditions for more coherent, sustainable social policies in the eurozone. They should be used to stimulate trust, not anger, among the people of the European countries on the continent. And a closer union can only move forward through a daring new initiative, the closer integration of social policies.

Methodology Appendix

Financing Social Protection

Social security contributions received consist of three major elements, disaggregated by source:
—Contributions by the employer for the employee
—Actual payments made by the household in the period to cover its share of pension and other provisions during the period (these payments may be made by employees, self-employed persons, or unemployed persons)
—Contribution supplements
Social security benefits paid are social benefits other than social transfers in kind; they include the following:
—Current transfers received by households intended to provide for the needs that arise from certain events or circumstances. Benefits are divided into two groups: (1) pensions, and (2) all other benefits, described as "non-pension benefits." These cover, for example, payments due in respect of sickness, unemployment, housing, education, or family circumstances.
—Social security benefits may be part of a social insurance or governmental social assistance scheme. Unlike social assistance, all social insurance schemes considered in this metric require formal participation by the beneficiaries. This participation is linked to employment and is usually evidenced by the

payment of contributions to the scheme either by the participants, the employer, or both.

Types of social benefits:

—Pensions—main benefit is a provision for retirees but includes other types of pensions as well (such as those for widows and the disabled)

—Non-pension benefits paid in cash—social insurance payments minus receivables from households that are not considered social benefits

—Does not include benefits in kind

"General government" is defined as follows:

—General government units include some nonprofit institutions and public enterprises not treated as corporations.

—Government units are defined as "unique kinds of legal entities established by political processes that have legislative, judicial, or executive authority over other institutional units within a given area."

—In an economy with multiple levels of government, it includes central, state, and local levels.

—Social security funds (where they are a distinct institutional unit, organized separately from other activities of government units) also constitute government units.

In determining if a nonprofit institution is controlled by the government, five indicators are considered (a single indicator could be sufficient to determine if control exists, but sometimes a number of separate indicators collectively are required for control): appointment of officers, contractual agreements, degree of financing by government, risk exposure, and other provisions.

Net Theoretical Replacement Rate (TRR)

The TRR measures the extent to which a pension system enables typical workers to preserve their standard of living when moving from employment to retirement. The calculation of the TRR takes into account social security contributions to statutory and supplementary pension schemes or funds.

Taxes and means-tested social benefits are included in the calculations. The net replacement rate is calculated as net of income taxes and employee contributions.

The choice of specific common assumptions about the hypothetical worker used for the calculation, such as the age of retirement and the length of the contributory period before retirement, inevitably imply that only a share of individuals are actually represented by this career scenario.

The TRR relies on nationally constructed models and projections to consider the full effects of enacted legislation.

Unemployment Benefits (UB)

The average replacement rate is calculated as unemployment expenditure per unemployed person over GDP in the labor force. The average replacement rate is a measure constructed by the author. It is unemployment expenditures in euros over the number of unemployed people divided by nominal GDP over the labor force.

UB generosity is computed using the following equation: UB generosity = $\sum_{i=1}^{k}$ nrr$_{UI_i}$ * duration$_{UI_i}$ + nrr$_{UA}$ * duration$_{UA}$ where nrr is the net replacement rate, UI is unemployment insurance, UA is unemployment assistance, and I represents different replacement levels for unemployment insurance over the period of unemployment.

References

Atkinson, Anthony B., Thomas Piketty, and Emmanuel Saez. 2011. "Top Incomes in the Long Run of History." *Journal of Economic Literature* 49 (1): 3–71.

Busch, Klaus, Christoph Hermann, Karl Hinrichs, and Thorsten Schulten. 2013. "Euro Crisis, Austerity Policy, and the European Social Model: How Crisis Policies in Southern Europe Threaten the EU's Social Dimension." Berlin: Friedrich Ebert Stiftung International Policy Analysis.

Ciccarone, Giuseppe. 2011. *EEO Review: Adapting Unemployment Benefit Systems to the Economic Cycle, 2011 Italy.* Luxembourg: European Employment Observatory.

Clements, Benedict, David Coady, Frank Eich, Sanjeev Gupta, Alvar Kangur, Baoping Shang, and Mauricio Soto. 2011. "The Challenge of Public Pension Reform in Advanced and Emerging Market Economies." Occasional Paper 275. Washington: International Monetary Fund.

de la Maisonneuve, Christine, and Joaquim Oliveira Martins. 2013. "A Projection Method for Public Health and Long Term Care Expenditures." Working Paper 1048. Brussels: OECD.

Dullien, Sebastian, and Ferdinand Fitchtner. 2013. "A Common Unemployment Insurance System for the Euro Area." *DIW Economic Bulletin* 3 (1): 9–14, Berlin.

Esping Andersen, Gosta. 1990. *The Three Worlds of Welfare Capitalism.* Cambridge, U.K.: Polity Press.

European Commission. 2012a. "The 2012 Ageing Report: Economic and Budgetary Projections for the EU-27 Member States (2010–2060)." *European Economy* 2. Luxembourg.

———. 2012b. "White Paper: An Agenda for Adequate, Safe and Sustainable Pensions." COM (2012) 55 final. Brussels.

———. 2012c. "Pension Adequacy in the European Union 2010–2050." Brussels.

———. 2013. "Social Europe: Current Challenges and the Way Forward." Luxembourg.

Gago, Elvira, and Cristina Serrano. 2011. *EEO Review: Adapting Unemployment Benefit Systems to the Economic Cycle, 2011 Spain.* Luxembourg: European Employment Observatory.

Ginest, Sandrine. 2011. *EEO Review: Adapting Unemployment Benefit Systems to the Economic Cycle, 2011 France.* Luxembourg: European Employment Observatory.

Heise, Arne, and Hanna Lierse. 2011. *Budget Consolidation and the European Social Model.* Berlin: Friedrich Ebert Stiftung.

IMF. 2013. *Fiscal Monitor.* October. Washington.

Judt, Tony. 2010. *Ill Fares the Land.* Berlin: Penguin Press.

Mistral, Jacques. 2006. "Market Forces and Fair Institutions: The Political Economy of Europe and the U.S. Reconsidered." Working Paper Series 138. Cambridge, Mass.: Harvard Center for European Studies.

OECD. 2011. *Pensions at a Glance: Retirement Income Systems in OECD and G20 Countries.* Paris.

———. 2012. *OECD Pensions Outlook 2012.* Paris.

———. 2013. OECD.Stat (database).

Pew Research. 2013. "European Union: The Latest Casualty of the Euro Crisis" (http://www.pewglobal.org/european-union-the-latest-casualty-of-the-euro-crisis/).

Stovicek, Klara, and Alessandro Turrini. 2012. "Benchmarking Unemployment Benefits in the EU." Economic Papers 454. Brussels: European Commission.

van Parijs, Philippe. 2013. "The Euro-Dividend." *Social Europe Journal* (July 3).

Venn, Danielle. 2009. "Legislation, Collective Bargaining and Enforcement: Updating the OECD Employment Protection Indicators." OECD Social, Employment and Migration Working Papers 89. Paris: OECD.

9

Visions for Europe: Democratic Legitimacy and EU Institutions

KEMAL DERVIŞ

The Europe that emerged from the catastrophic first half of the twentieth century was like a dream come true. It embodied a transformative vision, it opened the way for decades of peace and prosperity; it first imagined, and then created, strong institutions. For a long time it had democratic legitimacy, not because the nature of the decisionmaking mechanisms as such augmented democracy, but because the broad vision at the top was broadly in line with the aspirations and the understanding of the citizens.

The perceived decline in "democratic legitimacy" of the European institutions is due to a growing gap between what the citizens of Europe can *understand, follow, debate,* and *take into account when voting,* and the decisions and policies of their leaders and parliaments. Such a gap in contemporary governance is not unique to the EU; it exists at all national levels to various degrees. The gap has become extreme, however, in the case of the EU and unfortunately has been reinforced too many times by national politicians blaming the "complex EU bureaucracy" for things that go wrong at home.

The building of European institutions started when the six original countries signed the Treaty of Rome in 1957. At this writing in late 2013, there are twenty-eight members of the European Union, and about ten additional countries in close association, many of them prospective members, many relatively small such as Serbia, Iceland, Norway, and Switzerland, to name a few, but also the much larger Turkey, which started formal membership negotiations in 2005. The United Kingdom, a full but reluctant member, wants to "renegotiate" the terms of its membership.

The latest European Treaty was put in place in 2009 following the failure to ratify the proposed European Constitution. The Treaty of Lisbon represented a valiant attempt to adapt the European institutions to the new EU with close to thirty members, but it still carries the heritage of a structure put in place when there were many fewer member states.

The eurozone crisis led to an even greater level of institutional complexity: the creation of the European Stability Mechanism (ESM), the various stabilizing initiatives of the European Central Bank (ECB) (Long-Term Refinancing Operation 1, Long-Term Refinancing Operation 2, and Outright Monetary Transactions) (Draghi 2012a), and even a new intergovernmental treaty, outside of formal EU "law," to allow some further steps toward a more integrated eurozone, without having to have the United Kingdom sign up to them.[1]

With each enlargement, with each new treaty, and with each new mechanism to help Europe fight the crisis, the complexity of governance in the EU has increased. With increased complexity has come an increasing inability of the average citizen to understand how this governance works or is intended to work. It is *not* that in a formal sense democratic legitimacy has decreased. Each step forward could only be implemented with the approval of the democratic processes within the European democracies, although some decisions can be taken by weighted voting. The European Council assembles democratically elected governments. There have been gray areas at times, as we saw in the worries and deliberations of the Federal Constitutional Court of Germany in Karlsruhe. There have not been, and cannot be, however, purely technocratic agreements in Brussels that are not endorsed by the national political processes, even if by delegation and sometimes without the need for unanimity. Some agreements, moreover, are subject to formal approval by the European Parliament.

Legitimacy and Visions for Europe

Legitimacy has a *legal* dimension, but in politics it is even more about *perception.* Legitimacy comes from acceptance. The need for a clear and broadly accepted vision is crucial, therefore, for greater legitimacy. Such a vision existed in the

---

1. The Treaty on Stability, Coordination and Governance in the Economic and Monetary Union is available at http://europa.eu/rapid/press-release_DOC-12-2_en.htm.

1950s and 1960s: a vision of irreversible peace on the continent, after the horrors of two World Wars. Linked to that vision of peace was a vision of shared economic prosperity, which began to be realized by the late 1950s and gained momentum in the 1960s. These linked visions of peace and prosperity continued to be strong drivers in the 1970s and 1980s, and they were the source of the acceptance and legitimacy enjoyed by the "European integration project." Economic progress remained substantial, first spurred by postwar reconstruction and "catch up" with the United States, and then supported by increased trade integration thanks to the customs union and then the creation of the single market.

With the fall of the Berlin Wall, a new phase began. The original "peace project" got new impetus from the prospect of integrating Eastern Europe into it. The "unification" or "reunification of Europe" became a vision that generated a lot of grassroots support in the 1990s. It was a fairly simple vision that grew naturally from the original European peace project focused on French-German reconciliation. And after an initial period of economic stress, dislocation, and turmoil, most of Eastern Europe started experiencing rapid growth thanks to the market reforms and integration with the "West." This "unification vision," though complex in its implementation, was relatively easy to grasp, and it was broadly perceived as desirable.

From the 1950s to the early 2000s, the "European project" thus enjoyed strong legitimacy. The "peace and prosperity vision" contained a belief that increasingly greater integration would come. This was reflected in the move-ment from a customs union to a deeper single market and then to a monetary union for a large part of the EU. Throughout this period, the idea of an "ever closer union" did have the support of a majority of citizens, in most countries, and particularly in France and Germany. The older generation remembered the horrors of war and also the sharp increase in living standards that was associated with the EU for several decades. Many younger Europeans benefited from much greater mobility and from educational programs and exchanges such as the ERASMUS program. Later, the reunification of Europe was associated with the end of the cold war and the end of the danger of nuclear annihilation. It was a natural extension of the "peace vision." Moreover, there was little doubt in Eastern Europe that integration with the West would bring both more freedom and greater prosperity.

There were of course exceptions to this broad picture. An overwhelming majority of the British never liked the vision of an ever closer union. The Scandinavians too, were lukewarm, with the exception of the Finns, who had suffered much more than the other Scandinavians from the horrors of war.

Some Eastern Europeans retained nostalgia for the regimented, mediocre, but materially secure lives they had had before the disruptive transition to markets, competition, and the threat of unemployment. On the whole, however, the journey toward an ever closer union continued to progress, with a plurality of Europeans actively supporting it, and a majority going along with it, despite some growing doubts, as "Brussels" was being blamed for many things that were not quite working out. Although living standards did not improve as rapidly as they had at the start of the European journey, the vision remained fairly clear. The monetary union conceived in the late 1980s and early 1990s, which entered into full force in 1999 (wholesale monetary transactions) and 2002 (switchover in currencies), was in harmony with that vision. The fact that the details of how it was going to function had not been really thought through did not prevent its broad acceptance in continental Europe, precisely because it was a natural outcome of the "ever closer union vision" that still prevailed.

Renewed Vision or Decline

About ten years later, at the beginning of the second decade of the twenty-first century, the old vision has run out of steam. Both World War II and the cold war are distant memories. On the economic front, while there are well-performing countries in Northern Europe, there is an increasing popular perception that, on economic issues, Europe is more the problem than the solution (even if that perception is not necessarily grounded in reality).[2] In the South, the recession has been so deep that a majority of citizens are substantially worse off now than they were at the start of the century.

The eurozone crisis demonstrated that a monetary union cannot function well without much greater sharing of sovereignty among its members. The monetary union might be able to survive without greater fiscal, labor market, and banking sector integration, but it cannot thrive without such sharing of sovereignty. Something halfway between the original monetary union and a union that would incorporate sufficient financial, labor market, and fiscal integration would condemn the eurozone to mediocre growth and high unemployment for the foreseeable future. It is that kind of future that the IMF, for example, predicts in its latest reports. The southern periphery would

2. The Pew Research Center's May 2013 report, titled "The New Sick Man of Europe: The European Union," shows a decline in support for the European project and its institutions. The following are the percentage point declines between 2007 and 2013 of EU favorability within selected European countries: Germany: 8 percent, Britain: 9 percent, France: 21 percent, Italy: 20 percent, Spain: 34 percent.

experience only very little growth for the rest of this decade. Even the core, including Germany, would not thrive, because the eurozone countries are too integrated economically for some to truly succeed on a sustained basis, while others continue to suffer. Moreover, if too-large differences in economic and social outcomes were to emerge, they would again threaten the monetary union and let redenomination risks re-emerge, with ensuing negative consequences for economic performance.

At the same time, it is very clear that the United Kingdom, one of the three largest EU member countries, will not join the eurozone in the foreseeable future. Sweden, Denmark, and Norway (the latter not in, but closely associated with the EU) are also very unlikely to want to join. In Sweden, where political opinion was divided, it is now resolutely "anti-Euro." There is, therefore, part of Northern Europe that is likely to remain outside the eurozone. In the Southeast, there are other countries, such as Bulgaria, Romania, and Serbia, to name only three that may want to join the eurozone, in principle, despite the bitter lessons from Greece and the other crisis countries. But they will not be ready to join for a long time, and therefore will not be accepted for many years. Some of these "not yet eurozone" countries are already fully in the EU, while others would like to join the Union and have, in various ways, started the process of membership negotiations. And then there is Turkey, having started membership negotiations in 2005, apparently too big to be acceptable to the core EU countries as a member, but again too big for the same countries to want to exclude it from Europe and accept the geopolitical implications and consequences of such an open exclusion. As a result, Turkey-EU relations have been in a state of non-transparent uncertainty and limbo for decades, a situation that is becoming less and less tenable for both sides, but particularly for the new generation in Turkey.

Against this background, all kinds of very technical discussions and negotiations are constantly taking place, discussions and negotiations the average citizen has no hope of following and probably has no real desire to understand. To give some examples: there will be a banking union with supervision by the ECB at the eurozone level; non-members of the ECB such as the United Kingdom and Sweden may or may not be part of that supervision; there will be some kind of joint decision to intervene when banks get in trouble, but for years to come few joint resources to do it; and there will again be few joint resources to back a possible Europe-wide (or eurozone-wide?) deposit insurance scheme. This is a vision of a banking union that even specialists find difficult to comprehend, let alone the average citizen. The ECB will intervene and buy the bonds of countries if they get into trouble through its outright monetary transactions (OMT) program, but these countries will have to have an economic program agreed with the EU Commission, and perhaps also with the IMF. It is not clear what happens if the IMF and the EU disagree. When it was unclear exactly how the program could work, Mario Draghi's brilliant statement, "Believe me, it will be enough!," did scare those who would sell the program short (Draghi 2012b). Can such promises do that forever?

The euro is, by treaty, the currency of the EU, but the United Kingdom will not accept the euro, ever, and Sweden accepted it in theory but not in practice. Both countries are members of the EU, however. The European Parliament is the source of democratic legitimacy for the EU mechanisms, including for how the eurozone is managed and how the ECB conducts itself, but only some euro-parliamentarians actually represent countries that are in the eurozone. How can there be votes on eurozone matters in such a Parliament? The EU conducts trade negotiations with the United States and China; Turkey has to implement all the resulting agreements when it comes to U.S.-Turkey or China-Turkey trade, as if it is in the EU. But not only is Turkey not in the EU, it cannot even participate in the negotiations.

If Henry Kissinger tried to call the person in charge in the EU (an often referred to hypothetical phone call he apparently never thought of making), he would be even more bewildered now than in the past. Should he call the president of the Commission, the president of the European Council, the leader of the country chairing the EU for the current six-month period, the president of the Federal Constitutional Court in Karlsruhe (since that court could in theory nullify almost any agreement or treaty, although when tested, it has not done so), or simply Angela Merkel? Many may be tempted to answer, "Of course, call Angela Merkel!" But how tenable is it to have a Europe of close to thirty member states and about 450 million people for which the prime minister of one country with about 80 million people appears to make all the important decisions? How can Italian, Spanish, or French citizens relate to that?

The reality is that without a renewed vision, including a *simplified institutional structure* that the average citizen can understand and accept, democratic legitimacy cannot be strengthened in Europe. Moreover, without such legitimacy, European institutions and mechanisms will have great difficulty functioning effectively. The rise of overtly anti-European populism throughout the continent could lead to a European Parliament that is not supportive of Europe, as a higher participation rate of extreme populists, in comparison with disgruntled center-left and center right voters, will likely amplify the already substantial anti-European movement's representation well beyond its electoral strength in national polls.

Elements of a Renewed Vision

It is of course much easier to criticize the existing state of affairs than to propose solutions. It is also very tempting to argue that not much can be done practically, given political circumstances and legal constraints. The consensus view seems to be that Europe will continue to muddle through, make small steps toward greater coordination in the eurozone, leave the status of the non-eurozone members in limbo, create additional meetings of various sorts (such as the meeting of national parliamentarians of the eurozone countries, which met in the fall of 2013 in Vilnius), and perhaps even come up with a new intergovernmental treaty to substitute for needed change in the existing "European" treaties, since no one wants to touch those treaties. Some, such as Jean-Claude Piris, who was no less than the director of the General Legal Service of the EU, have argued that article 136 of the existing Treaty on the Functioning of the European Union already allows the eurozone to organize itself as a separate area of cooperation inside the EU (see Piris 2012). But his proposals would require unanimous agreement by all EU members to be put into practice. Moreover, the existing treaties are being interpreted in a rather conservative manner by those arguing for only minimal change.

A minimalist future is possible, perhaps even likely. Within such constraints, however, average annual economic growth is likely to remain very slow until the end of the current decade, unemployment will remain very high in the South, and Europe's weight and influence in the world will decline. The recent uptick in eurozone performance is real and reflects the usual, almost inevitable, course of a business cycle, but the recovery remains very weak. Moreover, social tensions within countries and tensions between the North and South may become unmanageable and could lead to a gradual but ultimately unstoppable unraveling of existing institutions. The populist extremes, which seem to be rising in number and intensity, could end up destroying a weakened European Union.

To create a better future, to roll back reactionary populism, a renewed vision is necessary. The renewed vision should be anchored in Europe's past achievements but look forward into the twenty-first century. It is such a vision that will permit the detailed institutional reforms that are needed. Often, when institutional and legal reforms are discussed, the specialists and bureaucrats are discouraged, because the path forward is both so complicated and so difficult to explain. Indeed, it will not be possible to move forward with difficult reforms, one by one in piecemeal fashion, against a backdrop of political confusion and lacking popular support. It is futile to expect the "vision" to emerge *from* the technical or institutional details. It must come *first:* once a vision is accepted by a strong majority of citizens, the technical and legal details can be worked out. Europe should not try to put the cart before the horse. The detailed institutional and technical arrangements should follow the articulation and acceptance of a renewed vision. Citizens do not actually want to know all the details. One of the biggest mistakes made before the French voted "no" in the 2005 referendum on establishing a European constitution was to send each household a copy of the draft constitutional treaty, a huge document including a lot of technical detail. Citizens do want, however, to understand the essential nature of the path they are being asked to embark upon. They also want to perceive the concrete benefits it will offer them. They need a narrative they can relate to. That is the essence of any political project. It is what Europe needs now.

What Path, Then, Should Europe Propose?

First, Europe can continue to stand for peace, and security through peace, but in the *context of today's world.* Peace is no longer about French-German reconciliation, or about the end of the cold war. It is now about a "global order" where the objective is to maintain and ensure peace worldwide, and to achieve this unless all other options are truly exhausted, through negotiations, compromise, and international rules that apply to all equally. Europe has been about building an ever larger area of peace. It can be the key player in extending that area to the world as a whole. A global vision of peace is something many, particularly the young, can relate to, and it can grow naturally from the peace vision of the past. It is also in line with the overwhelming trend toward more human interactions across the globe.

Second, Europe can redefine and strengthen the notion of prosperity as one of "human progress in many dimensions," a "good life" that includes much more than a single-minded pursuit of GDP growth.[3] At the high income levels most of Europe has already reached, such a good life can be achieved by having economies that realize moderate but stable GDP growth; enhance opportunities for economic mobility; increase the "agency" and "capabilities" of its people;[4] encourage flexible work lives; promote high levels of employment

3. See the "Better Life Index," OECD (2013), which tracks and compares well-being across countries since 2011. It is based on eleven topics identified by the OECD as essential contributors to material living conditions and quality of life.

4. "Agency" suggests a person's capacity to pursue a fulfilling life and the opportunities to exercise choice; "capability" is the subjective freedom of an individual to achieve various lifestyles (Sen 1999).

combined with sufficient time for family, friends, sports, and leisure; promote
life-long education and gradual retirement; offer flex-security in labor markets
(generous protection of workers, but without the insistence on maintaining
employment where there is no longer competitiveness); and provide quality
health care, a clean environment, support for diversity, and deep respect for
individual choices and privacy. Good economic performance must be rede-
fined in terms of concrete benefits that can be perceived by citizens as clear
improvements in the quality of their lives. In this context, income distribution
also matters. How does GDP growth alone help the quality of life or even the
income of a typical (median) household if more than 90 percent of the aggregate income increase accrues to the top 1 percent of households, as has been
the case in the United States after the 2008 crisis?[5]

Such an objective for achieving human progress and the "good life" can
complement the vision of peace. It is a vision that most Europeans, on the
center-left as well as on the center-right of the political spectrum, can relate to.
It does require a fundamental change in how good performance is measured,
away from one-dimensional GDP metrics and toward multidimensional human
satisfaction. European governments have been pioneers in formally augmenting
their national economic data with well-being and quality-of-life measures.
In 2008, France's president, Nicolas Sarkozy, instituted a commission chaired
by Nobel laureates Joseph Stiglitz and Amartya Sen to recommend specific
additional metrics to capture "a more relevant picture of economic performance
and social progress," metrics reflecting "societal well-being, as well as measures
of economic, environmental, and social sustainability." In 2010, British prime
minister David Cameron asked the Office of National Statistics in Britain to
incorporate similar metrics of well-being and quality of life into traditional
economic data and into policymaking.[6] The Better Life Index of the OECD
reflects a shared pursuit of measuring the "good life" across the spectrum of
political ideologies and countries in Europe.

There are two implications associated with this "peace and the good life
vision." The first is that Europe must be *large* and derive a lot of *soft power*
from its size. A Europe of 550 million people that stretched from the United
Kingdom and Norway to Turkey, from the Balkans to Portugal, with a market

---

5. Note that median per capita income in Northern Europe is the highest in the world, barring
some small oil sheikhdoms; median per capita income in the larger EU is about equal to that in
the United States.

6. See Graham (2011) for a discussion of recent initiatives to include well-being and quality-
of-life measures in policy deliberations by governments across the world.

and GDP that represented almost 30 percent of the world economy and was larger than any other, could have a great deal of influence worldwide and could insist on some global norms that are compatible with its preferences for human progress in all dimensions. It could insist more effectively, for example, that the world take measures against tax avoidance by international corporations that undermine the fiscal sustainability of social insurance and solidarity. It could insist more effectively on basic rights for labor and employment standards throughout the world economy, which in the long run would benefit all workers. It could carry real weight in climate negotiations, which in the long run would again benefit citizens around the world. It could be a better example of how to organize governance through weighted voting in a world where such "beyond national boundaries" governance will become increasingly necessary. Even a large Europe cannot replace the need for progress toward global governance. But a large Europe, if it acted with coherence, could weigh in on how global governance is built and practiced. A large and cohesive Europe could build a pan-European society in accord with its own preferences in connection with what constitutes a "good life" to a much larger degree than individual countries or a "small Europe" could. Such a society and renewed European model, performing well across many dimensions of human progress, could better compete globally not only in the material space but also in the space of ideas and values.

A large and inclusive Europe does mean, however, that European institutions must be quite flexible. It means that the principle of subsidiarity must be observed whenever practical: things that can be managed at the local level should not be interfered with from above. There is the need for a strong European Commission, but one that deals with essential matters, not one that decides whether restaurants can sell olive oil in reusable bottles. Local governments can do that. "Monetary union," on the other hand, does involve the need for a degree of sovereignty sharing that several European countries do not, and will not anytime soon, find acceptable. If Europe is to be large, and is to include countries such as the United Kingdom, Sweden, and also Turkey and Serbia, it will have to reconstitute itself into two distinct groups, two "circles": the group of countries that use the euro and want to be in the eurozone, and the group of countries that keep their own currencies. These two groups, *together,* would form the "large" Europe, sharing the single market, sharing many common policies, but not sharing the same currency. The eurozone would have to build its own legitimate governance inside the overall framework of the "large" European Union. There would have to be a eurozone budget, a subassembly of the European Parliament (which might include national parliamentarians) that would be a eurozone parliament, and a eurozone minister of finance, as there is already a European Central Bank president (for details, see Derviş 2013).

These elements are sufficient for a renewed vision: a large, coherent, and flexible Europe, oriented toward peace and inclusive human progress, delivering material prosperity and a high quality of life, strong enough that it cannot be pushed around, and large enough that it has a strong say in global governance. For it to function, it must encourage the eurozone to integrate further, while accepting as part of the larger union a group of countries that do not want to share sovereignty to the degree required by a common currency and a single central bank.

For such a vision, this outline, including the proposed institutional structure (eurozone, non-eurozone) is enough. If a large majority of Europeans finds this vision attractive, the lawyers, the specialists, the economists, and the "eurocrats" can then work on the thousands of more specific details needed to make it a reality and on a more detailed system of governance that functions and performs. There are all kinds of questions that will have to be answered, and a lot of work will indeed be required. If such a vision were to gain strong support, the work on details would be done and the resulting institutions would be able to function. Without a vision, however, the technicians and lawyers will spin in endless circles. Progress that might be achieved would likely be overwhelmed by unresolved practical problems and populist pressures.

Europe is thus at a crossroads. There is a need for political leadership and alliances across Europe to make it happen. A strong Franco-German driver remains essential, as it always has been. It should be complemented by a leadership in the United Kingdom that supports the "two circles" institutional vision, which responds both to the British need to retain more autonomy and to the eurozone's need for more integration. If such political leadership emerges with a renewed vision that is reasonably simple, clear, and appropriate for the times, Europe can again become the amazing success story that it was during the first fifty years after the launch of the most ambitious and peaceful regional integration project in human history.

References

Derviş, Kemal. 2013. "Europe in 25 Years." *Europe's World*, October 1 (www.brookings.edu/research/opinions/2013/10/04-europe-economy-future-dervis).

Draghi, Mario. 2012a. Introductory statement to a press conference at the European Central Bank in Frankfurt, September 6 (www.ecb.europa.eu/press/pressconf/2012/html/is120906.en.html).

————. 2012b. Speech at the Global Investment Conference in London, July 26 (www. ecb.int/press/key/date/2012/html/sp120726.en.html).

Graham, Carol. 2011. *The Pursuit of Happiness: An Economy of Well-Being*. Washington: Brookings Institution Press.

Pew Research Center. 2013. "The New Sick Man of Europe: The European Union" (www. pewglobal.org/files/2013/05/Pew-Research-Center-Global-Attitudes-Project-European-Union-Report-FINAL-FOR-PRINT-May-13-2013.pdf).

Piris, Jean-Claude. 2012. *The Future of Europe: Towards a Two-Speed EU*. New York: Cambridge University Press.

OECD. 2013. "Better Life Index" (www.oecdbetterlifeindex.org/).

Sen, Amartya. 1999. *Development as Freedom*. New York: Anchor Books.

Appendix: Economic Data for Select European Economies, 2000–14

Table A-1. *GDP Growth, 2000–14*
Annual percentage change at constant prices

	2000–07	*2008–12*	*2013**	*2014**
France	2.1	0.1	0.2	1.0
Germany	1.7	0.7	0.5	1.4
Greece	4.1	−4.4	−4.2	0.6
Italy	1.6	−1.4	−1.8	0.7
Portugal	1.5	−1.1	−1.8	0.8
Spain	3.6	−1.0	−1.3	0.2
Sweden	3.2	0.9	0.9	2.3
United Kingdom	3.2	−0.6	1.4	1.9
United States	2.6	0.8	1.6	2.6
Euro area (17)	2.2	−0.3	−0.4	1.0
European Union (28)	2.7	−0.1	0.0	1.3

Source: IMF, *World Economic Outlook* (October 2013).
*Estimated.

Table A-2. *Output Gap, 2000–14*

Annual average, percent of potential GDP

	2000–07	2008–12	2013*	2014*
France	1.6	−1.4	−2.5	−2.5
Germany	0.2	−0.4	−0.4	−0.2
Greece	2.0	2.0	−10.7	−9.5
Italy	1.7	−1.8	−4.8	−4.0
Portugal	0.7	−1.2	−4.5	−3.8
Spain	1.6	−1.7	−4.2	−3.6
Sweden	1.2	−0.9	−1.3	−0.8
United Kingdom	2.3	−1.5	−2.7	−2.4
United States	0.5	−4.6	−4.5	−4.0
Euro area (17)	1.1	−1.0	−2.7	−2.5
European Union (28)	—	—	—	—

Source: IMF, *World Economic Outlook* (October 2013).
*Estimated.

Table A-3. *Current Account Balances, 2000–14*

Annual average, percent of GDP

		2000–07	2008–12	2013*	2014*
France	Savings	20.3	18.5	18.2	18.7
	Investment	19.8	20.1	19.6	20.0
	Current Account	0.5	−1.7	−1.6	−1.6
Germany	Savings	22.1	24.0	23.5	23.8
	Investment	18.9	17.7	17.6	18.1
	Current Account	3.2	6.3	6.0	5.7
Greece	Savings	15.1	8.1	12.2	13.7
	Investment	23.6	18.0	13.2	14.1
	Current Account	−8.4	−9.9	−1.0	−0.5
Italy	Savings	20.6	17.1	17.4	17.9
	Investment	21.2	19.5	17.4	17.7
	Current Account	−0.6	−2.4	0.0	0.2
Portugal	Savings	15.4	11.2	15.6	15.6
	Investment	24.8	19.7	14.7	14.8
	Current Account	−9.3	−8.5	0.9	0.9
Spain	Savings	22.5	18.6	19.4	20.0
	Investment	28.3	23.4	18.0	17.3
	Current Account	−5.8	−4.8	1.4	2.6
Sweden	Savings	24.7	25.6	24.4	24.4
	Investment	18.2	18.8	18.7	18.9
	Current Account	6.5	6.8	5.7	5.5

(continued)

Table A-3. *Current Account Balances, 2000–14 (continued)*
Annual average, percent of GDP

		2000–07	2008–12	2013*	2014*
United Kingdom	Savings	15.3	13.1	11.3	12.2
	Investment	17.5	15.2	14.0	14.5
	Current Account	−2.2	−2.1	−2.8	−2.3
United States	Savings	18.4	15.4	16.7	17.4
	Investment	22.5	18.8	19.4	20.2
	Current Account	−4.7	−3.2	−2.7	−2.8
Euro area (17)	Savings	21.7	20.2	20.4	20.8
	Investment	21.2	19.6	17.9	18.1
	Current Account	0.4	0.5	2.3	2.5
European Union (28)	Savings	20.6	19.3	19.2	19.6
	Investment	20.7	19.2	17.7	17.9
	Current Account	−0.1	0.1	1.5	1.6

Source: IMF, *World Economic Outlook* (October 2013).
*Estimated.

Table A-4. *Trade and Current Account Balances, 2000–14*
Annual average, percent of GDP

		2000–07	2008–12	2013*	2014*
France	Trade	0.2	−2.3	−2.2	−2.4
	Current Account	0.5	−1.7	−1.6	−1.6
Germany	Trade	4.2	5.6	5.9	5.7
	Current Account	3.2	6.3	6.0	5.7
Greece	Trade	−12.2	−9.7	−2.2	−0.3
	Current Account	−8.4	−9.9	−1.0	−0.5
Italy	Trade	0.4	−0.7	2.6	2.8
	Current Account	−0.6	−2.4	0.0	0.2
Portugal	Trade	−8.8	−6.0	1.7	2.5
	Current Account	−9.3	−8.5	0.9	0.9
Spain	Trade	−4.1	−2.1	3.4	4.7
	Current Account	−5.8	−4.8	1.4	2.6
Sweden	Trade	7.3	6.2	5.8	5.9
	Current Account	6.5	6.8	5.7	5.5
United Kingdom	Trade	−2.5	−1.9	−2.5	−2.4
	Current Account	−2.2	−2.1	−2.8	−2.3
United States	Trade	−4.6	−3.6	−3.2	−3.3
	Current Account	−4.7	−3.2	−2.7	−2.8
Euro area (17)	Trade	1.6	1.5	3.4	3.6
	Current Account	0.4	0.5	2.3	2.5
European Union (28)	Trade	0.8	1.0	—	—
	Current Account	−0.1	0.1	1.5	1.6

Source: IMF, *World Economic Outlook* (October 2013); Eurostat.
*Estimated.

Table A-5. *General Government Debt, 2000–13*
Percent of GDP

		2000	2007	2012	2013*
France	Net	51.4	59.6	84.0	87.2
	Gross	57.4	64.2	90.2	93.5
Germany	Net	41.1	50.6	57.4	56.3
	Gross	60.2	65.4	81.9	80.4
Greece	Net	102.9	106.9	154.8	172.6
	Gross	103.4	107.2	156.9	175.7
Italy	Net	93.2	87.1	106.1	110.5
	Gross	108.6	103.3	127.0	132.3
Portugal	Net	41.9	63.7	112.4	117.5
	Gross	48.4	68.4	123.8	123.6
Spain	Net	50.4	26.7	73.5	80.8
	Gross	59.4	36.3	85.9	93.7
Sweden	Net	2.2	−17.4	−21.2	−19.4
	Gross	53.9	40.2	38.3	42.2
United Kingdom	Net	33.9	38.4	81.6	84.8
	Gross	40.5	43.7	88.8	92.1
United States	Net	34.4	46.5	84.1	87.4
	Gross	53.0	64.4	102.7	106.0
Euro area (17)	Net	53.7	52.1	72.2	74.9
	Gross	69.3	66.5	93.0	95.7
European Union (28)	Net	47.4	46.0	68.5	71.0
	Gross	62.1	59.3	86.8	89.5

Source: IMF, *World Economic Outlook* (October 2013).
*Estimated.

Table A-6. *General Government Fiscal Balance, 2007–14*
Annual average, percent of GDP

		2000–07	2008–12	2013*	2014*
France	Overall	−2.8	−5.6	−4.0	−3.5
	Primary	−0.2	−3.2	−2.0	−1.5
Germany	Overall	−2.3	−1.6	−0.4	−0.1
	Primary	0.2	0.6	1.7	1.8
Greece	Overall	−5.6	−10.4	−4.1	−3.3
	Primary	−0.1	−4.8	—	1.4
Italy	Overall	−3.0	−3.8	−3.2	−2.1
	Primary	2.4	0.9	2.0	3.1
Portugal	Overall	−4.1	−6.9	−5.5	−4.0
	Primary	−1.6	−3.7	−1.4	0.1
Spain	Overall	0.4	−9.2	−6.7	−5.8
	Primary	2.4	−7.5	−3.7	−2.6

(continued)

Table A-6. *General Government Fiscal Balance, 2007–14 (continued)*
Annual average, percent of GDP

		2000–07	2008–12	2013*	2014*
Sweden	Overall	1.3	0.1	−1.4	−1.5
	Primary	2.7	0.3	−1.3	−1.4
United Kingdom	Overall	−1.7	−8.4	−6.1	−5.8
	Primary	−0.2	−6.3	−4.7	−3.7
United States	Overall	−2.4	−9.7	−5.8	−4.7
	Primary	−0.5	−7.7	−3.6	−2.6
Euro area (17)	Overall	−1.9	−4.5	−3.1	−2.5
	Primary	1.0	−1.9	−0.4	0.2
European Union (28)	Overall	−1.8	−4.9	−3.4	−2.9
	Primary	0.8	−2.5	−1.1	−0.5

Source: IMF, *World Economic Outlook* (October 2013).
*Estimated.

Figure A-1. *Northern vs. Southern Europe Current Account Balances, 1999–2014*

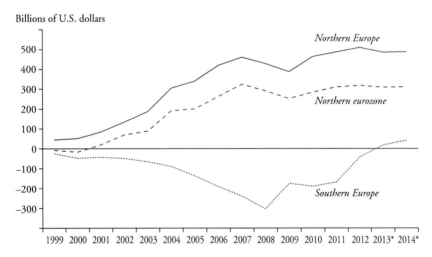

Billions of U.S. dollars

Source: IMF, *World Economic Outlook* (October 2013).
Note: The Northern eurozone includes Austria, Finland, Germany, and the Netherlands. Northern Europe includes the Northern eurozone plus Denmark, Norway, Sweden, and Switzerland. Southern Europe includes Greece, Italy, Portugal, and Spain.
*Estimated.

Figure A-2. *Degrees of Openness, 2000 and 2012*

Total trade as a percentage of GDP[a]

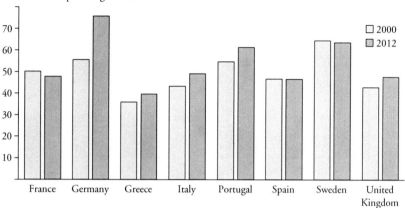

Source: Eurostat.
a. Total trade equals exports plus imports.

Figure A-3. *Total Leverage (Excluding the Financial Sector),
2000, 2007, and 2011*

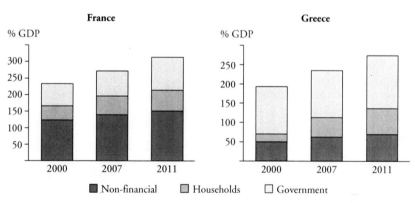

Source: Haver Analytics.

(continued)

Figure A-3. *Total Leverage (Excluding the Financial Sector),*
2000, 2007, and 2011 (continued)

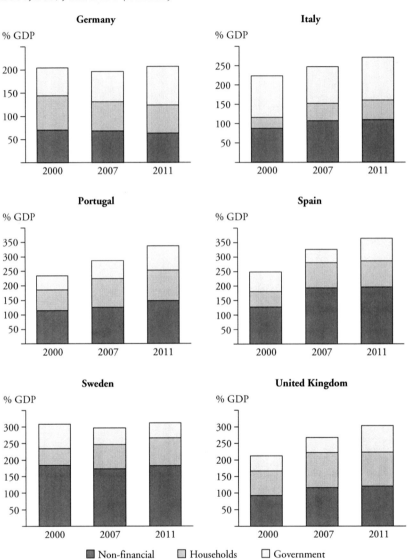

Source: Haver Analytics.

Figure A-4. *Labor Productivity, 2000–12*

Index: 2000 = 100

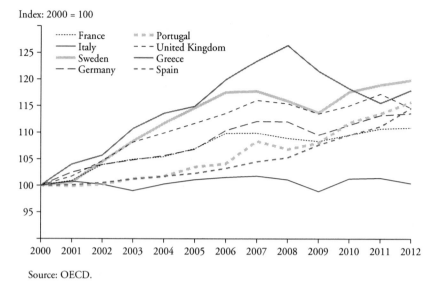

Source: OECD.

Figure A-5. *Labor Compensation, 2000–11*

Index: 2000 = 100

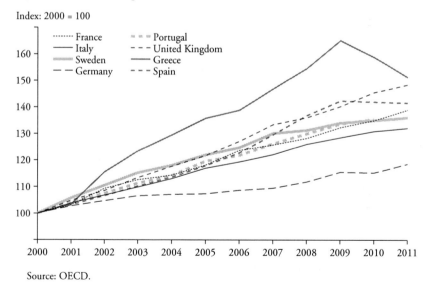

Source: OECD.

Figure A-6. *Unit Labor Costs, 2000–12*

Index: 2000 = 100

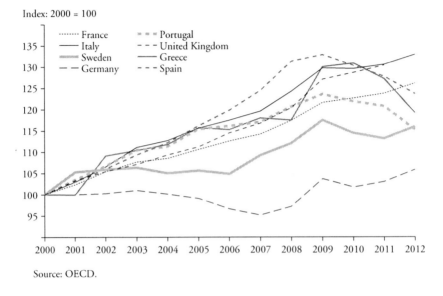

Source: OECD.

Figure A-7. *Unemployment, 2000–13*

Percent

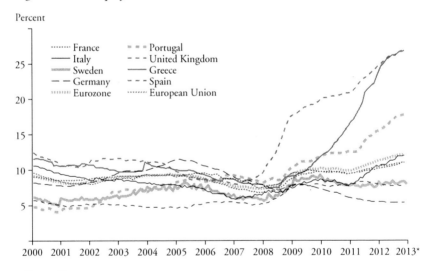

Source: Eurostat.
*Estimated.

Figure A-8. *Youth Unemployment, 2000–13*

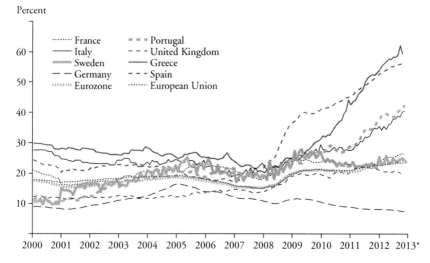

Percent

Source: Eurostat.
*Estimated.

Figure A-9. *General Government Expenditures, 2011*

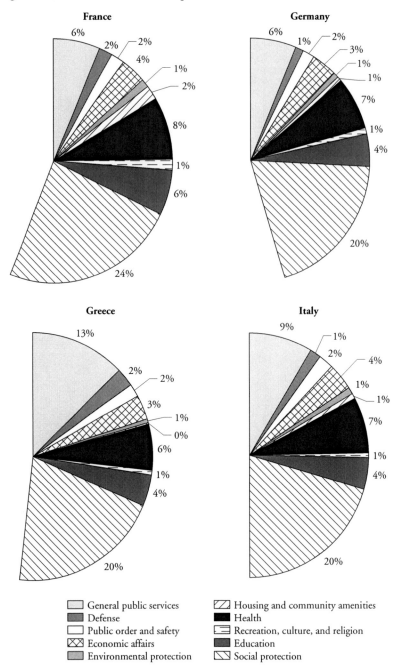

Note: Complete pie indicates total GDP.

(continued)

Figure A-9. *General Government Expenditures, 2011 (continued)*

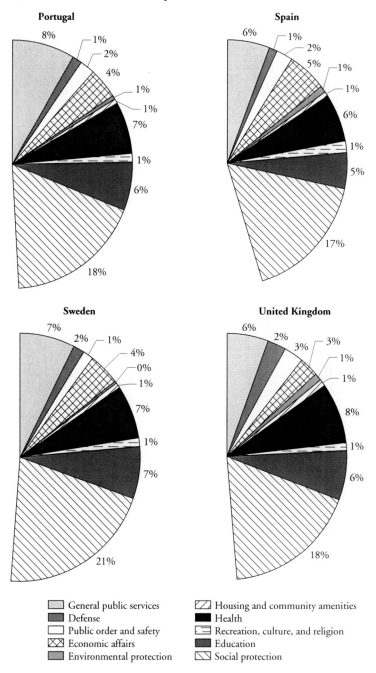

Source: Eurostat.
Note: Complete pie indicates total GDP.

Contributors

Kemal Derviş
Vice President and Director, Global
Economy and Development,
Brookings Institution

Douglas Elliott
Fellow, Economic Studies,
Brookings Institution

Friedrich Heinemann
Head, Corporate Taxation and
Public Finance, Centre for European
Economic Research (ZEW)

Domenico Lombardi
Director, Global Economy,
Center for International Governance
Innovation (CIGI)

Jacques Mistral
Nonresident Senior Fellow, Global
Economy and Development,
Brookings Institution, and Special
Adviser, Institut Français des Relations
Internationales

Michael Mitsopoulos
Coordinator, Infrastructures
and Entrepreneurship,
Hellenic Federation of Enterprises

Luigi Paganetto
President, Tor Vergata Economics
Foundation and the Centre for Eco-
nomic and International Studies (CEIS),
University of Rome "Tor Vergata"

Angel Pascual Ramsay
Director of Global Risks, ESADE
Center for Global Economy and
Geopolitics (ESADEgeo), and
Nonresident Senior Fellow, Global
Economy and Development,
Brookings Institution

Theodore Pelagidis
Professor of Economics, University
of Piraeus, Greece, and Nonresident
Senior Fellow, Global Economy
and Development,
Brookings Institution

Index

Lightning Source UK Ltd.
Milton Keynes UK
UKOW03f1144120514

231522UK00001B/6/P